THE DEVIANT IMAGINATION

THE DEVIANT IMAGINATION

Psychiatry, Social Work and Social Change

GEOFFREY PEARSON

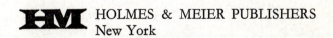 HOLMES & MEIER PUBLISHERS
New York

Published in the United States of America 1975 by
Holmes & Meier Publishers, Inc.
101 Fifth Avenue
New York, New York 10003

Printed in Great Britain

Library of Congress Cataloging in Publication Data

Pearson, Geoffrey.
  The deviant imagination.

  Bibliography: p. [232]-252
  Includes index.
  1. Deviant behavior. 2. Social service. 3. Social
control. I. Title. [DNLM: 1. Social behavior
disorders. 2. Psychology, Social. WM600 P36ld]
HM291.P38   364.2'56   75-9815
ISBN 0-8419-0209-7

For Jonathan and Kate

'This is abstract thinking: to see nothing in the murderer except the abstract fact that he is a murderer, and to annul all other human essence in him with this simple quality.'

George W. F. Hegel

CONTENTS

PREFACE

An article in the *British Journal of Psychiatry* in 1969 complained that some young patients were not listening to their doctor's orders and instead were reading the books of the psychiatrist Ronald Laing. It is an odd state of affairs when one doctor complains that another doctor's books are not good for his patients, particularly when those same books were probably confirming for his patients that he was no good for them.

This example is symptomatic of the turbulence and feuding which has been taking place in the social sciences, social welfare, psychiatry, social work and criminology since the 1960s. Theory and research into deviants, misfits, social inadequates, the disturbed, 'problem families', crooks, perverts, outcasts and oddballs took a sudden turn in that period. The question of what it is to be 'deviant', and what imagination it is which powers those who are called 'deviant', was raised in a critical form. Sometimes theory and research sided with the underdog deviant against his professional helpers and professional guardians. The question was posed whether these professionals were helping at all. And sometimes professionals were frightened by this turn of events, felt that it was not playing the game properly, and that it was mischievous, subversive, or even ignorant. Only rarely blessed with any kind of literate expression, these professional feuds were usually not written down and were passed on by gossip. But they were none the less real, and this book is an attempt to reach behind the written word and to make some of the problems which are posed for the field of deviance theory and social welfare articulate. In recent years the whole area has been spattered with question marks. This book addresses itself to those questions.

This is a book about *social practice* – specifically, about how social scientists, social workers, and so on, look at deviants and misfits. It is a social practice which consists not only of attempts to control, cure or correct deviants, but also of attempts to articulate the deviant's motives and to understand what the misfit's deviance says about the society in which he lives. This book is therefore about how theories are developed (by men), how they are read and received (by men), and how they might be implemented in action (by men). Theories do not fall out of the sky, and it is an assumption of this book that the men who make them are not at all unlike other men and that they share with other men blind-spots, weaknesses and ecstasies. If that is so, and if I am therefore also not unlike other men, it is wise to make a few preliminary confessions.

First, I have worked as a social worker, and I do not believe that it is possible to have done that and rest easy with theory and research which remains at the level of speculation without touching the day-to-day unhappiness of people called 'deviants' and 'clients'. Given that, however, the conclusion of the book is awkward, for it does not provide immediate solutions to social problems. Instead it arrives at the conclusion that there are no immediate solutions to social problems, at least without a comprehensive re-ordering of priorities in this society which is called a civilised society. It also concludes that social welfare is biased and unhinged in its appraisal of the deviant question, and this book is an attempt to open and continue certain areas of debate which might correct that bias. In order to do that it is necessary to forget for a moment the unhappiness of the deviant and explore the unhappiness of the professional.

The beginning of a book is perhaps an odd place to state its conclusion. But perhaps not: it has the advantage of announcing to the reader what he is letting himself in for. A common conclusion of studies in the social sciences is for the author to write that 'more research is needed'. But that kind of conclusion has become something of a bad joke and it is not my conclusion. That kind of conclusion should be recognised for what it is: a way of dodging the problem of arriving at a conclusion, burying one's head in the uncertainty which only scholars understand. Also, as a way of ending – or abandoning – a study, an appeal for more research begs another question: research for what? There is no shortage of research on deviance. The problem often is simply to know what to do with it. Commonly all the busy practitioner can do is forget it and 'get on with the job', and commonly all the researcher or academic can do is recognise that the conclusion of someone else's studies is not his own conclusion.

The reasons for this are simple enough. All conclusions embody theories and ideologies, and no amount of conclusive evidence can sway a reader from a theory or ideology which he finds persuasive. And for someone engaged in the practice of deviance-control, theories and ideologies which tickle his occupational defences or injure his professional self-esteem are not amusing. His job is not to juggle one theory off against another, and a theory which subverts his professional view of the world can give him little more than a headache.

Men choose from theories what they find useful, and they ditch what they cannot use or what discomforts them. They also sometimes see things in social-science literature which are not there. That is to say, they 'read in' things. The arguments of this book presuppose something of the nature of this relationship between what men read and how men read. They presuppose a theory of the relationship between social-scientific endeavour and literary endeavour, and a notion of social science *as* literature. My attitude is that men, as participants in the social world, do not read social-science books as they might read the theorems, proofs and calculus of mathematics. The marks which social-scientific literature leaves in its readers are partly made by implicit and unacknowledged literary and poetic devices. I do not assume that this is either a good thing or a bad thing; I simply assume that it is the case. Social science makes its mark when attitudes within its own texts makes links with, and resonate with, attitudes within its audience; but these attitudes are, nevertheless, rarely explicitly rendered. They are part of the attempt by men and women, through reading and writing, to come to terms with the experience of their lives.

The Deviant Imagination assumes and sets out to establish that learning about deviance and social control is not simply a question of memorising the formulae, aetiologies and prognoses of certain kinds of deviant act. Rather it involves an imaginative enterprise as to how men construct and conceive notions of social order, reasonableness, familiarity and events which go bump in the order of things. It is part of what Paulo Freire calls 'a difficult apprenticeship in naming the world'. The study of how and why men do things other than what they are supposed to do, and how other men think of this disorderly conduct, is also a study of how things might be other than they are. It touches a delicate nerve of the relationship between freedom and social order. In a strict sense each man must dream up his version of the world for himself and each man must find a place for his own deviant imagination.

This book would not have been started, and certainly not finished, without other people's encouragement, nagging, advice and love. For different things at different times I wish to thank Peter Barham, Irwin Epstein, Colin Fletcher, Anita Guiton, Derek Guiton, Laurie Hemingway, Geoff Mungham, Anne Murcott, the National Deviancy Conference, Norma Powell, Shaie Selzer, Ian Taylor, Jan Thomas and Paul Walton. There are, of course, many other people who have given help and friendship and they will know who they are. But there is nothing bad in this book which is the fault of any of these people, and if I didn't listen to them there is only one person to blame.

Cardiff, Wales   GEOFF PEARSON
June 1974

PART I
THE SMELL OF THEORY

'the recourse to "misunderstanding" as a means of explaining the effect of intellectual phenomena does not lead very far. It presupposes that there is an intrinsic substance, often simply equated with the author's intention, which exists independently of its historical fate; such a substance is in principle hardly identifiable. . . . Misunderstandings are the medium in which the incommunicable is communicated.'

Theodore W. Adorno

1

INTRODUCTION: TRADITIONAL IMAGES OF THE MISFIT

What follows is an account by Evans-Pritchard of the birth of a deformed child among the Nuer:

> one morning my Nuer servant Nhial came in some excitement to tell me that a woman of his village, where we were staying, had given birth to a hippopotamus and a male child, both dead. It was too late to see what had happened, but I was told that the hippopotamus had been placed in a nearby stream and the child, being a twin and therefore in Nuer eyes a sort of bird, had been placed in a tree. . . . The reason given for this particular twin-birth was that the woman's husband had killed several hippopotamuses and they had revenged themselves on him by stamping their likeness on one of the twins . . . the totemic mentality of the Nuer inclined them at once to perceive the form of a hippopotamus in what we would have regarded merely as a monstrosity.[1]

Commenting on this story, in fact not too accurately, Mary Douglas has this to say:

> when a monstrous birth occurs, the defining limits between humans and animals may be threatened. If a monstrous birth can be labelled an event of a peculiar kind the categories can be restored. So the Nuer treat monstrous births as baby hippo-potamuses, accidentally born to humans and, with this labelling, the appropriate action is clear. They gently lay them in the river where they belong.[2]

If we accept these comments, here a culture deals in an effort-less manner with a piece of contaminating evil. Unlike the Nuer we have no stream in which to lay events which go bump in the order of things. The relationship between deviance and conformity in urban-industrial civilisation is mediated by the highly complex machinery of the welfare state, the channel of the mass-communi-cations system and by theories which stress one cause or another of deviant happenings. Deviance is by no means entirely secularised, however, by this civilising vision and it still commands a place in moral discourse. It is possible to see relics of demon possession in theories of mental disorder, for example, and hang-overs from the idea of hereditary curse in genetic and chromosomal theories of deviance. In common-sense terms deviance, even in this civilisation which announces itself as the culmination of ration-ality, has monstrous qualities which can puncture that rationality and generate powerful emotions in sane, normal, conforming Everyman. If one attended only to the imagery of the mass media, for example, it would not be difficult to conclude that misfits and deviants were truly monstrous.

The face of the deviant changes over time. At this moment it is the terrorist bombers who have captured the imagination, in particular through the menacing face of the 'teeny bomber'. At other times it has been the drug addict, gangster, Hell's Angel, Mod, Rocker, Skinhead, pornography entrepreneur, football hooligan, racketeer, protesting student, spiv, high-jacker, mugger (and his elder brother the 'cosh boy'), people who steal babies from prams or men on strike. These are the cadres of the dramatic incident. They have been aptly called the 'folk devils' of our culture.[3] They appear, or are staged, very often as youth, and their activities have the character of scandal or menace.

At their back is a shadowy reserved army of misfits: mental patients, sexual deviants, petty thieves, 'delinquents' of all kinds, problem families, deprived children, unemployables ('shirkers', 'skivers' and the 'work-shy'), school truants, baby-bashers, alco-holics, etc. These are the bread and butter of the welfare profes-sions. And behind them, possibly more numerous and even more spectral, lie the 'non-deviant' deviants: licence dodgers, after-hours drinkers, parking offenders, drunken drivers, small-time tax-fiddlers, men who take home 'cabbage' from their work or, perhaps, their barbiturate-dependent wives.

I do not intend to foist an elaborate classification scheme upon the reader, which might force some appearance of order onto the heterogeneity of 'deviance'. In fact the list of misfits which I have offered does not even begin to test the limits of what might legitimately be regarded as 'deviance'. Simmons, for example, provides an amusing list of responses to a small research study which asked the question 'Who's deviant?':

The sheer range of responses predictably included homosexuals, prostitutes, drug addicts, radicals and criminals. But it also included liars, career women, Democrats, reckless drivers, atheists, Christians, suburbanites, the retired, young folks, card players, bearded men, artists, pacifists, priests, prudes, hippies, straights, girls who wear makeup, the President, conservatives, integrationists, executives, divorcees, perverts, motorcycle gangs, smart-alec students, know-it-all professors, modern people, and Americans.[4]

Deviance, Simmons concludes, 'is in the eye of the beholder'. There is a point, however, beyond which this exercise becomes trivial and Simmons seems to have crossed that limit: to call a card player, or an American, 'deviant' is to do something different than to apply the word to a prostitute, a rapist or a reckless driver. This kind of play with the word 'deviant' is a way of relating to the world in which men live. It is a stance which subsides into what gets called 'cultural relativism'. It suggests that all men are from some point of view 'deviant', but also from other points of view 'normal'. It implies that men live in a highly diverse, pluralistic society where there are many ways of going about life, and that from different perspectives different things are 'deviant' and different things are 'normal'. Depending where one starts out from this can either come as a startling insight or a commonplace truism.

Cultural relativism appears to be a very contemporary sentiment which overturns the idea that deviance is something locked away inside the heads of a few 'wierdos' or 'oddballs'. It is also, significantly, a sentiment which has surfaced recently, at the same time, historically, as deviants began to speak out on their own behalf through various client organisations, a move which has been called the 'client-rebellion'.[5] The purpose of this book is to take hold of this cluster of sentiments, render their implications explicit, and trace some of their connections with the traditional image of the misfit. We will not go very far without sketching some of the general features of this traditional image.

CONSTANCY AND DIVERSITY IN THE TRADITIONAL IMAGE

What is usually meant by the term 'deviant' is a place where impropriety, illegality and behaviour which is unexpected (and perhaps tinged with evil) come together. It is understood as an opaque mass compounded out of inadequacy, weakness of will, broken homes, the stresses of the city and 'modern living', poor judgement, lax discipline at home and school, the influences of television, working mothers, bad companions, illnesses, and so on.

There is a bewildering complexity among the theories which are thrown up to account for deviance, although this is not in any way peculiar to this particular academic domain. In his auto-biography, for example, Stephen Spender describes a common enough feature of how higher knowledge is thought, and how its growth and development is packaged in certain forms of thought:

> I do not know whether it is usual to teach philosophy as I was taught it. In the first lesson we were told that J. S. Mill's *Utilitarianism* meant the greatest happiness of the greatest number and that, for Mill, happiness was the criterion of moral value. In the next tutorial we were told that Mill was wrong because he had forced himself into the position where, according to his criterion, a very happy pig might be considered morally better than a moderately happy human being. Obviously this was outrageous. . . . Next please. The next philosopher is Locke. We were told what he thought and why he was wrong. Next please. Hume. Hume was wrong also. Then Kant. Kant was wrong, but he was also so difficult to understand that one could not be so sure of catching him out.
>
> This might be described as the Obstacle Race way of teaching philosophy. The whole field of human thought is set out with logical obstructions and the students watch the philosophers race around it. Some of them get further than others but they fall sooner or later into the traps which language sets for them.

It soon occurred to me that it was useless to enter a field where such distinguished contestants had failed.[6]

If we replace the names of philosophers with the names of criminologists, psychiatrists, social workers and sociologists, we have here a good picture of how the field of deviance traditionally conceives of itself and its development. Different sub-schools (biological, psychological, sociological) will construct a different course of obstacles, but the form is the same – with one important difference: progress is thought to be more evident in deviance theory than in philosophy. Thus, we are persuaded to think of early pre-scientific and moralistic conceptions of deviance being replaced in a steady fashion with scientific and objective theories. Also, we are persuaded to think of a linear course of development from theoretical dogmatism which stressed one-sidedly the importance of biology, psychology or social environment in the causation of deviance, towards more 'rounded' theories of multi-factorial causation. And there is a certain element of truth in all this.[7] What can be said without any hesitation is that in the gaze of social science deviance has been steadily displaced from the realm of moral discourse.

Without saying anything of the conclusions which they reach (or the questions which they leave unanswered) we can state the different emphases in different theories of deviance.[8] Some of those on the market stress heredity, chromosomal abnormalities and genetic predispositions. Others emphasise learning processes, conditionability or imitation. There are theories which focus on the deprivations of childhood, early traumatic experiences, family background and other immediate influences on the development of personality, motivation and behaviour. Other perspectives broaden the vision by enquiring into community, neighbourhood, ethnic or class dimensions of deviant conduct.

These different theories do not fall together into a unified whole. Some clash openly; others admit points of conciliation between themselves. Researchers poke around in their own corner, and advocates of one position are often quite ignorant of other theoretical views. And always research and practice are geared to assumptions which are specific to each theoretical standpoint. Results and data from one perspective, therefore, because of different assumptions and emphases, cannot be matched against (let alone welded *to*) results and data from another theoretical sub-school. Results, data, research, practice methods, theories pile on top of each other. In 1968 Bannister estimated that by the late 1950s 5000 academic papers had been written *on the single topic of schizophrenia,* and that since 1960 papers had been published at the rate of 300 per year with a growth rate of 10 per cent per annum.[9] Quantity does not dissolve, however, into quality and sometimes it seems that it has all become a game.

Undergirding this great diversity of explanation there are formidable constancies which must be engaged if the traditional image of the deviant is to be understood. These steady rhythms are what Alvin Gouldner calls the 'background assumptions' or 'domain assumptions' of theory:

Deliberately formulated social theories, we might say with deliberate oversimplification, contain at least two distinguishable elements. One element is the explicitly formulated assumptions, which may be called 'postulations'. But they contain a good deal more. They also contain a second set of assumptions that are unpostulated and unlabelled, and these I will term 'background assumptions'. I call them background assumptions because, on the one hand, they provide the background out of which the postulations in part emerge and, on the other hand, not being expressly formulated, they remain in the background of the theorist's attention . . . they are, as it were, 'silent partners' in the theoretical enterprise.[10]

'Domain assumptions' Gouldner continues 'are the background assumptions applied only to members of a single domain; they are, in effect, the metaphysics of a [theoretical] domain.'[11] Gouldner gives as examples of domain assumptions about the relationship of man and society 'dispositions to believe that men are rational or irrational; that society is precarious or fundamentally stable; that social problems will correct themselves without planned intervention; that human behaviour is unpredictable; that man's true humanity resides in his feelings and sentiments'.[12] It is this deep structure of social theory, Gouldner contends, which often governs the career of a theory. We can say that these root assumptions and root metaphors are commonly one of the most powerful dimensions of a theoretical construction; they are the crude resonances from which the more subtly worked, but superficial, face of theory derives as mere harmonics.

Theories of deviance demonstrate a remarkable ahistoricity. In texts covering more than a hundred years and different cultures the same themes and preoccupations recur. Sometimes the ahistorical character of texts simply reflects erroneous thought, as when in social-work texts quotations from Octavia Hill, the Charity Organisation Society of the nineteenth century, or Mary Richmond writing in the 1920s, are snatched out of their sociohistorical context in order to make some point in the present world. There is also, however, a rationality to this: writers are responding to the same rhythmic constances which *do* cut across history and across different theoretical tendencies.

The root constances of deviance theories represent themselves as a series of alternatives – for example, whether man is essentially good or essentially evil; or whether civilisation civilises men or distorts their spontaneous nature. Here another set of background assumptions concerns the question of simplicity and complexity in social life. They often present themselves as a contest between the corruption of city life and the innocence of the village green. Equally viable, but less fashionable, is a comparison of civilised urbanity as against rural idiocy and vagabondage.

The problem of how to phrase the relationships between social deviance and social order, reasonableness, unreasonableness and conformity is another recurrent theme. It poses itself as whether or not the misfit is to blame for nonconforming acts; or how to phrase the community's response to its deviant members: punishment, reform, care, isolation, destruction or public display and pillory.[13] A dominant constancy in this set of questions is to assume that deviance is a problem of deviants only: something to do with 'them' and not 'us'. Its opposing tendency is a recognition that there is also an inner voice which speaks of deviance in the dreams, reveries and entertainments of Everyman. It is difficult to articulate this relationship, but what is seen as monstrous is also embraced as a tasty feature of everyday life, at least during 'time off'. Some sports are thinly disguised ceremonies of violence: for example, Roland Barthes has de-coded the complex moral spectacle of wrestling.[14] The exciting portrayals of murder, robbery, sex-violence and trickery in popular literature, film and television are best-seller mixtures. And the dramatisation of sexual deviation, domestic violence and the loose living of movie stars and tycoons in the yellow press is also big business.

It is fanciful, therefore, to think of deviance only as something alien. The calculations would be difficult to make, but possibly in our culture less time, money and effort are spent controlling and minimising deviance than in promoting deviant enterprise and consuming the thrills second hand. The traditional image of the misfit, however, does not illuminate these matters. There the deviant imagination is firmly in its place. The boundaries between our orderly, reasonable world and the misfit's waywardness are secure: the relationship of the 'straight' world to deviance is understood only as one of many attempts at rational control.

A final set of constancies which insert themselves in the grid of deviance theories is whether to conceive of man as the creator of his collective life, or as the creature of his circumstances. And a vital, related ambiguity is whether the misfit is to be thought of as *this* man attempting to live *this* life under *these* specific circumstances, involving a set of choices which lead him outside the norm; or whether the misfit is essentially unlike other men, someone who is visited by a dark and terrible happening which thrusts him into lawlessness, immorality and unnaturalness.

These can be recognised as moral alternatives and in the traditional image of the misfit the dominant emphasis is to regard deviance as something to be purged: something pathological or under-socialised; something to be explained away in thought and swept away in practice.

THE DEVIANT VOICE, MORAL DISCOURSE AND CULTURAL CRITICISM

Theories of deviance rarely interrogate their own moral–political roots. Nevertheless, technical arguments about genes versus mothering versus the influences of social environment are often a play with shadows and the shadows of the debate are these same moral–political questions. Technical controversies over 'genes versus environment', for example, often give a sort of scientific sanctuary to questions such as 'Can deviants help it?' In different ways, therefore, the 'postulations' of the field of deviance contain (but also wrap up and make unanswerable) the dominant rhythms of the background assumptions.

In such a wide and dispersed area, however, it is difficult to attempt a characterisation without it turning into a bad caricature. When one says, therefore, that the emphasis in approaches to deviance has been to view it as an under-socialised waste product of civilisation, that is not the whole truth. The fundamental theoretical contributions of Freud's psychoanalysis, Durkheim's sociology, and even a behaviourism such as Skinner's, engage in explicit moral discourse.[15] Deviance is also viewed here as a realm of cultural criticism: lawlessness, neurosis, unreasonableness and nonconformity are grasped, although in different ways, as forms of unwitting protest and escape from the irrationalities of the dominant social order.

This theme of cultural criticism is carried fitfully throughout the traditional image of the deviant by a number of writers. In the 1940s, for example, Donald Taft argued that crime was an *inevitable* complement of American culture and a critical comment on that culture. In a society which emphasised competitiveness, acquisitiveness and success, and where the cultural accomplishment of equality and democracy was only 'nominal' Taft wrote that, 'such a culture must expect considerable crime which can be attributed to its own inherent qualities. In this sense we get the criminals we deserve'.[16] Willem Bonger is another, less well-known criminologist, whose work represents crime in a critical light against the 'egoistic' traits of capitalist societies.[17] Taft and Bonger were not alone. One of the general features of the complex structure of sentiments which their work reflects upon is highlighted by William Empson (who is not a criminologist): 'So far as the person described is outside society because too poor for its benefits he is independent . . . and can be a critic of society; so far as he is forced by this into crime he is the judge of the society that judges him.'[18] Within certain forms of moral discourse the misfit can rise above society which he is normally thought to be below.

Paul Goodman's *Growing Up Absurd* is a more recent expression of this cultural criticism, which fixes its attention on the problem of troublesome youth. Goodman notes that most authorities explain youthful deviance by stressing a failure in socialisation: 'They say that background conditions have interrupted socialisation and must be improved. And, not enough effort has been made to guarantee belonging, there must be better bait or punishment.'[19] Goodman, however, proposes a reversal of tactics in attempting to understand why young people do not feel that they belong in society:

> But perhaps there has *not* been a failure of communication. Perhaps the social message has been communicated clearly to the young men and is unacceptable.
>
> In this book I shall therefore take the opposite tack and ask, 'Socialisation to what? to what dominant society and available culture?' And if this question is asked, we must at once ask the other question, 'Is the harmonious organisation to which the young are inadequately socialised, perhaps against human nature, or not worthy of human nature, and *therefore* there is difficulty in growing up?' If this is so, the disaffection of the young is profound and it will not be finally remediable by better techniques of socialising. Instead, there will have to be changes in our society and its culture, so as to meet the appetites and capacities of human nature, in order to grow up.[20]

Goodman poses questions which have relevance to the whole problem of the status of the deviant imagination, and his work is perhaps the first indication of a new mood in the field of deviance which in the last ten or fifteen years has resurrected the spirit of cultural criticism across this area. Also the tone is new and different: it proposes that deviance is thought of not only as a capitulation to a bad environment, but also as a form of active protest against it.

The purpose of this book is to take hold of these new developments in deviance theory – criminology, social work, psychiatry – and to work through some of their assumptions. The book falls into two parts. The first maps out the scope and direction of the new deviance theories – that is, the 'anti-psychiatries' of Laing and Szasz and the new 'misfit sociologies' of the 1960s. But it offers more than a simple exposition: it also makes explicit the relationships between these new moves and the nature of the social world within which they arise. Most of these developments were not theoretical innovations of the period; they are old themes which are re-worked in a new climate of opinion. They represent a new and emerging consciousness among men and women in the professional world of deviance, and they should be seen as attempts to give voice to new and developing experiences of men in their world.

The first part of the book, then, turns a critical eye on some of the deformities of cultural style and theoretical style which were thrown up in the 1960s. These are also chapters which are intrigued by the question which is asked everywhere and never satisfactorily answered: 'What *were* the 1960s about?' The 1960s saw a great outrush of madness in urban-industrial civilisation, and the new deviance theories are symptomatic of a serious outburst of madness in social thought. Roger Bastide is one writer who has attempted to understand the nature of this recent (and easily forgotten) period of human history. His approach is stumbling; but then it is difficult ground.

The dimunition of social problems – social progress, that is – is thought of largely as a control of irrationality, including the irrationality of deviance. Bastide explores the antithesis of this position and he attempts to articulate the unspeakable relationships between social change, human imagination, all that the politics of progress conjure up – rationality, philanthropy, science, calculation, reasonableness – and madness. In an introduction to *Les Sciences de la Folie* – a collection of essays on nineteenth-century social philosophies – he writes that the book takes its point of departure, and inspiration, from the May events of Paris in 1968.[21] Bastide hints at the relationship between the romantic movement of the nineteenth century, the romanticism of the contemporary 'New Left' and the 'rediscovery' of madness in the 1960s: that is, the rediscovery of a 'method' in madness and other forms of deviant conduct. The first romanticism arises within the formation of industrial capitalism in the industrial revolution. The second romanticism, Bastide continues, comes at the time of capitalism's 'second revolution' which he calls '*la société d'abondance*' or '*la société de consommation*'.[22] The two mutations of the first and second industrial revolutions, he argues, produce strictly analogous results in social thought. An analogy is only an analogy, but there is certainly a contemporary ring to Fourier's pronouncement in this earlier period that if a science governed by reasonableness (*sagesse*) does not rid us of poverty and unhappiness, then give us 'sciences dictated by madness'.[23]

By way of introduction, then, or even perhaps as a warning, we can say that those aspects of contemporary social work, deviance theory and psychiatry which are discussed in the first part of this book have romantic qualities; they are also sometimes quite millenarial. The second part takes up some issues which are deposited by these swings in contemporary thought and practice. It looks at how the moral–political dimensions of deviance are handled in contemporary social-work theory; at the origins of the modern deviance-welfare field in the massive social changes of the industrial revolution and the rising domination of the factory system; and at how some notion of 'the simple life' is so often thought of as the only lasting solution to the deviant question. Taken as a whole, the book is part of an attempt to reappraise the nature of deviance theory and social welfare, and to return it where it belongs: out of the disguise of professional mystique and back into the difficult area of how men construct their lives together.

2

MEDICINE DE-FROCKED

Medicine is a highly legitimate business and its professional empire has colonised many strictly non-medical fields of interest. One of the most important, if not *the* most important, development in the field of deviance has been the 'medicalisation' and 'psychiatricisation' of social problems: crime, it is said, is an illness; youthful unrest is a maturational phase; political dissent is the result of personality quirks of 'mindless militants'; a poor employment record flows from a disorder of character; poor families, or 'problem familes', are low on something called 'interpersonal maturity'. Some critics will say that the worst thing to happen to deviance theory was medicine.

The power of medicine has carried great weight in the control of deviance, and vital to its authority is the fact that medicine – and all its associated vocabulary of 'treatment', 'diagnosis', 'therapy', 'sickness', 'illness' and 'cure' – is judged to be morally neutral. If deviance and social problems can be wound up in this neutral, scientific rhetoric, then uneasy consciences can be put to sleep: action taken against the misfit, which might in any other light appear morally ambiguous, is beyond all moral ambiguity when it is called 'treatment' or 'therapy'. In his book *The Child Savers* Anthony Platt notes that

> There has been a shift in the last fifty years or so in official policies concerning crime. The warrant has shifted from one emphasising the criminal nature of delinquency to the 'new humanism', which speaks of disease, illness, contagion, and the like. The emergence of the medical warrant is of considerable significance, since it is a powerful rationale for organising social action in the most diverse behavioural aspects of our society.[1]

In recent years there has been a move against this medical domination of deviance. It finds one of its most vigorous expressions in the school of 'anti-psychiatry' surrounding Laing, Cooper and others, and in the work of Thomas Szasz. Any assault on medicine is bound to be judged heretical by the liberal conscience since medicine has come to embody so much of the ethos of the humane, liberal approach to deviance control. In exploring some of the literature which has reversed this tendency to re-define moral problems (deviance) as technical problems (illness) this chapter engages this liberal, humane approach and its contradictions.

But if psychiatry can be said to have captured a hold on the liberal imagination, it does not drive away our common language which embodies quite different sentiments: 'nut doctor', 'funny farm', 'trick cyclist', 'loony bin', 'shrink'. The tenacity of this common-sense jargon alerts us to the danger and falsity of accepting a professional world-view (in this case a medical world-view) as the only possible view of that profession's activities. Psychiatry is not an unambiguous instrument of goodwill from all standpoints. Piedmont and Downey have shown, for example, that changes and liberalisations of psychiatric thought have not influenced public conceptions of what psychiatry is about; only mental-health professionals have seen these changes. The trick, as in the story of the Emperor's new suit of clothes, is to know what you are going to see, and only then will you 'see' it.[2] Insiders to professional codes and practices see revolutions in thought and humanisation in practice where Everyman sees problems of morality, propriety, offensive conduct, bunches of keys, asylum walls, and danger.

Much, if not all, of the literature discussed in this chapter is an assault on psychiatric practice and psychiatric theory. The implications reach much further than this, however, into the whole area of social welfare. Sometimes reflecting a tendency in our culture to medicalise everything, sometimes as an attempt to feed off the authority of the well-established professions, the 'semi-professions' – and in particular social work – adopt a quasi-medical terminology and thereby make a claim to a full-bodied professionalism with technical competence. It may be seen as a sort of magical appropriation of the legitimacy of medicine, but its social consequences are none the less real. And to the extent that they adopt a model of deviance as some kind of sickness, the whole of the social-welfare apparatus – social workers, psychologists, the courts, health visitors, the penal system, residential institutions for the elderly or for troublesome youth, probation officers – become the object of criticism of what is called 'anti-psychiatry'.*

'ANTI-PSYCHIATRY': SANITY AND CONFORMITY.

At the outset we stumble across the fact that if we wish to confront and understand the writings of Laing, Cooper and others who are called anti-psychiatrists, we must confront not only what is written, but also how it is read. There are a number of possible readings of the anti-psychiatry oeuvre. First, Laing offers a way of looking at mad, and specifically schizophrenic, experience: a way of looking which gives the schizophrenic a voice and attempts to untangle the code of his strange utterances. This way of looking does not surrender itself to the traditional psychiatric viewpoint, which regards these utterances as incomprehensible and invalid. Laing can be taken to be showing also the rudiments of a theory of schizophrenia which makes craziness the product of, or response to, social and family contexts which are 'schizophrenogenic'. In this sense, the schizophrenic is a victim of irrational social structures (family, hospital, school, and so on). Another reading of Laing takes him to be offering a theory of therapy which encourages dialogue between helper and helped, and challenges a rigid differentiation of roles in psychiatric practice. Here a critique of the psychiatric invalidation of deviant experience in practice complements the critique of invalidation in theory.[3] There is also a persistent theoretical endeavour in anti-psychiatry to render the structure of intra-personal experience *inter*-personally; that is, as a

* The term 'anti-psychiatry' was coined, I think, by David Cooper in the early 1960s, who practised it in what he called an 'anti-hospital' (Cooper, 1970). Strictly speaking it refers to the work of Laing, Cooper, Esterson and a number of others. Often it is employed more loosely to include Thomas Szasz and some of Erving Goffman's work. Peter Sedgwick (1972) also includes Michel Foucault. In my opinion Foucault's project is quite different from that of anti-psychiatry, and I exclude him from consideration here. Foucault's researches are hardly influential in the field of deviance, psychiatry and social work except in a scrambled form. I trace some of his ideas in a later chapter.

going-on *between* persons.[4] A further theme, made most explicit
in *The Politics of Experience*, is a critique of normality and
conformity in urban-industrial society. And a final reading,
related to this last example, is the idea of schizophrenic experience as 'hyper-sanity'; that is the idea of the schizophrenic as
a sort of cultural critic who points the way to a different and
liberating form of consciousness. Taken together these various
threads make it possible to read this anti-psychiatry scheme as an
attempt at a theoretical understanding which connects madness,
and deviant forms of experience, with social and political structure. And it is to this 'complete reading' of anti-psychiatry that
we must address ourselves, and not to a fragmented appreciation
of Laing-the-scientist, Laing-the-family-therapist, Laing-the-poet,
Laing-the-guru, or Laing-the-heretic.

At the root there is a flaw in the structure of the sentiments of
anti-psychiatry, and we can best approach this through the main
thrust of Laing's work, which is itself two-fold: first the family
theory of schizophrenia, and second the illumination of schizophrenic experience.

The family theory is apparently straightforward enough. It
derives in a large measure from the work and writings of family
therapists and family researchers: for example, Lyman Wynne,
Don Jackson, Theodore Lidz, and the communications theory of
Gregory Bateson.[5] Given the different theoretical and conceptual
armouries of these writers, they arrive at a surprisingly uniform
set of conclusions: in each instance crazy behaviour and experience is seen as something orchestrated to family contexts which
are themselves, in some sort of way, crazy. Communications and
personal exchanges in these families are described as blurred,
distorted, confused and confusing. There are reports in this
literature of therapists and researchers who feel that they are
going crazy themselves if they remain too long in the families of
psychotics.[6] Ross Speck takes matters further than most through
demonstrations of how psychosis can be a function of disharmony
and strain in whole social networks comprising thirty or forty
people and including family, extended kin, friends, neighbours,
workmates, employers, local shopkeepers, priests, and other
persons who are significant in the life of the identified patient.[7]
Speck engages this whole social system therapeutically with a
technique which he calls 'network therapy'.

These theories of the family origins of mental illness explode the medical model of mental disorder, which sees the problem as located firmly *inside* the patient (and nowhere else), and they locate the source of the 'sickness' in social and familial structures. Theories of family therapy, therefore, embody powerful moral imperatives as to where the action is, and as to how psychiatry traditionally masks social and family conflict through its focus on the individual patient.[8]

Anti-psychiatry makes a significant contribution to this social approach to mental illness. Laing and Esterson, for example, show how the crazy experience of eleven schizophrenic women can be seen to have some intelligibility if attention is given to what is going on in their family contexts.[9] And Morton Schatzman, in a re-analysis of Freud's famous study of Schreber's paranoia, shows how Schreber's symptoms correspond remarkably with his father's beliefs about child-rearing.[10] Paranoid people, to put the matter simply, might be responding to actual persecution in their families : there is a certain method in madness.

Anti-psychiatry's family theory, then, has close neighbours in some kinds of clinical psychology and the social psychology of the family. Its understanding of the nature of schizophrenic experience, however, stands alone. Although not quite : for anti-psychiatry's sentiments are formed within the *zeitgeist*, the political mood, of the late 1960s, and any approach to the work of Laing and Cooper which does not understand this will understand very little.

Stated very briefly, anti-psychiatry's position is that the requirements of normality, conformity and reasonableness – in a word 'mental health' – are a suffocation which stifles, blocks, and distorts the expression of a fully human consciousness. Learning to live at ease with urban-industrial society requires that men forget and repress much of their experience of a disturbing and destructive social system. And it requires that they bury much of their experience of their selves in the catechisms of conforming normality : being a 'good' boy; earning a steady living; bringing up a family quietly; consuming a properly regulated leisure-time; keeping one's nose to the grindstone. The abstract, joyless rationality of these notions of reasonableness leads anti-psychiatry to conclude that conforming men are lost souls.

Set against this, people who break-down or break-up might also be engaged in a break-through to a different and more complete experience of the self: mental illness is described as one way in which men and women disengage from the taken-for-granted routines of everyday life and undergo a disturbing self-reflection. This 'schizophrenic voyage', a voyage through inner space and time, is a perilous voyage in which it is easy to get lost. Psychiatrists who disturb this unwitting attempt to reconnoitre and reconstruct the self, with mind-flattening drug therapies, electroshocks, or psychotherapies which insist on conformity to outer (rather than inner) imperatives are, Laing insists, false healers. For, 'this voyage is not what we need to be cured of, but . . . it is itself a natural way of healing our own appalling state of alienation called normality'.[11] Therapies which interrupt the flow of the person through psychotic episodes simply leave him stranded at a point where he had disconnected himself from old patterns of normality without allowing the vital reconnections to occur. What is needed, then, is not a therapist, but a guide.

The 'schizophrenic voyage' can be recognised as a replica, at least in the way in which it is described, of the acid trip. Identical outcomes are proposed: a successful emergence from the voyage re-orientates and illuminates the self; a 'bad trip', on the other hand, can leave the person shattered, possibly for ever. In each case the outcome depends on the response of others: a careful guide can encourage break-through; a guide who tries to suppress and divert the alarming psychotic experience sponsors break-down.[12] Certain forms of meditation also act as a model for this psychotic self-exploration. David Cooper once described meditation as a form of 'armchair madness', and a number of similar novel healing techniques based on the encounter group, or the 'growth centre', utilise ideas culled from Eastern mysticism.[13] We cannot go far in this terrain without stumbling over some expression, or relic, of the 'counter-culture'.

If we extract the core from the sentiments of anti-psychiatry we are left with an unresolved contradiction: madness is at one and the same time both a product of a crazy, alienating family, *and* a legitimate, authentic mode of experiencing the world, which can heal. This contradiction and its influence can be traced throughout Laing's work. What is at issue in this contradiction is the relationship between madness, conformity and social structure; also the ways in which social institutional networks represent themselves, and insert themselves, at the level of individual experience. Anti-psychiatry, in other words, is reaching for a theoretical and practical synthesis of the *public* (or political) sphere and the *personal*. In a limited sense, it is the question of how the 'craziness' of the family of the psychotic relates to, and mediates, the 'craziness' of what Laing calls 'the total social world system':

> As we begin from micro-situations and work up to macro-situations we find that the apparent irrationality of behaviour on a small scale takes on a certain form of intelligibility when one sees it in context. One moves, for example, from the apparent irrationality of the single 'psychotic' individual to the intelligibility of that irrationality within the context of the family. The irrationality of the family in its turn must be placed within the context of its encompassing networks. These further networks must be seen within the context of yet larger organisations and institutions. These larger contexts do not exist out there on some periphery of social space: they pervade the interstices of all that is comprised by them.[14]

Within this scheme of interlocking irrationalities the traditional psychiatric strategy of invalidating the deviant's motives and experience as meaningless seems to serve specific functions within the structure of the system in which it occurs. . . . Hundreds of thousands of people are involved in this amazing political operation'.[15]

This is one aspect of anti-psychiatry's ambitious project to show how madness connects with social structure. Stated in a simple deterministic formula it would read: a crazy society increasingly drives people mad, and psychiatry conceals the fact. But Laing's is not a simple deterministic viewpoint. The 'madness' which our culture drives men into, in anti-psychiatry's view, is the strait-jacketed conformity of normal man, characterised by possessive individualism and a dream-like apathy which is likened to a hypnotic trance.[16] The 'madness' which psychiatry pays attention to, and discredits as meaningless sickness, is on the other hand embraced by anti-psychiatry as an unwitting attempt by a few to cleanse themselves, literally, of the wounds of civilisation.

The anti-psychiatry project, then, attempts to give voice to a

T.D.I.—B

politics of socialisation: that is, an account of how men are reared to conformity and how social inequalities, dominations, and intolerances are cultivated and maintained *within* individual consciousness. The schizophrenic stands as a symbol of how society handles individual perceptions of the world which differ from those of conforming man, and how it crushes dawning perceptions of how the world might be seen differently. Because he is different the schizophrenic becomes elevated to a semi-heroic status, both victim and critic of social systems; a victim who identifies in his irrationality the irrationality of the whole, and a hero who points to another rationality which is more completely human. This is a complexly structured sentiment, and the reader will find that its theme of the deviant as hero reappears throughout the field of deviance which this book elaborates. Part of the structure of its sentiment is the programme for the construction of a world which is both human and tolerant.

It is an easy matter to poke holes in this scheme, or even to make fun of it simply because it is so ambitious. But the relationship between institutional machinery and individual conformity (or deviance and social order) and how these are mediated through family, education, psychiatry, and the apparatus of the welfare state, is no joking matter. To understand both anti-psychiatry's strengths and weaknesses requires considerable effort. Indeed, to read Laing – especially when the reader's sympathies diverge from his – a reader must make himself or herself available in a rather special way; not only as a detached scientific–professional observer, but also as a participant in human affairs: critics who charge Laing with having *only* a poetic insight do him an injustice, but nevertheless get close to the bone. Taken as a whole anti-psychiatry raises the question of the deviant imagination: how and why people (including oneself) conform; how and why conformity is experienced (at least by some) as an impoverished life; how and why society conceals this question under a blanket of humane invalidation.

But this project does not realise itself in anti-psychiatry. The pieces do not fit together. In one of the most illuminating commentaries on Laing's work Richard Sennett describes what he calls an 'impasse' in anti-psychiatry's vision:

The analysis of schizophrenia on which Laing's work rests is that people are forced into what society calls insane behaviour when they try to take the world seriously; it is the essence of his argument that you do not become insane by some willful act or failure of your own. . . . [But] If I, a sane man, want to wake up, and I can't will myself into mental illness, what am I to do?[17]

Anti-psychiatry moves in, around, off, and back again onto this hook. For example, even though the claim of family therapy to our attention can only be understood as an insistence that certain kinds of family drive certain people mad, Laing is not happy to subscribe to these full aetiological implications. In a reply to critics in a new edition of *Sanity, Madness and the Family* Laing and Esterson write:

Eleven cases, it is said, all women, prove nothing. There are no controls. How do you sample your data? What objective, reliable rating scales have you employed? And so on. Such criticism would be justified if we had set out to test the hypothesis that the family is a pathogenic variable in the genesis of schizophrenia. But we did not set out to do this, and we have not claimed to have done so. We set out to illustrate by eleven examples that, if we look at some experience and behaviour without reference to family interactions, they may appear comparatively socially senseless, but that if we look at the same experience and behaviour in their original family context they are liable to make more sense.[18]

Laing has always been elusive and changeable on this point. One does not want to insist that an author stand still, but there is no indication of how one might de-code the flow and changes in his texts. In his 1961 preface to *The Self and Others* he writes:

The reader should remember . . . that I am not saying that other people *cause* madness, any more than a high hill can be the cause of heart failure in a sufferer from rheumatic heart disease. No aetiological theory of madness that I subscribe to is stated in this book.[19]

In a later, substantially re-written edition, which reaches a more positive emphasis on the family theory of schizophrenia at points, what is reprinted as 'Preface to the First Edition' is a totally re-written preface which omits these sentences altogether. In *The Politics of Experience*, where Laing's notion of schizophrenia as a healing voyage reaches its most mature expression, he nevertheless holds that schizophrenics are driven mad by the dominant structures of society:

> A child born today in the United Kingdom stands a ten times greater chance of being admitted to a mental hospital than to a university, and about one fifth of mental hospital admissions are diagnosed schizophrenic. This can be taken as an indication that we are driving our children mad more effectively than we are genuinely educating them. Perhaps it is our very way of educating them that is driving them mad.[20]

And elsewhere in that book, the 'hyper-sanity' of the schizophrenic is seen as the response of persons who are put in a double-bind checkmate: ' . . . it seems to us that *without exception* the experience and behaviour that gets labelled schizophrenic is *a special strategy that a person invents in order to live in an untenable situation*'.[21]

Laing is not simply being wayward or changeable. Anti-psychiatry's contradiction of the deviant-victim, who is also, somehow, a deviant-hero, expresses the central problem of the deviant imagination: whether to treat it as a lifeless, objectionable waste-product, or as an unlawful, odd, or even crazy mode of experience and conduct which makes a legitimate, albeit frightening, human point.

This ambiguity in anti-psychiatry's programme also echoes the contradictory plight of distressed and oppressed minorities who shout with the same voice, 'We're all right as we are, leave us alone!' *and* 'Take care of us; you've screwed us up – do something, we need your help!' In recent years a number of client organisations, or 'potential client' organisations, have formed in the United Kingdom and the United States. One thinks of the Gay Liberation Front and the various homosexual equality groups, the Child Poverty Action Group, Claimants' Unions, The Mental Patients' Union and the Mental Patients' Liberation Front, the PROP organisation (Preservation of the Rights of Prisoners), People Not Psychiatry, and the many 'community control' and 'neighbourhood control' programmes. These organisations are inevitably pinned on this contradiction, and only rarely do they avoid the ambiguous relationship to their own deviant status.

These ambiguities can be recognised as the other side of the liberal, humane approach to deviance and deviance-control. There the misfit must at one and the same time be held accountable for his actions, which are judged wrong *and* treated with compassion. The liberal-humane tradition is able to tolerate deviance only to the extent that it de-fuses its difference and labels it 'sickness'. The criminal, for example, can be treated with compassion only to the extent that 'he can't help it'. Gay people can just about be tolerated to the extent that their sexual bent is discredited as the result of bad genes, mothering which is 'too good', or in happy, uncondemning behaviourist terms as a fluke of conditioning 'which can soon be put right'. It is the same with crazy offensiveness, vagrancy, drug abuse, child neglect, and delinquency. There is a contradiction: *compassion* involves *invalidation* and to a large degree this contradiction is bound up with medical hegemony in the field of deviance. Medicine is the institution through which this contradiction is expressed in its most viable form; it shields the misfit from harsh punishment and abuse, while denying the authenticity or rationality in his action. The revolt of antipsychiatry is a revolt against the contradiction of humane psychiatric invalidation, but to the extent that the revolt of antipsychiatry only succeeds in reproducing these contradictions in an inverted form one must make the effort to understand why.

THOMAS SZASZ: HERESY IN THE THERAPEUTIC STATE

Laing and the anti-psychiatrists are not just proposing another theory of schizophrenia. Their work involves a confrontation with the medical–scientific viewpoint in psychiatric theory and practice. Thomas Szasz, often footnoted in the anti-psychiatry corpus, approaches the same question in a more direct fashion. If Laing has drifted around the terrain to which he stakes a claim, Szasz has ground the same axe relentlessly over ten years and nearly as many books.[22] Unlike the other anti-psychiatrists he does not take on psychiatry via a critique of conformity, but through a study of its diagnostic practices, its logic, and its role in political trials, assessments of criminal responsibility and welfare reform.

His point can be stated simply: the concept of 'mental illness' is a metaphor which approaches the status of a myth. Psychiatry is a moral–political con game, which confronts and re-arranges moral dilemmas by passing dud, pseudo-scientific cheques:

> Our adversaries are not demons, witches, fate, or mental illness. We have no enemy that we can fight, exorcise, or dispel by 'cure'. What we do have are problems in living – whether these be biologic, economic, political, or sociopsychological . . . mental illness is a myth, whose function is to disguise and thus render more palatable the bitter pill of moral conflicts in human relations.[23]

Szasz often seems to be misunderstood on this point. 'In asserting that there is no such thing as mental illness', he writes, 'I do not deny that people have problems coping with life and each other.'[24] His argument is that problems of human conduct have a moral and political character which is masked by psychiatric labels, and that medical terminology is quite inappropriate in the sphere of human conduct. In *The Manufacture of Madness*, for example, Szasz quotes another psychiatrist, Karl Menninger, who writes on the subject of homosexuality: 'We cannot, like Gide, extol homosexuality. We do not, like some, *condone* it. We regard it as a *symptom* with all the functions of other symptoms . . . '.[25] Szasz objects to this, and he insists that Menninger's choice of words gives the game away. He asks: what is there to 'condone', or not 'condone', if homosexuality is merely a symptom? Psychiatrists would not talk of 'condoning' the spots of measles or the fever of pneumonia. The word 'symptom' is a deception which conceals a hidden moral judgement about the propriety of homosexual conduct. Similarly, the complete vocabulary is the litany of the secular priests of the Therapeutic 'disease', 'doctor', 'patient', 'hospital' – is misplaced in psychiatry and obscures the moral–political grounds of psychiatric practice. The psychiatrist, Szasz argues, is a moral agent. His technical vocabulary is the litany of the secular priests of the Therapeutic State. Using homosexuality as a paradigm for the nature of psychiatric judgement Szasz writes:

> My contention [is] that the psychiatric perspective on homosexuality is but a thinly disguised replica of the religious

perspective that it displaced, and that efforts to 'treat' this kind of conduct medically are but thinly disguised methods for suppressing it. . . . [The psychiatrist's] medical role is but a cloak for that of the moralist and social engineer.[26]

Szasz does not object to the fact that there are moralists and social engineers, but he does object to the way in which psychiatry passes off moral enterprise as 'objective', scientific medicine. And to the extent that psychiatric forms of thought increasingly mask what are political judgements, he warns that 'although we may not know it we have, in our day, witnessed the birth of the Therapeutic State'.[27]

Some examples of what Szasz is getting at in this far-reaching claim will clarify matters. At the microscopic level of human intercourse, for example, he points to the way in which human difficulties of satisfying relationships between men and women are boiled down to a technological 'psychiatric-sexual myth' of simultaneous orgasm. This, he writes, 'is useful for fostering feelings of sexual inadequacy and personal inferiority. It is also a rich source of "psychiatric patients".'[28] At a macroscopic level, disputes over why men attempt political assassinations are reduced to medical–technical disputes about 'diagnosis': the moral and political reasons (however unpalatable) why subject men might wish to kill their leaders are simply junked in the medical model.[29] Similarly, right-wing political protests against the de-segregation of schools (again, however unpalatable to a liberal conscience) make sense to some people: within psychiatric logic and practice racism, however, is transformed into the quirk of an authoritarian personality, or even 'paranoia'.[30] The political opponents of racism, equally, couch their liberal appeals for racial equality in non-moral, pseudo-scientific terms. A Supreme Court decision in 1954 urged the desegregation of schools on the grounds that segregation was psychologically harmful to black children: but if one were a racist one might *want* to harm black children, or not care one way or the other. Technical know-how is, thereby, used to secure a pseudo-solution to the moral–political problem of racism by side-stepping it: rather than actually con-fronting the political issues, it 'dissolves' them in a neutral, objective language which has the deceptive appearance of being outside the arena of moral debate.[31] In an entirely similar fashion some forms of political dissent are psychiatrically invalidated as the work of 'head-cases' or 'mindless militants'.[32] And those who find the prospect of not working more personally meaningful than badly paid, routine, unskilled work are thought to be work-shy inadequates. In one psychiatric study, which takes the medical model to the limits of silliness, a man who did not work, and who could obtain more income from state benefits than from poorly paid labour, is described as a psychopath who suffers from an 'illness' which is called 'state benefit neurosis'.[33] The instrumental rationality of his action is entirely defaced, and the social inequality which this action is a response to is forgotten.

Szasz is a critic of social institutions, a would-be reformer of the psychiatric profession, and an iconoclast of the psychiatric enlightenment. He wants to argue that psychiatry restricts the human freedom to confront, and resolve where possible, moral and political problems. But he is aware of a paradox here, for the humane, liberal face of psychiatry has itself secured many reforms: medical judgements provide abortions for women on 'psychiatric' and 'social' grounds; they provide mitigating circumstances for some who break the law, sometimes acting as a buffer between law-breakers and harsher systems of justice. To some, 'psychiatric justice' appears as the pillar of a compassionate and rational system of law enforcement. But for Szasz these are not real freedoms. Psychiatry simply allows men to avoid the fact that they are not free and that life is not free of moral dilemmas. In the days of prohibition the bootlegger provided booze for a thirsty population, but he did not change the law which had criminalised the consumption of alcohol and make it freely available. So, in one of Szasz's more memorable phrases, the psychiatrist is a 'bootlegger of humanistic values': for example, abortions are secured for women on psychiatric grounds, but without a change in the law which would give women more control over their own bodies. The liberal–psychiatric reform of abortion laws ironically implies that one must be mentally ill 'to enjoy freedom from being coerced by the physiological consequences of the sexual act'.[34] The alternative to psychiatric decision-making which Szasz proposes is to 'develop fully and to confront frankly the socio-ethical issues involved in abortion (and other similar problems, such as birth control or the death penalty)'. Szasz's discussion of abortion-law reform is one of the most illuminating moments in his critique of the domination of the Therapeutic State, where mercy and exemption must be 'smuggled in under the guise of diagnosis and treatment' and the conclusion of the affair is a severe restriction of human freedom:

> By espousing and embracing legislation based on traditional legal and social attitudes, psychiatrists actually make it more difficult for people (themselves included) to come to grips with the really significant issues. I submit that efforts to 'liberalise' abortion laws by providing a broader spectrum of medical and psychiatric justifications for the procedure are, in effect, restrictive of human freedom and, therefore, truly anti-liberal. . . . [These measures] would only increase the number of times *other* people could provide abortions for women; they would not increase the number of occasions on which women could make this decision for *themselves*. Such measures, therefore, give assent to the proposition that it is good to deny people the right to determine for themselves how they should use their bodies.[35]

Here Szasz is arguing that the psychiatric mentality enslaves *all* men in its logic. Increasingly in his writings, however, he has come to place an emphasis on the manner in which psychiatry acts as a slavemaster of the State in controlling and suppressing deviant minorities. It is not surprising that he discovers that this therapeutic domination finds its mature expression in the courtroom. Physicians, he argues, inevitably become entangled in the social conflicts embodied in law and 'they are bound to help some and harm others', whereas their retreat behind a mask of professional neutrality only obscures this fact and 'serves strategic aims in an antagonistic relationship'.[36]

This, of course, is not the liberal-humane view of the relationship between psychiatry and the law. In American law the Durham Rule, based on the case of Monte Durham *v.* The United States 1954, holds that 'an accused is not criminally responsible if his unlawful act was the product of mental disorder or mental defect'.[37] Psychiatry appears to shield the deviant, and within liberal psychiatric opinion this is regarded as a landmark in the rise of a humane system of justice. As Leifer describes it:

> Defenders of this test, and others like it, claim that it represents

a scientific modernisation of the law. They claim that it establishes as the basis of criminal responsibility a question of fact – the mental illness of the defendant – and they claim that it permits the psychiatric expert to testify about matters of medical fact and opinion within his competence to assess.[38]

Szasz suggests that the crucial test of the justice provided by the Durham Rule is to be found not by interrogating the abstract operations of the principle, but by looking at what it does for (and to) the defendant:

> The triumph of psychiatric justice is symbolised not by the defendant's fate (who knows or cares about what happened to Monte Durham?), but by the judge's decision. The accused is a double victim: he is judicially sentenced and psychiatrically defaced. The judges are double victors: they revenge the (alleged) harm inflicted on society and establish themselves as heroic fighters for a utopian ideology.[39]

If the result of psychiatric justice, as in the case of Monte Durham (a poor black), is a prolonged period of psychiatric detention, then Szasz argues that the victim is not a 'patient', but a 'prisoner'. Psychiatric justice is a mystification, for although it takes sides in the struggle between the defendant and the State (and locks the defendant away) it hides this partisanship as a non-moral, scientific judgement:

> Clearly, the trouble with frankly recognising that a situation is adversary in character is that it helps the weaker party – the accused, the mentally ill, the socially oppressed – to defend himself. Thus, if what is wanted is an adversary proceeding better suited for repressing 'deviants' – whoever they might be – the thing to do is to have an adversary proceeding that is *not* an adversary proceeding. It is the best kind.[40]

Psychiatric strategies of confinement, therefore, are an effective means of concealing the fact of confinement and social antagonisms. 'We're only trying to help'; 'We know what's good for you'; 'We know you can't help it'; 'You're ill'; 'We're doing this for your own good'; 'Maybe things look bad now, but when you're better': the language of liberal concern, mitigating conditions, and psychiatric defacement. Psychiatric diagnoses, Szasz says in another context, are 'semantic blackjacks': we might add that they are instruments which knock the victim down without leaving a tell-tale bruise. Szasz draws the lesson of the forgotten Monte Durham: 'His criminal activity was not accepted as a reasonable strategy for him in a society where he was useless and expendable. Instead it was defined as a manifestation of craziness.'[41] Psychiatric liberalism, in Szasz's anti-psychiatric critique, is a highly masked form of social oppression: 'Modern liberalism – in reality, a type of statism – allied with scientism, has met the need for a fresh defence of oppression and has supplied a new battle cry: Health!'[42] It is thus with approval that Szasz quotes Albert Camus, who warns of the hidden face of benevolence: 'The welfare of the people in particular has always been the alibi of tyrants, and it provides the further advantage of giving servants of tyranny a good conscience.'[43]

THEORY AND SENTIMENTS IN ANTI-PSYCHIATRY

The ferocity of Szasz's critique is clear enough, and it appears to reach some agreement with the sentiments of Laing's anti-psychiatry. However, the two modes of anti-psychiatry emerge from what are quite different sets of assumptions. Laing's anti-psychiatry is a sort of fellow-traveller of the counter-cultural rebellion; Laing has been described as 'one of the main contributors to the theoretical and rhetorical armoury of the contemporary Left' with some justification.[44] Szasz's anti-psychiatry, on the other hand, emerges from an essentially conservative tradition. Although it is never made explicit in any satisfactory way in his writings, his philosophy is that peculiarly American blend of anti-collectivist rugged individualism which mixes a conservative political philosophy with a loose spirit of anarchism. Szasz is of the 'radical right'; Laing is of the 'soft left'. Conservative values and acid consciousness; fee-based psychotherapy and freak-out centre; Thomas Jefferson and the I Ching; Ralph Waldo Emerson and the teachings of the Tao: it seems at face value an unlikely match. Nevertheless, I wish to argue that there is more which brings Laing and Szasz together than holds them apart: the intersection of their projects is to be found in the *humanistic* thrust of their theories.

This humanism finds its expression in Szasz through the severe distinction which he draws between the logic and language of medicine, and the logic and language of a science of human conduct. Szasz takes the position that human conduct is essentially symbolic and rule-guided. It is not to be confused with the actions of physical objects or machines which are governed by clockwork-type laws. For Szasz's purposes the human body is a machine, and the logic and classification systems of medicine find their rationale there, and are, therefore, quite inappropriate for the study of human conduct.[45] Bodily symptoms and symptoms of mental illness belong to radically distinct phenomenal realms. To confuse the two areas is to commit what Gilbert Ryle has called a 'category mistake'.[46] Szasz spells out the implications of this conceptual error for psychiatry in what is a clear statement of his idea of the metaphorical and mythical nature of 'mental illness':

> One group of psychiatric disorders consists of physical abnormalities, like syphilis of the brain and toxic psychoses (for example, acute alcoholism). These are appropriately considered 'diseases'; but they are diseases of the brain, not of the mind.
>   Another group consists of personal disabilities, like fears, stupidities, and discouragements. Such so-called functional psychiatric illnesses may appropriately be considered 'mental' (in the sense in which we consider thinking and feeling 'mental' activities); but they are diseases only in a metaphorical sense.
>   A third group of psychiatric disorders consists of certain antisocial acts, like homicide or homosexuality. These are social deviations, and can be considered neither 'mental' nor 'diseases.[47]

The same distinction between bodily symptoms and symptoms of mental illness is made by Erving Goffman, whose work has often been claimed as part of the anti-psychiatry corpus. 'Signs and symptoms of a *medical* disorder', he writes,

> presumably refer to underlying pathologies in the individual organism, and these constitute deviations from biological norms maintained by the homeostatic functioning of the human machine. The system of reference here is plainly the individual organism, and the term 'norm', ideally at least, has no moral or social connotation.[48]

In *Asylums* Goffman suggests that the signs and symptoms of mental disorder, on the other hand, are instances of behaviour which is socially inappropriate:

> since inappropriate behaviour is typically behaviour that some-one does not like and finds extremely troublesome, decisions concerning it tend to be political, in the sense of expressing the special interest of some particular faction or person rather than interests that can be said to be above the concerns of any particular grouping, as in the case of physical pathology.[49]

Laing's anti-psychiatry makes substantially the same kind of distinction between the logic, concerns and methodology of the physical or natural sciences and those of the life sciences. One way in which this is expressed is through the distinction between *process* and *praxis*, here described by Esterson:

> The movement of an arm may be seen primarily as a pattern of flexion and extension of muscles and joints, or it may be seen primarily as striking a blow. In the first case its movement is explained in terms of anatomy and physiology, in the second in terms of the intentions of the person to whom the arm belongs. In the first instance we deal with process, in the second, praxis. The first stance is appropriate to the study of things and organisms, the second to a science of persons.[50]

The fault in medical–psychiatric thinking in these terms is that it treats praxis as if it were process, thereby losing the intelligibility of human action. Laing, in a typical juxtapostion of psychiatric thought and deranged thinking, writes that psychotics are 'people who experience themselves as automata, as robots, as bits of machinery, or even as animals. Such persons are rightly regarded as crazy. Yet why do we not regard a theory that seeks to transmute persons into automata, or animals as equally crazy?'[51]

Another way in which the same distinction is asserted is through a comparison of 'analytical' and 'dialectical' reasoning. This distinction involves anti-psychiatry's attitude towards subject–object relations in a science of persons; that is, its attitude towards the relationship between the observing scientist and the system observed. Both Cooper and Esterson spell it out at some length.

Dialectical reasoning is the principle of what may be termed *dialectical science*, which is to be distinguished from *natural science*. By dialectical science, I mean the study of the reciprocities of persons and groups of persons in contrast to the study of natural events. . . . Persons are always in relation. These relations are, in a sense, active. Natural entities, too, may be in relation. These relations are, in a sense, passive. Persons relate through establishing relations with each other and to natural events, while things and organisms appear not to relate so.[52]

Cooper's position is posed in similar terms:

In physical and biological science . . . observed facts are usually *inert* facts, that is to say they are grasped from the exterior by an observer who is not disturbed by them. . . . In a science of personal interaction, on the other hand, mutual disturbance of the observer and the observed is not only inevitable in every case *but it is this mutual disturbance which gives rise to the primary facts on which the theory is based* . . . .[53]

Thus, in a science of persons, if I am to study you, then part of my field of observation must be 'you-studying-me-studying-you'. This interchange is not properly grasped by 'analytical' reasoning, but only by a reflexive, 'dialectical' rationality. 'Dialectical understanding is understanding of the dialectic in and through the experience of reciprocal change wrought in oneself and in the system observed.'[54] The same issue is raised in even Laing's earliest work.[55]

The distinction which is asserted here is the same as that proposed by Szasz, although the language is different and has a 'European' flavour. Commentators on Laing's work have suggested that his departure from the traditions of psychiatric thought owes a considerable debt to his reading of European (that is, non-British) philosophers, and in particular the later work of Sartre.[56] However, this influence can be over-emphasised. The fact that we find the same methodological preoccupations in Laing's early work, for example, *before* his much celebrated reading of Sartre reduces the credibility of this claim. It is true, of course, that at a number of points in the anti-psychiatry corpus theoretical pledges are made to Sartre's work, and the book *Reason and Violence* represents an attempt by Laing and Cooper to make his later thought available to the English reader. Nevertheless, when Laing and Cooper actually *take hold* of Sartre for their own purposes, we are left with the remains of a theoretical meal; the implications which they draw for their field of interest are specifically (and only) humanistic:

> The difference between Sartre's position and that of many psycho-analysts is seen most clearly in relation to the question of the limits of psycho-analysis. At a certain point in the process of explanation, many psycho-analysts find it necessary to switch perspective from that in which the observer makes his observations from the heart of a relationship, an interactional situation of reciprocal influence and change, to that in which the analyst attempts to make judgements about the analysand (a person) from a position of complete exteriority in relation to a biological entity. The person disappears. Sartre, on the other hand, traces the life of the person to its own ultimate issues. . . . The reductive biologism prevalent in psycho-analytical thinking explains all, and it explains nothing. . . . It explains nothing in so far as the person with whom the psycho-analyst had supposed himself to be concerned has (in biological reductionism) evaporated from the field of discourse and we find ourselves talking about something else, indeed about no one. It is only through the discovery of a freedom, a choice of self functioning in the face of all determinations, conditioning, fatedness, that we can attain the comprehension of a person in his full reality.[57]

The terms of this argument are already familiar as the humanistic critique of the effects of imposing biological and mechanical categories on to the study of human subjects, and it is these humanistic tendencies – celebrating the intentionality, choice, purposefulness and moral condition of human conduct – which unite the field of anti-psychiatry. But anti-psychiatry does not have any monopoly over humanism, and its central theoretical thrust should be located within, and understood as part of, a larger humanistic revival which in recent years has opposed what it describes as mechanical, positivistic and reductionist emphases in social science, psychology and psychiatry.[58] In his book *The Broken Image* Floyd Matson has provided an overview of this area. Social science, he argues, has been won over to a Newtonian world-view: that is, a view of the world – physical, animal and human – as a Giant Machine which ticks according to the iron laws of physics. The dominant spirit of this mechanisation of man, as Matson describes it, was

> to force the objects of human inquiry and concern beneath the microscope of microscopic analysis, to reduce their content to the smallest measurable denominator or the single irreducible cause – without, at the same time, contaminating the observation with 'subjective' considerations. The ideal of the social scientist . . . was . . . merely to be a spectator at the grand performance of Nature – but a spectator with the mentality of a mechanic.[59]

Within this scientific paradigm the awkward, puckish qualities of human actors – their ability to make choices and fly in the face of constraining circumstances – could not be tolerated. B. F. Skinner, from the standpoint of a rigorous behaviourism, insists, for example, that 'we cannot apply the methods of science to a subject which is assumed to move about capriciously', and a working assumption of his psychology had to be that men did not have these changeable qualities.[60]

The humanistic opposition to this kind of statement, on the other hand, greets the capricious movement of human actors with something approaching joy: it stands as evidence that men *cannot* be pinned down, hemmed in, and manipulated; and it ensures that human qualities will always rise, phoenix-like, from the consuming fires of the experimentalist's laboratory.

There is more to this confrontation than a simple methodological–scientific argument. The humanistic position is embedded within, and embodies, a commitment to certain notions of human freedom. There is, for example, a hopeful wish for the full realisation of the potential of all human subjects. There is also a commitment to the idea that human beings are unique, individuated subjects; this also lends itself to a sort of pluralism – in the modern idiom everyone should do their own thing. The gentle humanistic psychology of Carl Rogers, to give an indication of the spirit of this tendency, has sometimes been seen as a highly subversive enterprise – and even a communist conspiracy.[61] And in one of its wilder moments (in Fritz Perls' *Gestalt Therapy Verbatim*) the relationship between self-realisation, conformity and society is described in the following terms: 'the basic personality in our time is a neurotic personality . . . we are living in an insane society and . . . you only have the choice either to participate in this collective psychosis or to take risks and become healthy and perhaps also crucified.'[62] This cluster of sentiments is evident in the 'reconstructive science of human behaviour' which Matson envisages as the humanistic alternative to Newtonian error: it will be a science which respects and vindicates 'Man's freedom of choice' and its guiding spirit will not be 'the measurement of organic mechanisms or the manipulation of conditioned responses but the understanding of personal experience in its complementary wholeness':

It will be a science activated, not by a rage for order, but by a passion for freedom . . . which regards men as actors as well as spectators, and accordingly perceives its own task as one primarily of participation (intersubjectivity) and only secondly of observation (objectivity). . . .

. . . a science which, in seeking to comprehend human nature and conduct, takes men's reasons and reasoning into account as seriously as it does nature's causes; one that makes of its inquiry into understanding and truth a reasonable dialogue, in which the other partner (the observed) has an equal right to be heard and even to be trusted. . . .

The reconstructive science of behaviour will dare to look upon all men as moral agents and upon their behaviour as the expression of a choice . . . .[63]

This is fighting talk. As this humanistic psychology confronts its non-humanistic counterpart, its libertarian political undertones are acted out under the guise of a theoretical–conceptual debate, and much of anti-psychiatry's own critical stance is informed by the same 'passion for freedom'. The broader ambition of anti-psychiatry, however, is to connect its humanism to its descriptions of psychiatric oppression. This presupposes a theoretical understanding of the social and political functions of psychiatric practice. The very fact that the psychiatry which anti-psychiatry opposes claims humanism for itself suggests that such a social theory is necessary to anchor and stabilise its own humanistic sentiments. Anti-psychiatry judges humanism in traditional psychiatry to be a 'bad thing'; but when its humanistic critique of medical logic in psychiatric thought and practice is interrogated *theoretically* and *politically* we encounter a serious theoretical vacuum.

PSYCHIATRY, HUMANISM AND THE STATE

The social-welfare apparatus in recent years has experienced some manpower problems. Particularly in social work, but also in the other helping professions, there has been strain and unrest among professionals and professional recruits, which finds its voice in various notions of 'radical professionalism'.[64] For those who wish to mount a political critique of welfare and deviance-control the anti-psychiatry viewpoint has seemed attractive. One of its main sources of power is that it is a scheme which talks of politics at the same time as it talks of professional practice, technical know-how and case-level studies. It promises a theoretical understanding (and a related practice) which connects the macro-politics of the State with the micro-politics of personal troubles and therapeutic or correctional activities. The politics of anti-psychiatry, however, is in need of demystification. The appeal which it undoubtedly does have for some professional malcontents is essentially one which is sentimental – that is, it reflects and voices the professional malaise rather than incisively analysing its structure and revolutionising its practice.

There is some overlap between the two main modes of anti-psychiatric thought in the way in which they attempt to think the connections between psychiatry and politics, but they are better treated separately. Laing's primary emphasis is on questions of the containment and freedom of personal experience; Szasz is more inclined to interpret politics as a question of civil liberties.

The 'Laingian' position, as I have noted, has a close affinity with the philosophy and politics of the so-called New Left. There one finds attempts to understand the relationship between the personal and the political, and a brief statement of that position helps to clarify the politics of Laing's anti-psychiatry. Wilhelm Reich's work, for example, lays out the rudiments of a psycho-analytical theory of political domination. He ties the study of the repression of sexuality to attitudes of political apathy and authoritarianism. 'The family', he writes, 'is a factory for producing submissive people.'[65] Until men and women are free of this family-induced political neurosis they will be afraid of freedom and will cling to authoritarianism and externally imposed controls. A different approach to the same problem of how political control is mediated through personal experience is offered in the writings of Herbert Marcuse and the Frankfurt School, whose work I will examine in a later chapter.[66] There is also the writing of Erich Fromm – who was also once a member of the Frankfurt School – and Norman O. Brown, who both, again in different ways, approach the problem of the personal and the political. Although all these writers share the psycho-analytical perspective of the anti-psychiatry school, however, there is *no* attempt written down in the anti-psychiatry corpus to come to grips with the work of the 'Freudian Left'.[67] The tenuous relationship of anti-psychiatry to this tradition can be judged by the fact that Marcuse – by popular acclaim the 'guru' and theoretical mentor of the New Left – is only briefly encountered by Laing in a footnote. Laing jots out a gnomic, single-sentence 'summary' of Marcuse's position and writes: 'This is not my view';[68] which is simply 'out-guru-ing' the guru. No serious reading of Laing's anti-psychiatry can mistake the superficial nature of its political theory.

The relationship between politics and psychiatry is secured in this anti-psychiatry by the trick of analogy. When psychiatry and the State appear together in anti-psychiatry their relationship is theoretically un-anchored, placed side-by-side rhetorically: which is more dangerous, we are asked, 'a little girl of seventeen in a mental hospital' who thinks that she has an Atom Bomb inside her, or world statesmen 'who boast and threaten that they have Doomsday weapons'?[69] Esterson sets the masking and blurring of social contradictions by governments side-by-side with the blurred communications of the families of psychotics; or he suggests that the psychiatric invalidation of schizophrenics as non-persons 'parallels' the treatment of Jews, Reds and Niggers.[70] Schatzman asks, without offering an answer, how the irrationality of families who persecute their offspring find their rationality in wider social networks; he also hints, in the nearest approach to

Reich in the whole of the anti-psychiatry literature, that there might be links between child-rearing practices which produce paranoia and the child-rearing ideologies of totalitarian states.[71] Cooper states, flatly, that the inability of men to live with the whole flux of their experience 'conditions the possibility' of the war in Vietnam.[72] Laing writes that psychiatric invalidation 'seems to serve specific functions within the structure of the system'.[73] But that is all: there is no politics of psychiatry worked out in Laingian anti-psychiatry.

Thomas Szasz's politics of psychiatry shares some of the weaknesses of Laing's anti-psychiatry. His accounts of how psychiatric procedures infringe individual liberties, although it strikes to the heart of Institutional Psychiatry's self-satisfied liberal humanism, are generally linked to a wider notion of psychiatry's political functions with little more than vivid flourishes of the pen. There is one aspect of his approach, however, which requires more elaboration. An image which Szasz uses to sling his view of the relationship between psychiatry and the State around is that of the witch. In Szasz's writings the mental patient and the witch are historical correlates: the search for the witch is the search for the limits of social order and 'reasonableness' itself. The witch is a shape of the devil, psychiatry is the measure of our reasonableness: psychiatry is a witch-hunt.

Szasz's originality is not in his comparison of witchcraft and mental illness, and, by various techniques, it can spot and purge the is that witches were mentally disordered people who went un-diagnosed because of the immaturity of medical knowledge, and that witch-finding, witch-spotting and witch-pricking represented a primitive, pre-scientific 'psychiatric' practice.[74] To this end, the *Malleus Maleficarum* – a manual for witch-finders – has been described as an early psychiatric textbook of diagnosis and treatment. In a dramatic reversal of this view Szasz proposes that psychiatry, on the contrary, is a modern secular version of witch-mongering. Whereas the Inquisition held that witches were possessed by demonic forces, had various techniques for extracting confessions and other techniques for decontamination, modern psychiatry holds that mental patients are possessed by mental illness, and, by various techniques, it can spot and purge the symptoms of disorder. The social function of both institutions, Szasz argues, is 'to validate the self as good (normal), by invalidating the Other as evil (mentally ill)'.[75] This identity of function, he holds, is obscured only by the fact that a scientific world-view has replaced a religious cosmology: 'medicine replaced theology; the alienist, the inquisitor; the insane, the witch. The result was the substitution of a medical mass-movement for a religious one, the persecution of mental patients replacing the persecution of heretics.'[76]

Szasz pursues his unlikely analogy in a manner which is both compelling and imaginative, tying together 'the former need for witch finders, witch prickers, and inquisitors, and the present need for psychiatrists, psychologists, and social workers'.[77] In the light of this view progressive developments, such as community mental-health programmes which urge 'preventive case-finding', only represent an acceleration of the pursuit of psychiatric heresy. And Szasz is quite alive to the fact that his own theory of the 'myth of mental illness' (comparable to the grave heresy of not believing in witchcraft) marks him out in official psychiatric terms as a madman.[78] The persecution of scapegoats, Szasz argues, is a mechanism by which a society confirms the value of normality and conformity without having to put those values to the test in social practice. Szasz writes that 'man's *refusal* to sacrifice scape-goats – and his willingness to recognise and bear his own and his group's situation and responsibility in the world – would be. a major step in his moral development'.[79] The implication would seem to be, although this is not spelled out, that society should be liberated *from* psychiatry.

There is some ambiguity in Szasz's position here. On the one hand he holds that the persecution of 'The Other' is a *universal* human need to sustain an image of the self as good through the expulsion of evil. At one point he even describes this as a 'reflex'.[80] At other times, however, he suggests that psychiatry selects its victims specifically from among the powerless – women, blacks, the poor – and that psychiatry therefore represents the State's control of these groups. Thus, in a feminist critique of psychiatry, Phyllis Chesler is able to use Szasz's arguments to suggest that '*state* mental asylums are the "Indian Reservations" for America's non-criminally labelled poor, old, black, Latin and female populations'.[81] And Szasz writes himself that:

As witchcraft claimed its victims mainly from among certain

classes, so does mental illness. The public madhouses of the seventeenth and eighteenth centuries were full of society's *miserables*; the state mental hospitals of the nineteenth and twentieth centuries have been full of poor and uneducated people. Why? Because the social control and subjection of these people is one of the chief aims of Institutional Psychiatry.[82]

And in another inflammatory moment Szasz describes mental hospitals as 'the POW camps of our undeclared and unarticulated civil wars',[83] which is not at all the same thing as an inevitable, universal human reflex.

There are two deep sources of trouble reflected here in Szasz's witch motif and the theory of the political functions of psychiatry which he builds around it. First there is the question of its credentials as a *history* of the politics of psychiatry. Any history which must resort to *timeless* universal human needs in order to piece itself together is suspicious and will inevitably raise questions against itself.[84] Nevertheless, Szasz has got hold of the fact, which is a penetrating observation, that the emergence of the Modern Age involved a profound mutation in social thought and social practice, and that the emergence of modern psychiatry must be understood as part of that transformation; and he is proposing that he offers a history of the emergence of psychiatric thought, culminating in the Therapeutic State. However, this mutation involves more than just a transition from witchcraft to psychiatry: particularly Szasz neglects the shifting organisation of wealth and production, and the changing conception of citizenship, labour and pauperism which this necessitates.[85] Szasz's witch motif ignores the huge differences in the structure, organisation, scale and pre-occupations of agrarian society and industrial society. His history, in short, is profoundly ahistorical, and at the root of the witch-craft analogy, for all its intriguing depths, is another crippling theoretical weakness.

Secondly, Szasz falls back on a distinction between state mental hospitals and private-practice psychotherapy which his theoretical critique of psychiatry does not warrant at all. This is admittedly a very incoherent movement in Szasz's thought, and all one can do is make informed guesses in relation to the problem. The general drift of his writing, however, seems to be only that he wants to separate the social-control aspects of psychiatry from those other areas of psychiatric concern where clients freely enter bargains with psychiatrists in order to resolve some unhappiness in their lives. This second area of psychiatry can then become a 'liberated zone' in which therapy can go on uncontaminated by the moral–political dilemmas which his analysis has unearthed; while the social-control functions of psychiatry can return to their proper place: that is, the courts, prisons, police departments, and reform schools. On this point David Matza says in an interview:

> Szasz is a conservative. I think that would be the implication of his work and I think he'd want it to be. I'm not sure if I'm being fair now, but I think Szasz thinks everyone who has done something wrong should go to prison. . . . He thinks that the whole idea of mental illness isn't helpful at all and that we shouldn't get into the question of intent or the question of insanity. If a guy does something, it doesn't matter whether he's crazy or not crazy, he ought to go to prison. . . . I think Szasz is different from Goffman. If Goffman has an ideology – I don't know if he does – he would be humanist. Goffman would be for the patient; he wouldn't want the patient to go to prison – that's just the worst of all total institutions.[86]

Matza's hesitancy is justified: it is not at all clear what Szasz is getting at other than a division between *two entirely separate* functions of psychiatry, as he sees them. Making a distinction between 'Institutional Psychiatry' and 'Contractual Psychiatry' or 'Private Psychiatry' – for which the model is fee-based psycho-analysis or psychotherapy – he states that his criticisms of psychiatry refer only to Institutional Psychiatry. Institutional Psychiatry 'rests on coercion and . . . [its] function is to protect society', whereas Contractual Psychiatry rests on 'co-operation and . . . [its] function is to protect the individual client'.[87] Robert Leifer, whose position is close to that of Szasz, makes a similar division between 'ethnicizing' and 'educative' psychiatries. Ethnicising therapy is an instrument of social control, 'moulding . . . behaviour so that it conforms to prevailing cultural patterns';[88] Leifer portrays this model – 'bad guy' psychiatry – as inextricably bound up with the exercise of social power. Educative therapy, on the other hand, 'is designed to help the individual master society, rather than help society to master the individual':

According to the educational model, the therapeutic transaction consists of a relatively harmless exchange of information. The patient speaks freely of his history, thoughts, dreams, and activities, and the therapist reveals to him hidden aspects of self. The insight that he gains will enable the patient to be a whole person, better integrated, more able to actualize his potential, and more able to participate creatively in social relationships.[89]

The point which Szasz's critique of psychiatric practice had established, however, is that moral and political considerations insert themselves in the question of who decides, and why, what is 'creative', 'integrated' and 'real'. But his 'Contractual Psychiatry' does not appear to interrogate itself on these matters. Szasz can still find time to poke fun at psycho-analysis – 'beware the psycho-analyst who analyses jokes rather than laughs at them'[90] – but his own recommendations for therapy are not made the object of scrutiny, and they seem to somehow lift themselves magically free from the hidden operations of power and influence which are well documented for even the most non-directive therapies.[91] Sedgwick is unkind enough to suggest that 'the whole literary oeuvre of Szasz and Leifer is an attempt to justify one important way in which they earn their living',[92] and certainly there is a failure of nerve (or wallet) somewhere in Szasz's critique which ends in a *cul de sac* as the Magna Carta of fee-based, private-practice psychotherapy. Taken in its kindest light, Szasz's recommendations are a renewed appeal to the spirit of humanism in professional psychiatry, although that is a spirit which his own work has done much to discredit.

This abrupt closure to Szasz's critical thinking signals a failure in anti-psychiatry's programme which was to encompass the relationships between psychiatry, deviance and the State. In all its modes anti-psychiatry simply retreats *from* the State and State-funded psychiatry into both theoretical and practical enclaves where it can do what it will. The journal *Radical Therapist*, which has criticised this kind of retreat as the arrival of a new 'hip professionalism', ceremonialised its own attempt to come to terms with the problem in a change of name: to *Rough Times*.[93] But even its own highly militant brand of 'radical psychiatry' occasionally falls back into an appeal to humanism: an appeal to the therapists to *heal* rather than selling his skills 'like a vendor of fried chicken'.[94] Thus criticism gives way to moralism, for the definition of what it is to 'heal' was the whole point of the critical spirit of 'radical psychiatry'.

The retreat takes a number of forms, but it is always predicated on a distinction between the 'bad' psychiatry practised by the many and the 'good' psychiatry practised by a few. For Szasz 'contractual psychiatry' is 'good' psychiatry. The excellent document of the work of Laing's Philadelphia Association provided by Peter Robinson's film *Asylum* shows what proper psychiatric practice looks like to Laingian anti-psychiatry (if it is still possible to talk about any *one* such thing).[95] The Philadelphia Association project resurrects the meaning of 'retreat' and 'sanctuary' for the word 'asylum' and is a continuation of the work at Kingsley Hall.[96] Dissolving the roles of 'helper' and 'helped' to a large degree, the place to live which is an 'asylum' is a home for a few who could not live elsewhere. It is a pioneering effort to create the living space in which madness can hopefully learn to live with itself without recourse to mental hospitalisation. And one cannot complain if it helps. But meanwhile the mundane business of psychiatry – which Szasz, Laing, Cooper, and the various 'radical' psychiatries condemn wholeheartedly – grinds on. And at one crucial moment in *Asylum* a troublesome member of the community is warned that he will return to the 'bin' if he does not quieten down. One reads of the same problem of having to turn over people who are too troublesome to 'bad guy' psychiatry in Michael Barnett's account of the People Not Psychiatry network, which is another of the alternatives to psychiatry which have grown in the shadow of the anti-psychiatry movement.[97] 'Alternative psychiatry' offers an alternative to psychiatry only for a few who conform to the alternative norms which it embodies.

The point in raising the question of these lapses is not to abuse the practical help which the alternative psychiatry movement might offer to its clientele. They are lapses which might even be described as a vindication of one argument in the anti-psychiatry platform: madhouses are places where people go (or are sent) when they become too frightening (or frightened) and too troublesome to be contained by their surrounding living groups. Hospitalisation is a 'political' act, we might say: a way of resolving, at least temporarily, a conflict of interest or viewpoint. Mental hospitals contain the uncontainable.

Or do they? 'Mental hospitals: localization of a resource we've yet to exploit' writes John Cage in the spirit of the romanticism of anti-psychiatry.[98] It is, of course, not only anti-psychiatry's romanticism, and critics of anti-psychiatry who level against it the fact of its romanticism forget that other men at other times have been fascinated with the 'resource' of madness and its uncanny promise of crazy genius, unlicensed imagination and illumination. Michel Foucault's *Madness and Civilisation* is, in part, a study of how the heroism culturally embodied within madness fluctuates through European history.[99] But the other side, the irony of John Cage's aphorism, is that the 'resource' in mental hospitals which is not yet exploited is human labour power. Dream or waste product? – this is the question of the deviant imagination. The distinction between 'good' psychiatry and 'bad' psychiatry ignores that question and simply perpetuates it: a few (usually if they can afford to pay fees) can pursue the 'dream'; the many must be recycled as social waste-products in the 'bin'.

The medical model in psychiatry conceals all this: the social practice of psychiatry is committed to the extinction of madness and its troublesome questions, not its elucidation. The human dilemmas of what this thing madness is, and how it is caused, and whether it is a curse or a special kind of grace, and what this thing madness might be saying to us, the sane ones, is not part of the world of modern psychiatry. Modern psychiatry is preoccupied with technology, whether this takes the form of dosage levels, psychotherapeutic theoretical disputes, or voltage levels. That, unless history makes mistakes, is what the history of modern psychiatry describes to us. The 'medical model' is a firmly legitimated institution of social practice in western civilisation: it is not merely a theoretical error, and one of the mistakes of anti-psychiatry is to think that it is and debate it in those terms: so that when theoretical error is corrected, and the historical clock put back, it is imagined that the house of psychiatry will fall. When Ernest Becker, for example, whose work has a close affinity with humanistic anti-psychiatry, sets out the reasons for medical dominance in the study of schizophrenia, it is seen as the result of an ironic, uneven development in thought: interest in the care and correction of the insane arrived *before* the theorists who could tell us properly what it was all about. The study of deviance, according to his account, has fallen into bad company and the villain is medicine, which has 'redoubled efforts to keep man under medical wraps and dress his behavioural disorders in Greco-Latin cant':

> Thus the science that knew least about total symbolic man and most about the animal body fully established its sacrosanct domain. We are coming to know that it had no business there.
>
> In 1860, those who could have shed light on the malfunction of the symbolic animal had not yet arrived and developed their anthropological, sociological, and psychological ideas. Only towards the end of the nineteenth century did Darwinism become fully assimilated, and only then did it become possible to understand the development of the human organism in evolution and in culture. Baldwin, James, Dewey, McDougall, George Mead, and a host of others had enough to do in systematising their ideas about human uniqueness; it could hardly be expected that they would lay claim to the domain staked out by Kraepelin, Bleuler, Charcot, Freud, Jung, Adler, and other medical psychologists. The result of this lopsided jurisdictional development was that human malfunction has continued to be treated largely in nineteenth-century disease categories up to the present day.[100]

Becker dreams of a 'post-psychiatric world' where, through a liberation of thought from mechanisation, man enters a promised land where he can 'truly create and truly love'.[101] Szasz hopes, if a little ambiguously, for a society free of medical totalitarianism. Laing sees a self-exploration in the labyrinths of psychotic breakdown which 'could have a central function in a truly sane society'.[102] But medical psychiatry does not blow away.

All these writers are drawn by their critique of the medical model into a consideration of moral and political issues which seem much wider than the day-to-day business of doing psychiatry. It is not that these writers are dragging morals and politics into the arena of psychiatry: they are already there in the nature of the medical model itself. For if the mechanisation of man and the medicalisation of deviance is a 'mistake' then it is a mistake which coheres with little difficulty within industrial capitalist society and the industrial sectors of the communist world. A history and a critique of psychiatric thought, and the social institutions which both embed thought and embody it, must take account of this fact. When a voice is given to the unexpressed sentiments of the medical model they are found to embody a notion of *a purified social order*. When medicine inserts itself into an understanding of social *dis*order, as it does in the medical model of deviance, it expresses an ideology of social order as a *natural phenomenon*. Conformity – rather than being viewed as a *social* accomplishment – is elevated to the status of 'health'.[103] Nonconformity is disqualified as 'sickness'. This embodies a notion of a purified community and a purified identity because one cannot be both ill and well at the same time, although a person can both conform (in some things) and deviate (in others). A view of conformity and deviance as a social accomplishment, which is what any critique of the medical model entails, raises the uncomfortable questions of how men construct and maintain social order and how they might reconstruct it. And these are political questions. Medicine puts these matters out of sight and out of mind: social order is taken for granted; one does not need to know why men conform, only why men fail to fulfil their place in the *natural* order of things. When its hold over the imagination is punctured, however haphazardly, a whole Pandora's box of questions are scattered about. The forest of confusion which is found in the antipsychiatry corpus is not just muddle-headedness.[104] Nor is it just the medical bogey-man who has put things out of focus. What all this jumble of half-formed criticism and speculation needs to be grasped as is a fundamental ambiguity of *deviant conduct*. Medicine simply masks these ambiguities; anti-psychiatry unearths a few of them. But when they are unmasked they remain ambiguities.

In the gaze of anti-psychiatry some of the contradictions of the medical model are exposed to view. The moral and political implications of deviance and deviance-control, which were buried beneath the magical authority of medicine, are put back into discourse. But that is all. The body politic of medicine is exhumed, but the corpse is not dissected.

3

THE MISFIT SOCIOLOGIES: SCHOLARSHIP, COMMITMENT AND DEVIANCE-CONTROL

Psychiatry, and its anti-psychiatric opponent, is both a theory and a practice of deviance and deviance-control. Whatever else there may be to divide the field, it contains a commitment to the relief of human suffering; and that commitment is understood as both a theoretical undertaking and its practical realisation. This is not the case in the wider social science of deviance. There a division of labour rips theory and practice apart. In a sort of 'mandarin' attitude to social science, action is something which leaves a taste in the scholar's mouth; and action in the field of deviance is left to do-gooders, meddlers and 'social administration'.

The theme of this chapter cuts across the various axes of this division of labour: scholarship and commitment, objectivity and partisanship, 'pure' social science and 'applied' social science, research and action, 'theory' and 'practice'. It engages an out-growth of deviance theory which lends itself to partisanship with the deviant underdog and action on his behalf, but which also raises a number of significant questions against both the theory and practice of deviance-control. It is an area which gives a voice to the deviant and approaches the politics of his containment.

It is all too easy to trivialise the tensions between scholarship and action in social science. The organisational relationship of sociology, social work and social administration in British universities, for example, sponsors gossip, trivia and mutual re-crimination. Often the three disciplines have been packed into multi-purpose departments where a sociological hegemony has watched anxiously, and sometimes jealously, over the apparently limitless and exponential growth of vocational courses in what is called 'applied social studies'. And although sociologists have studied the organisational contexts, professional ideologies and work habits of almost every conveivable occupation – dentists, janitors, physicians, topless go-go-dancers, boy prostitutes, lawyers, architects, jazz musicians and pool-hall hustlers to name only a few – they have been reluctant to engage in self-scrutiny. The problems of the social scientist are left to common-sense judgement. Typified as problems of personality, working relationships and other delicate parochial matters, however, the relationship between pure and impure social science is misrepresented. Behind 'common room sniggerings about "girls who want to do sociology because they like people" '[1] lie important conceptual divides. 'Mandarin' social science, quite simply, has viewed social-welfare concerns as marginal.

It is vitally important that this is grasped as more than an ivory-tower attitude. To describe the strain between scholarship and action in social science as the attempt by a theoretical discipline to maintain its 'purity' is to have only a partial hold on the problem. The tension has to do fundamentally with the theoretical and conceptual status of the deviant imagination; it is not only a question of distaste for action or commitment. Intellectuals who are committed politically, for example, are not necessarily less distant from matters of deviance and welfare than the mandarin, who is in any case something of a straw-man. In traditional Marxism, for example, deviants (the 'lumpenproletariat') are irrelevant to politics; no less irrelevant in fact than boxing or gardening, as one Marxist critic makes clear:

> Marxism has . . . a view that abolishes this field [crime and deviancy] as a coherent object of study. There is no 'Marxist theory of deviance', either in existence, or which can be developed within orthodox Marxism. Crime and deviance vanish into the general theoretical concerns and the specific scientific object of Marxism. Crime and deviance are no more a scientific field for Marxism than education, the family, or sport.[2]

Hirst's fire was drawn in the above quotation by a blend of social science which has emerged within the last few years and which suggests that this is not the case at all, and that the field of deviance is central both to the theoretical concerns of sociology, and to political theory. This area of scholarship is an odd theoretical cocktail, constructed out of sociology, psychiatry, criminology, social administration, media studies, law, social work, political science, cultural criticism, social psychology, and even some strands of popular culture and music. This interdisciplinary misfit finds its focus in the study of deviants, but it is more than an inter-disciplinary exercise. In a useful review of research in this area Schur has lumped many of the strands together as 'the labelling perspective', although the sociology of labelling is only one of its elements.[3] Within the same domain one finds what passes for 'phenomenology', and also a sort of 'Marxism'. Anti-psychiatry has left its mark, and Schur, again, points to the affinities with existential psychology.[4] To add to the mix, one of the central contributions in the area owes a considerable debt to Durkheim.[5] Here, clearly, is an area of high theoretical dispersion, a *zeit-geist* of sorts which allows for an apparent harmony between some widely differing perspectives. It is also, rightly or wrongly, a theoretical jig-saw which has earned the reputation of being 'radical'. Hirst, quite aptly, refers to it as 'a general ideological tendency in the social sciences; a tendency far more marked in its wide-spread and spontaneous manifestations than in particular published works'.[6] I call this space, which opened out in social thought in the 1960s, *misfit sociology*.[7]

I do not intend to review or summarise this far-reaching body of work. Reviews, summaries, critiques, and expositions of different elements of the misfit paradigm are already widely available.[8] What needs to be done instead is to expose some selected threads of misfit sociology with a particular eye to their critique of welfare. It can also be assumed at the outset that this is a highly confused and dispersed theoretical domain, but I will not try to put its theoretical house in order. In the previous chapter I approached anti-psychiatry's critique by beginning some sort of criticism of its theoretical base, but the tactic must be altered in relation to the broader vision of misfit sociology. Anti-psychiatry directly assaults psychiatry and social welfare; misfit sociology's critique of welfare is much more highly veiled. To render its critique articulate its literature must be read in a particular way, and this requires not only a *theoretical* reading, but an *imagina-tive* reading. My selective summary of misfit sociology, which

follows, is intended to lay the basis for this imaginative reading,
which continues in the next chapter. In particular, it is necessary
to understand how a body of research which could in some lights
appear to be a constructive contribution to liberal social reform
instead emerges as a highly explosive perspective which has the
smell of a 'radical' politics.

MISFIT SOCIOLOGY

The fountain-head of much of misfit sociology's divergence from
the traditional view of the deviant is found in one of the most
quoted pieces of sociological writing:

> The [traditional] sociological view . . . defines deviance as the
> infraction of some agreed upon rule. It then goes on to ask
> who breaks rules, and to search for the factors in their
> personalities and life situations that might account for their
> infractions. This assumes that those who have broken a rule
> constitute a homogeneous category, because they have committed
> the same deviant act.
>
> Such an assumption seems to me to ignore the central fact
> about deviance: it is created by society . . . *social groups
> create deviance by making the rules whose infraction consti-
> tutes deviance*, and by applying those rules to particular people
> and labelling them as outsiders. From this point of view,
> deviance is *not* a quality of the act the person commits, but
> rather a consequence of the application by others of rules and
> sanctions of an 'offender'. The deviant is one to whom that
> label has been successfully applied; deviant behaviour is
> behaviour that people so label.[9]

This is the catechism of 'labelling theory'. It is a remarkably
ambiguous statement, overlaid with implication and open to a
number of diverging interpretations. It was not the first statement
of its kind, however, by any means. Lemert, for example, had
suggested earlier that it was potentially unfruitful to think of
crime and deviance leading to social control, and 'that the
reverse ideas, that is, social control leads to deviance is equally
tenable and the potentially richer premise'.[10] In a statement which
also anticipated Howard Becker's, Kitsuse wrote:

I propose to shift the focus of theory and research from the forms of deviant behaviour to the *processes by which persons come to be defined as deviant by others*. Such a shift requires that the sociologist view as problematic what he generally assumes as given – namely, that certain forms of behaviour are *per se* deviant and are so defined by the 'conventional or conforming members of a group'.[11]

Kai Erikson suggests in similar terms that 'deviance is not a property *inherent in* any particular kind of behaviour', and elsewhere that 'the critical variable in the study of deviance . . . is the social audience rather than the individual actor'.[12]

The focus of deviance theory is turned in these statements in two directions. The first is towards a study of the *rules* which must be broken for a deviant act to be said to be committed. It is rather an obvious thing to say, but if there were no rules of social order we could not even think of deviance as such. The second switch of focus is towards the *reaction* which an audience has towards deviant action. These re-orientations towards *rules* and *audience reaction* are two quite distinct implications of the labelling perspective (or 'societal reaction theory' as it is sometimes called) although the two are frequently conflated, perhaps because they both turn the attention away from the individual misfit's assumed pathology towards the social construction of deviance.

The stress on audience reaction lends itself to a social psychology of 'deviance amplification'. This takes many forms. Lemert's distinction between 'primary' and 'secondary' deviation is a case. 'Primary deviation' refers to the initial act of deviation which might flow from any number of causes; it is judged to have only marginal implications from the point of view of the individual's self-conceptions and his ordering of his place in the world. Lemert defines 'secondary deviation' as the *added* deviant behaviour which follows from being apprehended and labelled as a deviant; it is 'a means of defence, attack or adaptation to the overt and covert problems created by the societal reaction to primary deviation',[13] and it involves a re-ordering of the self-concept. Jean Genet in *The Thief's Journal* captures the sense beautifully: 'I owned to being the coward, traitor, thief and fairy they saw in me.'[14] The concept of secondary deviation is a formal statement and extension of the folk wisdom that if a man goes to prison he will learn a lot of bad habits and lose his 'self respect'. There is, as David Matza puts it, an 'irony' in this set of statements.

> Their irony, stated simply, is that systems of control and the agents that man them are implicated in the process by which others become deviant. The very effort to prevent, intervene, arrest, and 'cure' persons of their alleged pathologies may . . . precipitate or seriously aggravate the tendency society wishes to guard against.[15]

One of the most convincing demonstrations of the argument is Scott's research on the blind.[16] It is a common belief – and apparently a correct one – that blind people share certain personality characteristics and clusters of attitudes. Scott argues that common-sense, folk-lore explanations of this rely on the idea that blind men are different in this sense because they live in a different world which gives blind people 'a peculiar purity and innocence of mind'.[17] A hardly more sophisticated view, which Scott calls the 'psychological explanation' suggests that the 'blind personality' comes from the common modes of adjustment to the shock and horror of becoming blind. Scott demonstrates, however, through his research on how blind-welfare agencies process blind people, that they are socialised by others into their personality and attitudes.

> The disability of blindness is a learned social role. The various attitudes and patterns of behaviour that characterise people who are blind are not inherent in their condition, but rather, are acquired through ordinary processes of social learning. Thus, there is nothing inherent in the condition of blindness that requires a person to be docile, dependent, melancholy, or help-less; nor is there anything about it that should lead him to become independent or assertive. Blind men are made, and by the same processes of socialisation that have made us all.[18]

Crucial to this socialisation process are the programmes, strategies, and belief systems of welfare agencies and the workers who man them. As the blind man is made, so he comes to adopt the expert's view of what blindness is about, and crucially, *who he is*. 'Such organisations', he writes, '*create* for blind people the experiences of being blind.'[19] Furthermore, the way in which a blind agency acts towards its clients, and the different variants of *stigma* which it peddles, depends on 'political, economic and sociological pressures that arise inside and outside the agency'.[20] The secondary deviation of blind men, in short, is in part a product of political, economic and social forces.

The impact of audience reaction on deviant behaviour is developed in relation to other areas of deviance by other writers. Reiss in his study 'The Social Integration of Peers and Queers' shows how boy prostitutes are able to maintain a heterosexual identity although engaging in acts of fellatio with customers. The system of norms and values which operate among his prostitute peers, who constitute in this case the significant audience, enable him to avoid the tag of 'queer' and also to avoid self-definition as a prostitute.[21] Becker has also shown how the values of the culture of drug-users enable a drug-user to avoid seeing his deviant acts as a deviation, and to keep himself clear from the spectre of a 'dope fiend'.[22] More commonly, however, misfit sociology has focused on how the deviant is 'bottled' by the labelling process. Jock Young in his study of the relationship between marijuana users and public fantasies of marijuana smoking argues that in the process of arrest, and also in the situation of the court, 'the policeman because of his position of power inevitably finds himself negotiating the evidence, the reality of drug-taking, to fit these preconceived stereotypes'. The policeman, Young suggests, because of his isolation in the community and his heavy reliance on peer (colleague) support, 'is peculiarly susceptible to the stereotypes, the fantasy notions that the mass media carry about the drug-taker', and these actually become a reality in the course of police action :

> changes occur within the drug-taking groups involving an intensification of their deviance and in certain important aspects a self-fulfilment of these stereotypes. That is, there will be an amplification of deviance, and a translation of stereotypes into actuality, of fantasy into reality.[23]

In *Being Mentally Ill* Scheff also emphasises the importance of public stereotypes of madness in the creation and consolidation of a career as a mental patient.[24] In another study Scheff shows how the psychiatrist's preconceptions of what his client's reality is — and these will depend to a large extent on the theory of human behaviour to which the psychiatrist adheres — can be powerfully enforced so that the client accepts as his own reality the reality as defined by the psychiatrist.[25] Balint's work on medical practitioners — although conducted from outside the misfit paradigm — also suggests that physicians have what he calls an 'apostolic function', so that the doctor *teaches* the patient, by subtle hints and cues, how to be sick, what symptoms are appropriate in his case, and the where, when, and how of pain.[26] Kitsuse and Dietrick employ a deviance-amplification model in relation to juvenile delinquency,[27] and the fluidity of the concept is demonstrated by the way in which Leslie Wilkins — who had earlier done work on the 'contaminating' and 'criminalising' influence of penal institutions — presents a general theory of deviance in terms of a cybernetic model of feedback systems.[28]

In fact 'deviancy amplification', contrary to all appearances, is not necessarily the same as the labelling perspective. Deviance-amplification is a model which can be applied to a whole range of diverse phenomena — confidence on the stock market, the ecological balance of commensal and antagonistic animal species within a given area, some features of the stability of electronic systems, etc.[29] — phenomena, that is, which are not necessarily human or symbolic. The vital element of labelling theory, however, is the symbolic component: the way in which people are 'tagged', pigeon-holed, bottled, stamped, labelled, stigmatised; how they come to bear the mark of Cain.[30] The labelling position insists that societal reaction leads both to an increase in deviation, and to a symbolic re-ordering of self and the world. In his account of Genet's criminal career, Sartre exposes the central sentiment:

one day, when ten years old, Genet was playing in the kitchen. Quite suddenly, in a spasm of anguish, he felt his aloneness, and plunged into an ecstatic state (absente). His hand entered an open drawer. He became aware that someone had entered the room and was watching him. Under the look of this other person Genet 'came to himself' in a sense for the first time. Until that moment he had lacked an identity. Now he became confirmed. All at once he became a certain Jean Genet. He was blinded and deafened. He was an alarm bell which kept on ringing. Soon the whole village would know the answer to the question 'Who is Jean Genet?' Only the child himself remained ignorant. Then a voice announced his identity . . . 'You are a thief!'[31]

Genet is hurled into a life of crime by a 'dizzying word' which *fixes* him. Anticipating our imaginative reading for one moment and reading, as it were, in between the lines, in the misfit paradigm deviance is not the 'fault' of the deviant; he suffers, if he suffers at all, 'from contingencies'.[32]

Already in my account the two sides of the labelling perspective – *rules* and *audience reactions* – have merged considerably. It is something which cannot be avoided: the literature which is reviewed conflates the two at every turn. The focus on *rules*, however, is more explicitly developed in studies of the organisational practices and routines of the agencies of social welfare and law enforcement, and studies of the way in which 'typical cases' are viewed by these organisations.[33] Organisations generate official statistics and rates of deviance out of their routine work, which gears their operations to selected 'problem areas'. In studies of these processes the economics and politics of policy formation are seen to saturate not only public and official conceptions of deviance, but also the nature of deviation itself: rule-making, the public imagery of deviance, and the deviant's symbolic re-ordering of his universe coalesce. We have already seen indications of this in Young's work on marijuana use, and Scott's research on the making of blind men. Schur, in a statement on social policy relating to opiate addiction, similarly argues that many of the problems of addiction are *created* by social policy which influences dramatically the marketing of drugs, their availability, price, and purity.

certain aspects of addict behaviour (notably addict-crime, involvement in trafficking, development of addict-subculture) cannot directly be attributed either to the effects of the drugs or to psychological characteristics of the individuals involved. Rather the presence or absence of such behaviour appears to be determined largely by the nature of the societal reaction to the addict.[34]

One particular aspect of social-policy formation which has been given some attention is that of the 'moral crusade'. Examples of moral crusades are the Temperance movement in the United States, the anti-vivisection movement, the recent campaign to widen the definition of 'pornography' in the United Kingdom, and the classical case of the creation of the Marijuana Tax Act. 'Rules are not made automatically', writes Howard Becker, they are the product of some kind of enterprise.[35] Even delinquency, as Anthony Platt puts it, had to be 'invented'.[36]

Becker's analysis of the moral crusade hinges around the notion of 'moral entrepreneur'.

> The prototype of the rule creator . . . is the crusading reformer. He is interested in the content of rules. The existing rules do not satisfy him because there is some evil which profoundly disturbs him. He feels that nothing can be right in the world until rules are made to correct it. He operates with an absolute ethic; what he sees is truly and totally evil with no qualification. Any means is justified to do away with it. The crusader is fervent and righteous, often self-righteous.[37]

As Becker goes on to suggest, although rather limply, the moral entrepreneur is also often a humanitarian. Dickson has argued, against Becker, that the focus on the lone crusader is in danger of missing the bureaucratic aspects of moral crusades and the need for bureaucratic organisations to perpetuate themselves and find work.[38] David Musto, in his explorations into the origins of narcotics control in the United States, takes matters further and provides a dramatic account of rule improvisation.[39] Through careful research he shows how law creation was influenced in the early twentieth century by far-reaching political conflicts, and how specifically in relation to cocaine the process of law-making was related to conflicts between Southern and Northern States. Cocaine was used, he says, as an excuse in the South to move against the black population in a series of reprisals. Although cocaine use had been something of a commonplace – until 1903 it was a constituent of Coca Cola; a former surgeon general of the army swore by it and took a dose with every meal; and it had been the official remedy of the American Hay Fever Association – it was the alleged connection between cocaine and the Southern negro population which precipitated its criminalisation. The 'cocaine-crazed Negro brain', as one writer in the *Literary Digest* described it,[40] was alleged to be responsible for attacks on white women and other horrible crimes. Musto argues that the massive repressive measures taken against blacks in the South in the early twentieth century, including their disenfranchisement, was the motor power behind the move against cocaine. The cocaine scare legitimised reprisals against blacks; Southern police departments used it as the reason for increasing their fire-arm power, employing the bizarre excuse that cocaine use made people immune to smaller calibre bullets.[41] Musto writes that, 'the fear of the cocainised black coincided with the peak of lynchings, legal segregation, and voting laws all designed to remove political and social power from him . . . evidence does not suggest that cocaine caused a crime wave but rather that anticipation of black rebellion inspired white alarm'.[42]

The political ramifications of this movement seem considerable. Eventually, Musto writes, it was used also by Northerners in their struggle against Southern politicians, and he demonstrates a certain amount of government complicity in stirring up feelings about cocaine for its own ends, which did not have to do with the social welfare of blacks. Hamilton Wright, who worked for the State Department on the American Opium Commission, wrote to the editor of the Louisville *Journal Courier* in 1910: 'A strong editorial from you on the abuse of cocaine in the South would do a great deal of good (but) do not quote me or the Department of State'.[43] Cocaine had become a pawn in a much bigger game. 'In each instance' Musto argues 'there were ulterior motives to magnify the problem of cocaine among negroes, and it was almost to no-one's personal interest to minimise or portray it objectively.'[44] Musto's work on rule-improvisation and rule-enforcement can be set alongside current preoccupations with drug abuse. It raises the question of whether modern drug control would have its particular orientation and vigour if the drug problem were not popularly associated with the control of 'troublesome youth', or even whether drug-control has got much to do with the problem of drugs as such.

Directly paralleling these findings is Stanley Cohen's work on the 'moral panic' surrounding the Mods and Rockers in the United Kingdom in 1963.[45] In an analysis which provides much

more substance to the influence of the mass media in the generation of moral panics and the definition of social problems than
Musto's work, Cohen arrives at the same conclusion: that the
reaction against the Mods and Rockers should not be split off from
its wider social and political roots. Fighting on the beaches of
Brighton, and amphetamine use among youth was only a screen,
onto which were projected the images of a much larger moral
drama. Troublesome youth were the 'folk devils' of a scenario
which depicted the strain of a society emerging from the austerity
of the 1930s and the immediate post-war years. Quoting a
magistrate who described delinquency as 'trying to get at too
many things too easily . . . people have become more aware of
the good things in life . . . we've thrown back the curtain for them
too soon', Cohen writes:

> The Mods and Rockers . . . touched the delicate and ambivalent
> nerves through which post-war social change in Britain was
> experienced . . . messages about 'never having it so good' were
> ambivalent in that some people were having it too good too
> quickly. . . . Resentment and jealousy were easily directed at
> the young, if only because of their increased spending power
> and sexual freedom. When this was combined with a too-open
> flouting of the work and leisure ethic, and the (as yet) un-
> certain threats associated with drug-taking, something more
> than the image of a peaceful Bank Holiday at the sea was being
> shattered.[46]

One should not neglect the fact – indeed it is highly important –
that much of the literature which I have exposed so far concerns
exotic, fringe, even 'bohemian' deviance. There is little, or no,
mention in misfit sociology, for example, of property crime. But
here is a significant point: the deviant imagination for which
misfit sociology was reaching, albeit unwittingly, was not the
imagination of gain and acquisitiveness; it was the imagination of
personal expression. These emphases and blind-spots in the
literature of misfit sociology need not so much to be *read*: they
need to be '*psychoanalysed*'.

In this discussion of how social problems are socially generated
and defined I have focused on the symbolic *imagery* of deviance,
and the way in which a conversion takes place so that what might

have been seen as unobjectionable, or at least ambiguous, comes to be understood as evil. There is also a literature concerning the construction of statistics, official rates of crime, and notions of typical crime. I will not discuss this in any detail. The same sentiments invade the research: social-control agents are seen as *unwittingly* fiddling the statistics and cooking the books, translating common-sense fantasies into numerical realities; enforcing the law selectively against the working class, blacks, the poor and long-haired youth; realising in their practice Everyman's worst dreams.[47] In every sense in the literature of misfit sociology, deviance is 'in the eye of the beholder'. It is in the gaze of the public official that deviance is created, and if he would only close his eyes the problem would go away. In a late work of the misfit paradigm Edwin Schur describes the policy implications of the perspective as 'radical non-intervention': *'leave kids alone whereever possible'*.[48]

If one major sentimental thrust of misfit sociology is that deviants are not to blame, a second major accomplishment resurrects the deviant's authenticity and integrity, discovers his 'free will', and lifts him free from imputations of 'pathology' and 'wrongheadedness'. The most lucid expression of this shift is provided by David Matza in his commitment to *naturalism*, the aim of which is to be loyal to the phenomena under study, and not to ditch that loyalty in the name of some version or another of scientific method. The faithfulness of naturalism, however, can only be approximate. 'The very act of writing or reporting commits the author to a *rendition* of the world, and a rendering is a sifting'.[49] In deviance research naturalism commits the researcher to the attempt to enter the world of the deviant, 'to comprehend and illuminate the subject's view and to interpret the world *as it appears to him'*.[50] Matza calls this stance *appreciative*, and he compares it with the *correctional* research stance in criminology, which is concerned to understand deviance only to the extent that it wishes to correct, cure, or annihilate it. The correctional perspective, that is, 'explains' before it has learned to describe:

> The purpose of ridding ourselves of the phenomenon [of deviance] manifests itself most clearly in an overwhelming contemporary concern with questions of causation, or 'etiology'. The phenomenon itself receives only cursory attention. The

ultimate purpose of liquidation is reflected in this highly dis-
proportionate division of attention between description and
explanation.[51]

Howard Becker in different language pictures a similar problem in the sociology of deviance. Having described how when
studying 'normal' or 'legitimate' occupations a sociologist will
look at the different points of view of, say, doctors, patients,
nurses and aides, he goes on,

> But somehow when sociologists studied crime they didn't under-
> stand the problem that way. Instead, they accepted the common-
> sense notion that there must be something wrong with criminals,
> otherwise they wouldn't act that way. They asked, 'Why do
> people go into crime? Why don't they stop? How can we stop
> them?' The study of crime lost its connection with the main-
> stream of sociological development and became a very bizarre
> deformation of sociology, designed to find out why people were
> doing bad things instead of finding out the organisation of
> interaction in that sphere of life. . . . I had approached the
> problem differently, the way I'd learned to do in studying
> occupations. . . . So I approached deviance as the study of
> people whose occupation, one might say, was either crime or
> catching criminals.[52]

This seemingly benign and liberal attitude of appreciation,
however, has a kick in it. Matza describes appreciation, for
example, as a 'fateful decision'; 'it eventually entails a commitment – to the phenomenon and to those exemplifying it – to render
it with fidelity and without violating its integrity'.[53]
Matza singles out Becker's well-known study, 'Becoming a
Marihuana User',[54] for extended discussion as a prototypical case
of the naturalist stance, thus illuminating the whole of the work
of misfit sociology which is characterised by an approximation to
this method, employing a 'participant observation' methodology,
studying deviants from the inside in micro-social detail, and –
as Taylor, Walton and Young put it – 'telling it like it is'.[55] This
constitutes a vital break with the established traditions
of criminologival theory and research which always rest finally on
preconceived assumptions that deviants are bad, evil, or sick, or

that they were gullible and had been led astray. In either case their motives and meanings could be discounted.

I will not extend the discussion of the appreciative research stance here; it will assert itself at later stages of my argument as one of the core assumptions of misfit sociology. One more thing needs to be said, however, in so far as 'appreciation' entails certain theoretical moves, principally a criticism of positivistic and deterministic views of deviant action. In an earlier work, *Delinquency and Drift*, Matza developed some of the implications of a break with positivism.[56] For our present purposes the most important of these is the rejection of the notion of the 'constrained delinquent' who is 'fundamentally different from the law-abiding'.[57] The difficulty with this positivist claim, as Matza sees it, is that it accounts for too much delinquency. If the delinquent were as different from conventional youth as positivism requires and 'constrained through compulsion or commitment', delinquency would be 'more permanent and less transient, more pervasive and less intermittent than is apparently the case'.[58] Put rather bluntly, positivistic and deterministic theories of delinquency do not allow for the fact that the delinquent grows up and does not remain committed to a criminal career. The delinquent is not constrained, argues Matza, either by inner or outer compulsion; he merely 'drifts' into delinquency, 'guided gently by underlying influences',[59] influences which may 'accidentally' and 'unpredictably' carry him into, or deflect him from, the delinquent path.

Matza makes a firm distinction here between mundane 'drifters' who do not become adult criminals – and who constitute the majority of delinquents – and a minority who are, by some process or other, constrained, compelled, or committed. Taylor, Walton and Young charge him with avoiding through this distinction the 'full implications of his sociology of motivation', indicating a root contradiction in his critique of determinism.[60] And although this criticism is itself unfair to Matza's subtle analysis of the relationship between compulsion and willingness,[61] it is true that Matza slithers around these issues in a manner which is not always helpful. There is no doubting, however, the sentimental imperative of Matza's position, which is that when the blinds of positivism are pulled away all men are revealed as potentially law-breaking. The common-sense gulf between 'us' and 'them', which is supported by positivist criminology to a considerable extent, is dismembered in misfit sociology: 'it becomes apparent', writes Matza, 'that *any-one* can be a marihuana user and that *no one* has to'.[62]

DE-REIFICATION, RADICALISM AND THE CRITIQUE OF WELFARE

Here are two projects in misfit sociology – the labelling focus on rules and rule-making, and the 'phenomenological' focus on faithful, insider accounts of deviant action – somehow, mysteriously, linked to the appearance of radicalism. A number of attempts have been made to formulate what it is about the misfit paradigm which holds its pieces together, and at the same time constitutes a break with the traditional image of the deviant. Each of them is in one way or another unsuccessful; partial holds are secured on misfit sociology's 'break', but the whole enterprise is never convincingly contained within these schemes. In Howard Becker's formulation the crux of the matter is a reassertion of 'the connections between the study of deviance and the growth of sociological theory and method'.[63] Paul Rock echoes this when he describes how interactionist sociology 'destroyed the absurd barrier which has hindered the application of normal sociology to this once reserved area of crime'.[64] Sociologists, that is, within what I call the misfit paradigm, refused to take for granted common-sense notions of deviants which had previously hindered the application of sociology to this 'sacred' and 'mysterious' area. In Jock Young's attempt at a formulation this same sentiment is described as a break with 'moral absolutism'; that is the assumption of an absolute consensus of opinion, life-style and morality within society which is surrounded by a deviant, non-conforming fringe. The 'absolute monolith', Young argues, is replaced by a sociological relativism which finds 'deviance' everywhere.[65] Equally, Cohen writes of what he calls the new 'sceptical' approach to deviance which refuses to take as *given* the consensus view of deviance.[66] There is truth in all four statements, but they only grasp one side of the problem. Most importantly, they conflate the theoretical break of misfit sociology and its 'politics' of underdog sympathies. In a sense they *describe* the nature of the shift, but they do not help us to *understand* it any better.

Another side of the rupture between the misfit paradigm and traditional criminology, psychiatry and welfare which is often pointed out as the essence of the matter is the break with positivism. We have already seen how Matza takes off from a critique of positivism in criminology, and there are reflections of this in the statements by Becker, Young, Rock and Cohen. Also, for Taylor, Walton and Young in *The New Criminology* labelling theory 'is part of a larger movement in criminology and sociology against the legacy of positivistic or absolutist notions of crime, deviance and social problems'.[67] Edwin Schur coins a frightful word to capture the theoretical emphasis in the new approach to deviance: 'neo-anti-determinism'.[68] In his earlier work Schur also saw a theoretical 'convergence' between the small-scale, microscopic study of deviant action in misfit sociology and the modern trends in sociological theorising – phenomenology and 'ethnomethodology' – which he calls the 'microsociology of meaning'.[69] There is no doubt that misfit sociology must be located in relation to the 'tidal wave of phenomenology'[70] which hit social science in the 1960s. It is also true that superficial links can be traced between the two – as Schur demonstrates through attention to the work of Harold Garfinkel, the founder of 'ethnomethodology', and Jack Douglas, Aaron Cicourel, and others. However, this does not take us much further forward. When Douglas – a phenomenologist – writes that 'the sociology of deviance has for some years been the most creative and turbulent area of sociological theory',[71] he is expressing a similar sentiment to Howard Becker, *but from an entirely different position*. So what, then, unites these different positions? What holds deviance, phenomenology, and underdog sympathies in the same space? What magical formula keeps the juggler's trick in the air?

The central unifying tendency within misfit sociology is the attempt *theoretically* to throw off the shackles of a pre-defined and officially categorised social reality; that is to say, there is a dissolution of *reification* in social science and its view of the moral and social order.

'Reification' is a central concept both in the work of Marx and in the phenomenological movement. For Marx the concept is developed predominantly in the context of his discussion of the *fetishism* of the commodity: the process whereby the actual social relations of production become disguised, and the relations between men involved in production come to appear as the relations between things (commodities):

A commodity is therefore a mysterious thing, simply because in it the social character of men's labour appears to them as an objective character stamped upon the product of that labour; because the relation of the producers to the sum total of their own labour is presented to them as a social relation, existing not between themselves, but between the products of their labour . . . the existence of things *qua* commodities and the value relations between the products of labour which stamp them as commodities, have absolutely no connexion with their physical properties . . . it is a definite social relation between men, that assumes, in their eyes, the fantastic form of a relation between things.[72]

Reification is a concept which has extensions and applications beyond the analysis of commodity production. As Berger and Pullberg suggest: 'there are not only fetishized commodities, but there is also fetishized power, fetishized sexuality, fetishized status . . . [correspondingly] theoretically formulated and thereby mystified in reified political science, reified sociology, reified psychology, and even scientistic philosophy'.[73] Berger and Luckmann provide the following account of the concept of reification:

To what extent is an institutional order, or any part of it, apprehended as a non-human facticity? This is the question of the reification of social reality.

Reification is the apprehension of human phenomena as if they were things, that is in non-human or possibly supra-human terms. Another way of saying this is that reification is the apprehension of the products of human activity *as if* they were something other than human products – such as facts of nature, results of cosmic laws, or manifestations of divine will. Reification implies that man is capable of forgetting his own authorship of the human world. . . . The reified world is . . . a dehumanized world. It is experienced by man as a strange facticity, an *opus alienum* over which he has no control rather than as the *opus proprium* of his own activity. . . .

The objectivity of the social world means that it confronts man as something outside of himself. The decisive question is whether he still retains the awareness that, however objectivated, the social world was made by men – and, therefore, can be remade by them. In other words, reification can be described as an extreme step in the process of objectivation, whereby the objectivated world loses its comprehensibility as a human enterprise and becomes fixated as a non-human, non-humanisable, inert facticity.[74]

De-reification unites the many threads of the misfit paradigm. Deviance is thus revealed as a *socially constructed* event. Crime rates, the imagery of deviance, and deviant action are animated and given life as events in the social, man-made world. In his statement of the labelling thesis, to give a clear example, Jerry Simmons writes:

Deviants do not exist in nature, but are man-made categories. This means that deviance is not an inherent attribute of any behaviour but is a social process of labelling. *Society is the creative force behind the deviant*. This does not mean that there is really no such thing as deviance or that the deviant is just an innocent bystander. It means that society is an active partner in producing the phenomenon called deviance and that we must look at the work of both partners if we want to understand.[75]

It is also in its de-reifying tendencies, and not in some superficial relationship to 'micro-sociology', that misfit sociology finds its suggestive links with phenomenology and ethnomethodology, both of which engage in a profound exercise in de-reification. Ethnomethodology, at least in one of its versions, attempts to uncover the background workings of the 'familiar', taken-for-granted, reified social world. Garfinkel writes:

Procedurally it is my preference to start with familiar scenes and ask what can be done to make trouble. The operations that one would have to perform in order to multiply the senseless features of perceived environments; to produce and sustain bewilderment, consternation, and confusion . . . anxiety, shame, guilt, and indignation; and to produce disorganised interaction should tell us something about how the structures of everyday

activities are ordinarily and routinely produced and maintained.[76]

Garfinkel's ethnomethodology sets out to understand how
social order is 'accomplished' in everyday activities. The major
focus of its critique of mainline sociology is that it does not know
itself theoretically, and only knows the world through a set of
concepts (class, role, status, deviance, norm, structure, and so on)
which have no established connection to the real world. Sociology,
it therefore reckons, cannot go beyond a common-sense view of
the reified world. However, ethnomethodology's claim that it
makes a revolution in sociology is not upheld everywhere.[77] Also,
disputes about its status have a tendency to become quarrelsome.
These are arguments which must be left to fend for themselves:
here the more modest undertaking is to establish the character of
ethnomethodology's links with the misfit paradigm, and to assert
that its inspirations establish it as one of the misfit sociologies.

For phenomenological enquiry, the study of deviance according
to Warren and Johnson 'is simply the observation of the meanings
of morality and immorality as acted out in everyday life'.[78] It concerns how moral rules are constructed, how they are maintained,
and how infractions of these rules are handled. The natural attitude
of the common-sense world tells us that as members of society we
can judge quite easily the difference of right from wrong. Pursuing
the argument of a phenomenological sociology, however, Jack
Douglas suggests that in concrete situations morality is not so
unproblematic. The construction and use of moral rules cannot be
relied upon in any absolute sense; these matters depend on contexts
in which problem situations arise, or upon their 'situationalness':

> when we actually observe everyday social activities we find that
> the members of our society do not, in fact, find it easy to agree
> on what is right and wrong, moral and immoral. . . . In accord
> with the assumptions that morals are nonproblematic, they do
> tend . . . to assume that morals are obvious, but only in the
> abstract, independently of any concrete situations in which the
> individual is actually involved.[79]

Under the conditions of a reified morality, Douglas argues, moral
rules become 'highly routinised . . . *absolutised* or *objectified*; that

is, made independent and necessary (absolute) but . . . thinglike or objects not subject to individual interpretation'.[80] It is the implicit de-reification of this reified, thinglike morality in misfit sociology which makes for its uneasy tensions with welfare professionalism, and lends it one aspect of its appearance as a radical sociological critique of welfare.

The welfare professional lays claim to his authority from two sources: he claims to possess a measure of *technical competence*, and he lays claim to *moral veracity*; that is, to being a 'good person'. De-reification robs him of both these props to professional legitimacy, for a reified morality is the glue which binds together professional ideology. While morality stands 'out there' it seems divorced from human agency – at once thinglike, spiritual and unquestionable. In traditional theories of deviance this reified edifice is embodied in the way in which deviance (the breaking of moral rules) is treated as 'immaturity' and 'social disorganisation'. This reified appearance of morality is a source of *absolute* legitimation for those who maintain it. Furthermore, the act of servicing a non-human, non-humanisable moral entity has the appearance of a *technical* and *morally neutral* activity, rather than a morally and politically committed *persuasion*. In one of the essays in *Toward a Rational Society* Jürgen Habermas draws a distinction which has use here. He identifies two kinds of rule: those of a 'purposive-rational' character (*zweckrational*) and 'consensual norms'. Purposive-rational rules imply predictions which are conditional upon observable events; their validity depends on either empirically grounded propositions of analytically correct propositions (for example, tautologies, mathematical statements). Consensual norms, on the other hand, are valid only in so far as they are agreed mutually between persons or parties.[81]

Habermas considers the nature of violations of these two different kinds of rule. Violations of technical, purposive–rational rules he calls *incompetence*: punishment is 'built in', so to speak, through failure and rebuff by reality. The violations of consensual norms he calls *deviant* behaviour: punishment and sanctions only operate by convention and through human agency. 'Learned rules of purposive-rational action', writes Habermas, 'supply us with *skills*, internalized norms with *personality structures*.'[82]

The domination of reification in social order, it seems, causes *deviant* acts to assume the appearance of *incompetent* acts; that is, behaviour which is susceptible to change by *skilled* intervention as compared with persuasive, coercive, or educative intervention. Under the conditions of a reified social reality, the *technical competence* and *moral veracity* of the welfare professional become merged; deviance appears to have its rightful place in the domain of technical accomplishment. The intervener, furthermore, looks like someone who possesses an armoury of technical skills, rather than someone possessed by a persuasion.

De-reification subverts this technocractic conception of morality, deviance and order and returns it to the realm of moral discourse where social problems are re-discovered, or re-membered, as moral dilemmas. And with it goes the sure-footed professionalism which saw life as a 'problem-solving process', described misfits as people whose 'coping mechanisms' had failed, and characterised its own activity as technical and unobjectionable.

It is easy to see how this theoretical de-reification might be experienced as a violent assault by social-welfare professionals, especially social workers who have had the most intimate contact with misfit sociology, and whose official, political and moral authority is in any case less securely legitimised than, say, psychiatry. It is less easy, perhaps, to see how this might be experienced as a politically radical critique of social work. And yet it is. One social-work educationalist, Brian Munday, has provided a sharp example of this reaction to the misfit paradigm. In an article entitled 'What is Happening to Social Work Students?' Munday discusses student troubles and unrest in social-work education programmes. It is an account of a professional Dante descending into the inferno: students 'highly motivated by very left-wing values' are exposed to a training programme in which 'sociology' conducts 'general attacks on traditional beliefs in society' and assails them with 'a variety of academic material that is threatening, undermining and often downright depressing', teaching that 'it is our system that is at fault'.[83] One would be forgiven for imagining a revolutionary Marxism, spilling out of the seminar room and taking to the streets. Fortunately, Munday names the sources of this insurrectionary inspiration: 'The ideas of writers like Matza, Becker and Cicourel are intellectually fascinating and persuasive, but quite ominous for the social worker.'[84]

We can get a better hold on this reading of Becker, Matza and

Cicourel – which is a *visceral* reading – if we follow how the theoretical de-reification works itself out in the pages of misfit sociology. The challenge which de-reification places before social welfare is not a technical challenge. It does not have to do with the effectiveness of the social worker's skills. Rather, it undermines the technocratic professional's claim that deviance is an area only for technical discussion. It, literally, robs him of the ground on which he stands as a technically accomplished professional. A key idea of Becker's is the notion of the 'hierarchy of credibility' which suggests that the higher up a person is in any organisational hierarchy, the more he knows about it: 'in any system of ranked groups, participants take it as given that members of the highest group have the right to define *the way things really are*'.[85] In the tradition of misfit sociology, such a credibility hierarchy is suspended: the definitions of reality offered by prisoners and mental hospital inmates are as valid, and interesting, as those offered by prison governors or psychiatrists. This is necessary for research, Becker insists, because conventionally the perspectives of those lower down are ignored and discredited. But to the welfare professional and policy-maker a suspension of the hierarchy of credibility takes away a further prop from his moral veracity. As David Matza indicates this theoretical shift expresses itself also through the appreciative stance, and it is not nearly as harmless as it might at first appear:

> To appreciate the variety of deviant enterprises requires a temporary or permanent suspension of conventional morality, and thus by usual standards inescapable elements of irresponsibility and absurdity are implicit in the appreciative stance. Deviant enterprises, and the persons who engage in them, are almost by definition troublesome and disruptive. How silly and perhaps evil, therefore, seem the appreciative sentiments of those who have been guided by the naturalist spirit. These appreciative sentiments are easily summarised: we do not for a moment wish that we could rid ourselves of deviant phenomena. We are intrigued by them. They are an instrinsic, ineradicable, and vital part of human society.[86]

The tendency finds a particularly strong expression in the work of Goffman. Alvin Gouldner has offered an account of this side of Goffman's work in which he notes that Goffman's world is one where all appearances and social claims – however eccentric, lowly, disreputable, or quirkish – 'are endowed with a kind of equal reality'. Gouldner writes:

> in short, it has no metaphysics of hierarchy. In Goffman's theory the conventional cultural hierarchies are shattered: for example, professional psychiatrists are manipulated by hospital inmates; doubt is cast upon the difference between the cynical and the sincere; the behaviour of children becomes a model for understanding adults; the behaviour of criminals becomes a standpoint for understanding respectable people; the theatre's stage becomes a model for understanding life. Here there is no higher and no lower.[87]

Gouldner notes that this dissolution of the 'metaphysics of hierarchy' carries the implication of being *against* existing hierarchies and is 'infused with a rebel vision critical of modern society'. Consequently, 'some among the rebellious young may see it as having a "radical" potential'.[88] In similar terms John Horton has commented on how phenomenology and the ethnomethodological programme seem to constitute 'a kind of cultural phase of sociological radicalism . . . with charismatic leaders, possessed followers, and a language which only insiders pretend to understand'.[89] Both Gouldner and Horton, however, are deeply suspicious of these radicalisms. Gouldner reckons that, if ambiguously, Goffman provides not a critique of society, but 'an *avoidance* . . . [and] an accommodation to existent power arrangements';[90] in Horton's view phenomenology represents a similar side-step:

> For the student and practitioner the field has the esteemed advantage of looking radical, providing a ready key to knowledge, yet preserving individualism and the freedom to do phenomenology under any regime whatsoever. . . . [But] . . . 'Beautiful people' found ugly by the pigs may learn that power is not merely a phenomenological label.[91]

Gouldner is even more sharp in his criticism of Howard Becker's 'school' of sociology:

It is a sociology of and for the new welfare state. It is the sociology of young men with friends in Washington. It is a sociology that succeeds in solving the oldest problem in personal politics: How to maintain one's integrity without sacrificing one's career, or how to remain liberal although well-heeled.[92]

If Becker's sociology is a new kind of careerism, however, it is a 'cool' careerism which 'finds itself at home in the world of hip, drug addicts, jazz musicians, cab drivers, prostitutes, night people, drifters, grifters, and skidders: the "cool world". Their identifications are with deviant rather than respectable society.'[93] But the position avoids 'erect partisanship', says Gouldner, and is only a new variant of an enlightened liberalism. It criticises the welfare state, but only the low-level officials who manage caretaking institutions; it does not challenge high-level officialdom which shapes the policy and character of these institutions, welfare budgets and research funding. Becker asks the question, 'Whose side are we on?', and Gouldner replies that Becker's school 'is indeed taking sides; it is a party to the struggle between the old and the new elites in the caretaking establishments'.[94]

It is difficult to assess Gouldner's criticisms of Becker, for he gives no clear indication of the structuring of welfare elites which he has in mind when he makes these fierce stabs. It can be said, nevertheless, that superficially these remarks miss the far-reaching critical sense of misfit sociology which I have begun to expose here: misfit sociology does not only criticise the 'bent' copper, but also enlightened, liberal-welfare practice. In order to see Gouldner's criticisms in a better light we must arrange them against the implications of misfit sociology's de-reification of welfare practice.

Much of misfit sociology, and in particular the labelling perspective, would appear to be well suited as platforms for a liberal reform strategy in social welfare, stressing preventive, non-punitive and non-stigmatising approaches to welfare. There has, however, been little attempt formally to weld the elements of the misfit paradigm to social-policy formation. Both Schur and Young have made gestures in that direction, but that is all.[95] In trying to account for the failure of labelling theory to influence psychiatry, Roman has placed emphasis on the tone of the labelling perspective, in terms not too far removed from those adopted by Gouldner: 'work such as Goffman's *Asylums* and Scheff's *Being Mentally Ill* cast psychiatrists into the role of clear-cut "bad guys" who know or care little about human nature or welfare'.[96] This, he says, has reduced communication between the fields of psychiatry and sociology, and has tended to reduce the credibility of the criticisms. In an interview Howard Becker describes his experience of this:

> I run into this a lot. People ask me, 'Why do you look at things from the point of view of medical students or people who smoke dope? What do they know about it? Why didn't you ask people who know about these things? Why don't you accept what the good people or the people in the hospital say?' It is the same criticism Erving Goffman gets. 'Why does Goffman go around acting as if the people who run the mental hospitals are out to do the patients in?' That's the way the criticism is put. I don't think it's valid. What he does is not take it for granted that their pious protestations are correct. If they are doing wonderful things, he will see it. If they are not doing them, he won't see it.[97]

There is more, however, to the suspension of a hierarchy of credibility than simply keeping one's eyes open and 'keeping an open mind'. In refusing to take at face value the cherished myths and beliefs which professions hold about themselves, Becker argues, one is simply being honest, open and scientific. Behind this apparently innocuous stance, however, lies an antagonism which is deeper than an unconventional sentimentality or underdog sympathy. The critical appraisal of deviance, morality, order and deviance-correction which misfit sociology provides points through the professional's routine, taken-for-granted world to a world of moral and political uncertainty. De-reification shows up the professional's complicity in creating the problems which he solves; the dissolution of the metaphysics of hierarchy gives the underdog misfit a voice in what consensus welfare had imagined was an already settled debate.

Peter Berger has suggested, it is worth noting here, that a de-reifying social science is one which *inevitably radicalises*. Those assumptions which are neither reflected upon nor challenged – the taken-for-granted world – have the function of legitimising specific institutions of power and interest. Berger suggests that any threat to the taken-for-granted quality of legitimating thought patterns can quickly become a threat to the institutions which they legitimate: 'Sociology, willy-nilly and by its own intrinsic logic keeps generating such threats. Simply by doing its job, sociology puts the institutional order *and* its legitimating thought patterns under scrutiny. Sociology has a built-in debunking effect . . . at least in certain situations, then, sociology can be political dynamite.'[98] Berger does not make it clear how this 'mind revolution' can 'quickly' become a real restructuring of the world; nevertheless, in his conception of a sociological conspiracy against the enterprise of common-sense he is raising important, if limited, issues.[99]

Misfit sociology undermines the *given* qualities of the field of deviance. That old catch-phrase, 'You can't legislate morality' is dis-membered. Morality can be, and *is*, legislated; moral crusades *are* events in the world; patterns of stigma *are* constructed by professionals and passed on to their clients who *do* conform. 'Deviance', in the pages of misfit sociology, is something socially and morally constructed. Professional ideology is mesmerised by this de-reification which appears to take away the facticity of deviance, dissolving it in a whirl of transaction.

Spitzer and Denzin, for example, summarise a lengthy review of the sociology of psychiatry by saying, 'in short, mental illness should be recognised for what it is – a social reaction to a certain type of behaviour'.[100] Spitzer and Denzin thus provide a definition which seems to deny the existence of madness. Coulter, taking exception to this formulation of the labelling perspective, suggests that 'either this statement was simply a *slip in expression* [my emphasis], or it reveals some quite profound misunderstanding of what is at issue'.[101] There is no slip. Misfit sociology provides such a profound *loosening* of the concept of deviance as a *given* that it can sometimes even disappear altogether. Goffman, in an early paper which argues that acts recognised as deviant in one context may be quite unobjectionable in another, writes: 'I know of no psychotic misconduct that cannot be matched precisely in everyday life by the conduct of persons who are not psychologically ill nor considered to be so.'[102] Matza, in his interview with Weis, picks up this 'slip' in the misfit paradigm:

I think that labelling theory suffers from another weakness, and that's due to its radical subjectivism. . . . Some so-called labelling theorists . . . write as if there were no real crime going. Some of the writers on mental illness, like Thomas Scheff, write as if there is no such thing as mental illness. . . . And some of the writers on witchcraft, like Kai Erikson, who is very good, except that you're not quite sure whether he acknowledges any actual witches. . . . The label 'witch' is important, but there *were* witches; the label 'mental illness' is important, and makes things even worse; but there is definitely a reality called madness; the label 'thief' is important, but there are thieves.[103]

This 'radical subjectivism', as Matza calls it, is part of a wider movement of thought both in social science and in the world. The radical subjectivism of misfit social-thought labelling theory, 'appreciative' research, anti-psychiatry, and the attendant phenomenological tidal wave – echoes the radical subjectivism of political undercurrents in the 1960s – the student protest movement, the libertarian New Left and the rise of 'personal politics' (Women's Liberation, Gay Liberation), the 'counter-culture', hippies, and the Underground. Matza recognises that 'some of the so-called American phenomenologists have a kind of affinity, an intellectual affinity, with the ideology of "hippies" '.[104] Stanley Cohen, in an 'autobiographical' sketch of the reception of misfit sociology by radical intellectuals writes: 'we all sensed something in the sceptical, labelling and societal reaction perspectives, the anti-psychiatry school and similar currents, which struck a responsive political chord.'[105]

It is to these 'intellectual affinities' and 'political chords' – which are the unwritten, but lived history of the misfit sociologists and anti-psychiatrists – to which I turn in the next chapter, where I situate misfit social thought in the moral and political mood of the 1960s. Hagan is a recent critic of labelling theory, who has suggested that its compelling qualities, and the fact that it gathered support, flow from its iconoclastic nature and the fact that it reverses and denies certain assumptions which are cherished by social scientists.[106] In reaching this conclusion Hagan takes his inspiration from a theoretical paper by Davis, who develops what he calls a 'sociology of the interesting'.[107] Davis's argument, briefly, is that what makes an audience 'sit up and take notice' about a theory is not its truth, or its explanatory power, but whether it is found *interesting* and the things which make theory interesting, he suggests, are the ways in which it denies and reverses taken-for-granted assumptions. However, the popularity of misfit social thought, its mood and its 'smell' cannot be captured by this kind of formal debate, which abstracts the processes of theory-production and theory-reception from the context of the social world in which it emerges. If misfit sociology represents a move against positivism, for example, then it was a move made by many who knew little of the positivism which they were moving against: misfit social thought moved men as men, not only as theorists. 'The roots of sociology' Alvin Gouldner writes 'pass through the sociologist as a total man, and . . . the question he must confront, therefore, is not merely how to *work*, but how to *live*.'[108] The very fact that the theoretical programme of misfit social thought was available for many years before its abrupt emergence as an 'interesting' theory underscores the fact that we must pay attention to its socio-historical roots.

Misfit sociology held the key, or so it appeared, to a particular life problem of the social scientist who had rejected the un-committed persuasions of 'mandarin' social science, but was equally reluctant to embrace the traditional and 'discredited' channels of liberal social-welfare reform. Stanley Cohen, again, writes:

> going through various degress of disillusionment with such activities . . . talking or doing something about deviance seemed to offer — however misguided this may look to an outsider — a form of commitment, a way of staying in, without on the one hand selling out or on the other hand playing the drab game of orthodox politics, whose simplicities were becoming increasingly irritating.[109]

Specifically, misfit sociology enabled some social scientists to put together *politics*, *social science* and *compassion*; to effect some partial solution to the problem of the relationship between their lives as social scientists and their lives as men and women. The misfit paradigm also glimpses something of what it means to understand the politics of deviance-control, the politics of con-formity, and the politics of welfare. But, significantly, that under-standing is in great debt to the political undercurrents of the 1960s.

It is possible that misfit sociology and anti-psychiatry represent only a historically limited solution to the problems of the developing political consciousness and commitment in the social-welfare field, a solution which temporarily dissolved the antagonisms between scholarship and action, objectivity and partisanship. In order to begin to understand both the limitations and the enduring qualities of misfit sociology and anti-psychiatry, it is necessary to look at the world in which they rose to popularity, to enter the murky waters of the 'counter-culture' and read off its codes.

4

'THE GREAT REFUSAL':
THE PERSONAL AND THE
POLITICAL

Deviance and politics come together in misfit sociology and anti-psychiatry. In an attempt to clarify the nature of the imagination of these new approaches to deviance there are a number of objectives in this chapter. First, I will briefly discuss some of the utopian and personal politics of the 'New Left' in the 1960s and its characterisation of modern society as one-dimensional doom. This is the atmosphere in which the misfit paradigm matured, and I will trace the correspondence between this view of society and its politics and the tenor of the misfit sociologies and anti-psychiatry. In the one-dimensional society *personal* protest was depicted as one of the last remnants of human and political hope: deviant acts become a fulcrum on which to move the earth. Finally, from this full-bodied imaginative rendering of the misfit social thought I will look at how the relationship between the 'personal' and the 'political' which it throws into relief is handled, particularly by the new political criminology, which is highly critical of the misfit paradigm.

'FUCKING IN THE STREETS'

The sub-heading is necessary, if awkward. The politics of the 'counter-culture' is shocking and libidinal. The sub-heading brings us, crudely, to the point. Behind such mindless slogans as 'Fuck your way to freedom' rests the pivot of the claims of the counter-culture and the New Left to serious attention: that political action and personal action cannot be torn apart. Vaneigem writes, for example: 'People who talk about revolution and class struggle without referring explicitly to everyday life, without understanding what is subversive about love and what is positive in the refusal of constraints, such people have a corpse in their mouth'.[1] We must make here a similar pronouncement: all claims to talk of the politics of personal distress, the politics of deviance, and the politics of the machinery of the welfare state within which personal distress is handled must come to terms with the scandalous imagination of the counter-culture. For it is there that the relationship between what is 'personal' and what is 'political' finds some articulation.

There are a number of variants on the theme of the personal, the political and their relationship.[2] But we must take Herbert Marcuse as the voice of the New Left. Marcuse's vision of 'one-dimensional society' is one where men have come to relinquish critical thought; it is a society which perpetuates itself not through open force but through the creation of false needs which gently contain its subjects:

A comfortable, smooth, reasonable, democratic unfreedom prevails in advanced industrial civilisation, a token of technical progress. . . .
    The people recognise themselves in their commodities; they find their soul in their automobile, hi-fi set, split-level home, kitchen equipment. The very mechanism which ties the individual to his society has changed, the social control is anchored in the new needs which it has produced.[3]

With biting sarcasm Ernest Becker has characterised the spirit and consciousness of conformity and reasonableness in modern society as the consciousness of the busy consumer:

His bright and smug consumer face shines benignly through our advertising in his many poses: counting the pennies saved and winking wisely; beaming with pride over shirt sleeves that extend the proper half inch beyond the jacket cuff; transported into heavenly raptures by zippers that do not catch or by laundry soap that makes just the right amount of foamy bubbles.[4]

This is the Cheerful Robot, as C. Wright Mills called him,[5] living in a society which represents itself as the spectacular culmination of human history and social progress.[6] In it we are said to have reached the comfortable promised land which occupied the dreams of our fathers. There is no room in this world for complaint or social protest, for the good society has already arrived and its arrival is concretely embodied in the wonders of technology which liberate men from hardship into affluence, from puritan conformity into 'permissiveness', and from wage slavery into leisure. The arrival of this conception of society carries with it certain implications for the understanding of deviant conduct. The spectacle of this transition into a 'new society' has also possessed the thought of social theorists of many persuasions. It has been called 'post-industrial society', 'post-capitalist society', 'managerial capitalism', 'leisure-time society', 'consumer society', the 'affluent society', 'advanced industrial society', 'mass society', the 'service-class society', the 'personal service society', and the 'technetronic society'. Brzezinski, who coined the last of these terms, states a clear position: 'social problems are seen less as the consequence of deliberate evil and more as the unintended by-products of complexity and ignorance; solutions are not sought in emotional simplifications but in the use of man's accumulated social and scientific knowledge'.[7] John F. Kennedy was one of the politicians – Harold Wilson in his enthusiasm over the white heat of technology was another – who appeared to applaud and embrace these sentiments:

Today these old sweeping issues have largely disappeared. The central domestic problems of our time are more subtle and less simple. They relate not to basic clashes of philosophy or ideology, but to ways and means of reaching common goals. . . .
What is at stake . . . today is not some grand warfare of rival ideologies which will sweep the country with passion, but the practical management of a modern economy. What we need are not labels and clichés but more basic discussion of the sophisticated and technical questions . . . subtle challenges for which technical answers – not political answers – must be provided.[8]

Quite simply, civilisation had arrived; ideology is at an end; science will provide. Everything which is outside this is unthinkable: 'the movement of thought is stopped at barriers which appear as the limits of Reason itself'.[9] Notions of utopia in this sense become fanciful obstacles to 'real' progress. The rise of professionalism and technicalism in the field of deviance and welfare should be understood as part of this more general process.

In an almost uncanny anticipation of Marcuse's one-dimensional society which had closed in on itself, Max Horkheimer wrote in *Eclipse of Reason*: 'Modern mass culture, although drawing freely on stale cultural values, glorifies the world as it is. Motion pictures, the radio, popular biographies and novels have the same refrain: this is our groove, this is the rut of the great and the would-be great – this is reality as it is and should be and will be.'[10] The appearances of modern society, Horkheimer argued, were that it was in a state of constant change and renewal; but: 'Though everything changes, nothing moves.'[11] This encloseure of the totality in one-dimensional, uncritical thought and practice led Horkheimer, Adorno, Marcuse and other members of the Frankfurt School of 'Critical Theory' into a profound political pessimism. They judged that there could be no real hope of a truly free society; against the massive forces of social order – themselves highly irrational – even individual subjectivity was threatened. Adorno wrote that: 'To write poetry after Auschwitz is barbaric.'[12] This was the pessimism, on the other side of which there was a vague hope that the search for politics and political change might continue if it attended to individual (and not collective) forces. In one of the fragments in his *Minima Moralia*, subtitled the reflections and experiences of a 'damaged life', Adorno wrote: 'some of the liberating forces may even have converged in the sphere of the individual. Critical Theory lingers there without a bad conscience'.[13] If there was to be social change, consciousness of the human condition must somehow surface. But how could it emerge when, as Marcuse was to write, the stabilising control of political forces was now 'anchored in the instinctual structure'?[14]

At about the time when Horkheimer and Adorno were reaching the low trough of their pessimism, George Orwell was writing *Nineteen Eighty-Four*. The criminal code of Oceania reached to the soul: *thoughtcrime, facecrime, ownlife*. 'Nothing was your own' reflected Orwell's hero Winston Smith 'except a few cubic centimetres inside your skull.'[15] Memories of freedom in Oceania are conjured up only by an old paperweight, the taste of chocolate, and the smell of good coffee.[16] 'Rebellion meant a look in the eyes, an inflection in the voice';[17] making love to Julia in the open air 'was a political act'.[18] The political theory of the Frankfurt School, Orwell's desciption of freedom in *Nineteen Eight-Four* and the rebellion of the counter-culture collide: dissent must come from *outside* one-dimensionality if it was to mean more than making furtive love, and protest must come from *inside* the human subject. '*If there is hope*', Winston Smith wrote in his illegal diary, '*it lies in the proles*.'[19] The 'proles' of Oceania, of course, are not the 'proletariat'. Although they constitute an oppressed class, they are not oppressed in their spirit, their emotions and their life-style. As Orwell describes them they lie outside society and they are the location of an unlicensed libido. It was in this setting that Orwell saw revolt as visceral – 'in your stomach and in your skin there was a sort of protest, a feeling that you had been cheated of something that you had a right to'[20] – or it was contained in 'isolated acts of violence such as killing somebody or blowing something up'.[21] In the structure of the sentiments of Orwell's Oceania we are in the land of the Yippies, the hippies, Weathermen, flower children, Mad Dog and the Angry Brigade. It is a land, that is, where deviance is politics.

In the western world a succession of events overturned the easy complacency of the 'end of ideology' thesis; these events constitute the turbulent (but easily forgotten) history of the 1960s. And in particular it was the arrival of the counter-cultural rebellion from the most unexpected source – white, prosperous, middle-class youth – which is often taken as a kind of support for Marcuse's analysis of political domination. For here were people protesting not against material hardship, but against the emotional containments of affluence, a feeling that affluence was not all that there was to life and that public success in the affluent world might be personally meaningless. The counter-culture did (and does) excite a great deal of comment, but one should not run away with the idea that it represented a unified, broadly-based social movement. It was (and is) probably much smaller and less integrated than many commentators (especially journalists) have implied. But that does not mean that it was about nothing, for the counter-culture did touch the nerve of a wide number of contemporary concerns. Paul Breines describes the New Left's revolt as saturated with 'the virtually subcutaneous dread of conformity, boredom, bureaucracy, and psychological, sexual, and cultural modes of exploitation which informs . . . [its] life-style'. Breines continues that this 'suggests that it arose from precisely that dimension of society in which America proclaims to have realised its ideals'.[22] It was Marcuse's political theory, moreover, which Breines identifies as the thing which made possible an understanding of the relationship between 'personal hang-ups' and 'social structure' which is so central to the New Left's philosophy: through it the New Left discovered 'the politics of its own unhappiness'.[23]

But the New Left did not understand 'politics' in any traditional sense and in some of its moments it moved completely outside the official language of political discourse, a language experienced to be as constricting as Orwell's *Newspeak*. For example, Jerry Rubin of the Yippies writes of the Berkeley Free Speech Movement:

> A dying culture destroys everything it touches.
> Language is one of the first things to go . . .
> Language *prevents* communication.
>
>   CARS LOVE SHELL
>   How can I say
>   'I love you'
>   after hearing:
>   'CARS LOVE SHELL'
>
> Does anyone understand what I *mean*?
> Nigger control is called 'law and order'.
> Stealing is called 'capitalism'.
>
> A 'REVOLUTION' IN TOILET PAPER.
> A 'REVOLUTION' IN COMBATING MOUTH ODOR!
> A 'REVOLUTIONARY' HOLLYWOOD MOVIE!
> *Have the capitalists no respect?*
>
> But there's one word which Amerika hasn't destroyed. One word which has maintained its emotional power and purity.
> Amerika cannot destroy it because she dare not use it. It's illegal!
> It's the last word left in the English language:
> FUCK!!!

One bright winter day in Berkeley, John Thomson crayoned

on a piece of cardboard 'FUCK WAR', sat down with it and was arrested within two minutes. . . .

The Filthy Speech Movement had been born.[24]

Marcuse gives some theoretical dignity to these pranks of the Yippies: obscenities, he writes, must be seen as part of the 'Great Refusal' in the sense that they constitute 'a methodological subversion of the linguistic universe of the Establishment'.[25] And John O'Neill is another who attempts some articulation between the counter-culture's joyful, theatrical celebration of 'political delinquency' and the area of discourse which is formally conceived of as 'politics'.[26] One of the dominant themes of the New Left was its attempt to reach beyond formal politics and unearth the political significance of commonplace, everyday events.

At this point the exploration of the New Left must stand back on itself: is this not childish and ridiculous? The question is not rhetorical. The answer is that it *is*, precisely, 'childish' and 'ridiculous'. The 'counter-culture' is also silly, outrageous, sloppy, and mindless: it stops serious thought dead in its tracks. One of the words which it commonly uses to describe itself is 'mind-blowing'. The revolt of the counter-culture is a visceral revolt which embraces the playfulness, the childishness, and the polymorphous perversity of the infant. In its genteel moments – the 'Human Potentials Movement', encounter groups, 'Growth Centres', and so on – it involves breaking the taboos of the middle-class living room under the paternal gaze of the encounter-group 'trainer'. The 'Growth Centre' is an indoor love-in where you keep on your clothes; in so-called 'sensitivity-training' the subject 'expands human awareness' – or so it is claimed – but without the use of illegal drugs. The impulse appears to be the same – 'psychic jailbreak'.[27] Where the hippie might talk of being 'high', the encounter movement offers 'joy': both reach back to a promise of childhood which has not been fulfilled.[28]

In a 'Political Preface' to an edition of *Eros and Civilisation* Marcuse notes that the revolt of the New Left does not only involve traditional political issues and demands – poverty, civil rights, war – but also 'the refusal to speak the dead language of affluence, to wear clean clothes, to enjoy the gadgets of affluence'.[29] He asks: 'Can we speak of a juncture between the erotic and political dimensions?'

T.D.I.—D

even the attempt to formulate, to articulate, to give word to protest assume[s] a childlike, ridiculous immaturity. Thus it is ridiculous and perhaps 'logical' that the Free Speech Movement at Berkeley terminated in the row caused by the appearance of a sign with the four-letter word. It is perhaps equally ridiculous and right to see deeper significance in the buttons worn by some of the demonstrators (among them infants) against the slaughter in Vietnam: MAKE LOVE, NOT WAR.[30]

It is ridiculous *and* right, argues Marcuse, to penetrate the counter-culture, and to give it theoretical articulation. In the later phase of his writings he returns to an old theme of the Frankfurt School: a biological basis for political rebellion which lay in the libido, 'a stratum of human existence stubbornly out of reach of total social control'.[31] And this old preoccupation linked up with the new youthful protest, for the revolt of youth, Marcuse argued, represented a 'new sensibility' which implied the necessary break from the constraining false needs of one-dimensionality and a restructuring of human nature: 'that is to say, different instinctual needs, different reactions of the body as well as the mind'.[32] The 'new sensibility' of the counter-cultural deviant imagination was, for Marcuse, a highly significant political event. In order to understand why it is that Marcuse places this emphasis on the personal side of political change, and how his theory reverberates with modern deviance theory in a much more fundamental way than is usually recognised, it is necessary to understand a little of the 'Critical Theory' of the Frankfurt School.

THE FRANKFURT SCHOOL AND THE DEVIANT IMAGINATION

The corpus of the Frankfurt Institute of Social Research is breathtaking in its scope. At one time or another the Institute's membership included not only Adorno, Marcuse and Horkheimer, but also Erich Fromm, Walter Benjamin, Leo Lowenthal and many others. Nathan Ackerman – the grand old man of family therapy – did some of his earliest work under the aegis of the Institute, for example.[33] Most commentators agree that the School's most compelling work was completed before the end of the Second World War, both in Germany and later in American exile.[34] Until quite recently, however, the major corpus was untranslated and ignored in the English-speaking world. In approaching the Frankfurt School, none the less, language is only a superficial barrier: more formidable are its intimate relationships to European, and specifically German, philosophy and social thought. The English-speaking world is also an English-thinking world, and a wide gulf separates Critical Theory from English and American social science.[35]

The Frankfurt School were into every nook and cranny: a critique of philosophy; an attempt to integrate psycho-analysis into their broader social theory; the sociology of art, music and popular culture, and so on. The corpus ranges from the sublime – the critique of the Enlightenment, or the societal implications of Schoenberg's twelve-tone scale – to the apparently ridiculous – the astrology column of the *Los Angeles Times*.[36] Until recently, however, the only well-known work of the Frankfurt School was its highly atypical study of the authoritarian personality, which represents its foray into the quantitative methods of American social science.[37] The re-emergence of a wider interest in this Critical Theory flows from its almost magical anticipation of the political outbursts of the late 1960s – the focus on 'personal' politics, the 'ecology' crisis and, of course, the New Left. It is only this aspect of Critical Theory which I wish to map out here.

The Frankfurt School's history can be understood, to a large degree, as a move away from Marxism. In part this is a move which stems from a simply human disillusionment in the face of the failure of the German socialist movement in the 1920s, and the rise of Hitler and Stalin; in part it stems from a theoretical break with Marx. A furious debate has surrounded the question of how to separate these two parts; I will not enter into that debate here.[38] The most important side, however, *for the theory of deviance*, is undoubtedly the Frankfurt School's critique of the Enlightenment, and their development of the concept of man's relationship to nature – both external nature and internal (human) nature.

The historical decline of religion and a spiritual view of nature was accompanied by the rise of science. This secularisation of man's view of nature is generally conceived of as a dissolution of super-stition and myth. It was the aim of the Enlightenment, write Horkheimer and Adorno, to liberate men from fear and establish their sovereignty. In the secular gaze of science nature becomes de-animated, an object; the relationship of man to nature, Bacon insisted for example, was that 'we should command her by action'. Horkheimer and Adorno write:

> The concordance between the mind of man and the nature of things that he had in mind is patriarchal: the human mind, which overcomes superstition, is to hold sway over a dis-enchanted nature. Knowledge, which is power, knows no obstacles. . . . What men want to learn from nature is how to use it in order wholly to dominate it and other men. That is the only aim. . . . There is to be no mystery – which means, too, no wish to reveal mystery.[39]

This is the view of nature supplied by the Enlightenment. It is a view – *our culture's view* – of man's relationship to nature in which nature has only a commercial value: that is, stones are good or bad bricks; meat is good or bad food; the *raw* is always something with a potential to be *cooked* and exploited for men's ends. As Horkheimer wrote in an earlier piece: 'the assimilation of food largely dominates the organic life of plant and brute beast'.[40] Critical Theory contends that the view of man's relation-ship to nature as one of dominance is a one-sided view; and it contains a trap, in that it falls prey to its own mythology: the religious myth that God rules the world is simply replaced by the secular, scientific myth that man controls nature. The final yield of this trap is that man's own nature becomes the subject of domina-tion by man. As Martin Jay has expressed this inversion: 'The instrumental manipulation of nature by man led inevitably to the concomitant relationship among men.'[41] But, only among men; also within men: human nature becomes something to be *expunged*, in the same way that external nature must be expunged and controlled. The final result of this process is well represented in the work of B. F. Skinner: men must progress 'beyond human freedom and dignity', for human nature is something too treacher-ous to be lived with in the modern world.[42] Just as capriciousness must be excluded from Skinner's orderly laboratory, so wayward-ness must be expelled in his view of a perfect, stable society.

The emancipation of the Enlightenment – which we understand as social progress – according to Horkheimer and Adorno thus inevitably turns into its opposite: into a containment and a restriction of man, his nature and his sensibilities:

Animism spiritualised the object, whereas industrialism objectifies the spirits of men . . . the conventionalised modes of behaviour are impressed on the individual as the only natural, respectable, and rational ones. He defines himself only as a thing, as a static element, as success or failure. His yardstick is self-preservation, successful or unsuccessful approximation to the objectivity of his function and the models established for it.[43]

Returning to this theme thirty years later, Marcuse writes that politics, therefore, must drive to the very heart of human sensibility: men are contained 'not only in the mind, the consciousness of men, but *also in their senses*; and no persuasion, no theory, no reasoning can break this prison, unless the fixed, petrified *sensibility* of the individuals is *"dissolved"* . . . – broken in a *second alienation*: that from the alienated society'.[44]

This tricky talk of a 'double alienation' should not be allowed to cloud the issue. It is more, for example, than an indication of Marcuse's theoretical debt to Hegel – who also writes of an 'alienation of the alienation'. In fact it describes perfectly the process which is traced in Kenneth Keniston's empirical research into the 'radicalisation' of youth. First succeeding in the system, these young people find alienated achievement lacking in human value, and then break from it.[45] And so it is that Marcuse celebrates the deviant counter-culture and its 'revolution in manners' as a break from one-dimensionality. The counter-culture, quite simply, is seen as an attempt to radicalise *sensibility* through experimentation with different patterns of sexuality, altered forms of family living, mind-blowing drugs and life-style. The counter-culture has been described as the 'New Mutants';[46] Marcuse sees them as throw-backs from, and against, the Enlightenment, engaging in a revolution of total sensibility. To take the manifesto of the White Panthers as an example of this: 'Our culture, our art, the music, newspapers, books, posters, our clothing, our homes, the way we walk and talk, the way our hair grows, the way we smoke dope and fuck and eat and sleep – it is all one message, and the message is FREEDOM. . . .'[47]

Collisions come thick and fast between the New Left's 'politics of everyday life' and the Frankfurt School critique of the Enlightenment. The superficial idiocy of a search for the connections between a highly theoretical, difficult and sometimes frosty German philosophy and the anti-intellectual pranks of a movement which at one time took as a slogan 'Don't trust anyone over thirty' cannot be denied. The difficulty, however, is not finding the convergences which press from all sides; the difficulty is containing them in thought. How, for example, does one contain (and articulate) the relationship between the Frankfurt critique of man's domination of the natural and animal world, which presses against the concern with the 'ecology crisis', and 'freak foods' and vegetarianism?[48] Or the formidable resemblance between the critique of the Enlightenment and Theodore Roszak's 'hippie mysticism', which arrives at much the same conclusion of man's destructive relationship to a 'de-sacralised' nature? Roszak traces the source of political and human difficulties in the industrial world to a refusal to admit the elemental nature of man's relationship to the natural world: man denies nature a place in the world, except as a passive object, at the eventual cost of denying his own place.[49] But, then, Roszak proceeds not from Critical Theory, or anything resembling it, but from a reading of the Romantics in which he proclaims: 'Blake, not Marx, is the prophet of our political horizon.'[50] And, again, in a moving fragment titled 'Man and Animal', Adorno and Horkheimer move from an account of the cruel domination of animals to how woman represents a more earthy 'nature' than man, which unfolds as an analysis of male-domination which foreshadows much of modern feminism.[51] Women's Liberation, the politics of life-style, and the extension of human sensibilities: the themes of the 1960s reverberate in the pre-war writings of the Frankfurt School. And equally, the critique of the Enlightenment and scientific rationality brings Critical Theory into proximity with crime, madness and the deviant imagination.

Critical Theory was not afraid to go to the lowest levels of human endeavour in its search for the mechanism of social control. 'It is not that chewing gum underlines metaphysics', wrote Horkheimer, 'but that it *is* metaphysics – this is what must be made clear.'[52] And here, in the silent, inarticulate depths of the imagination – hidden away within banality – Critical Theory might pursue its goal. The human Ego – defined from the beginning by Descartes as an instrument to dominate 'the passions' – was an agency which had only self-perpetuation at heart: 'the ego is indulgent to agreeable and wholesome emotions but is stern with anything conductive to sadness.'[53] The conscious ego, insisted Horkheimer, Adorno and Marcuse (who knew their psycho-analysis) was not to be trusted as an indicator of the political and historical mood. As one of the new generation of critical theorists has expressed it: Critical Theory 'must plumb the psychic depths for sounds of sadness and revolt'.[54]

In a footnote to *Eclipse of Reason* Horkheimer quotes with approval the following lines from Poe:

> That individuals *have* soared above the plane of their race, is scarcely to be questioned; but, in looking back through history for traces of their existence, we should pass over all biographies of 'the good and the great', while we search carefully the slight records of wretches who died in prison, in Bedlam, or upon the gallows.[55]

And in his history of the Frankfurt School Martin Jay reveals that Horkheimer also included the quotation in a letter to his friend and colleague Lowenthal, where he wrote: 'During the last years I have never read any sentences which were closer to our own thoughts than these.'[56] Earlier in *Eclipse of Reason*, in a chapter with the title 'The Revolt of Nature', Horkheimer had worked through the themes of the critique of Enlightenment: domination of nature involved the domination of man, which entailed self-renunciation. Horkheimer suggests that: 'Resistance and revulsion arising from this repression of nature have beset civilisation from its beginnings, in the form of social rebellions . . . as well as in the form of individual crime and mental derangement.'[57]

But here Critical Theory is in conflict with itself. *If* crime, madness and deviance are sometimes the containers and expressions of man's revolt against his own containment, then that goes too close to a *positive* expression of thought for the Frankfurt School: Critical Theory is committed to *negative* thinking. Adorno was, possibly, the most emphatic of the Frankfurt School on this point. In one of his most often quoted aphorisms in *Minima Moralia* he wrote that 'the whole is the untrue'.[58] Any attempt to grasp this false totality in a theoretical synthesis risks falsity. Equally in the one-dimensional society any anticipation of utopia or freedom was at risk of being untrue to itself; Critical Theory must content itself with being an expression of *negative* thinking which teases out the contradictions, discontinuities and disharmonies in the world. Critical Theory must be a 'melancholy science' rather than a 'joyful' one: Adorno wrote that 'the splinter in your eye is the best magnifying-glass'.[59] Correspondingly, there was a ban in Critical Theory on giving a description of liberation (utopia) which has been compared with the Jewish ban on naming God. The implication that the deviant imagination contains some hints of rebellion goes too close to breaking this ban; Critical Theory must leave the suggestion dangling in its negative, fragmentary form.

If Adorno places the strongest emphasis on this point, Marcuse goes nearest to breaking the ban.[60] And yet, although he embraces the revolt of the New Left and the 'new sensibility' of the 'hippies' as something which 'herald[s] a total break with the dominant needs of repressive society',[61] he asserts strenuously that he has never at any point understood the counter-cultural rebellion as a force which can liberate mankind.[62] *And yet* – contradictions abound in this difficult area of Critical Theory – 'playpower' *might* contain some indications of our hopeful future, for, Marcuse writes, a hopeful future *might* see a convergence of work (labour) and play.[63]

I have said enough to indicate the difficulties of interpretation in this area. The deviant imagination in Critical Theory's gaze *might* contain some clues to the alternative society; it might also contain the sounds and sadness of revolt; but it might also indicate only a memory of some 'natural', asocial tendency in human beings. Thus, in a piece with the inflated title 'A Theory of Crime' – where Adorno's influence is particularly felt – Horkheimer writes with Adorno that the criminal 'represented a trend which is deep-rooted in living beings, and whose elimination is a sign of all development: the trend to lose oneself in the environment instead of playing an active role in it; the tendency to let oneself go and sink back into nature'.[64] The contradiction is fully expressed here. Horkheimer and Adorno also write in this piece, which is full of bitterness and sarcasm, that prison is simply a reflection of the unfreedom of Everyman in totalitarian society.

Critical Theory goes beyond formal political analysis to understand how politics inserts itself in the lives of individual subjects. Thus, Horkheimer and Adorno write: 'Europe has two histories: a well-known, written history and an underground history. The latter consists in the fate of the human instincts and passions which are displaced and distorted by civilisation.'[56] In its attempt to read the 'hidden history' of the containment of human spontaneity and passion Critical Theory poses the question of the deviant imagination and its relationship to politics. Can we therefore think of deviance as a contained freedom? The question mark, which is the emblem of Critical Theory's *negative* thinking, refuses to close itself into a full-stop.[66] But in the heat of world events in the 1960s the many-sided negativity of Critical Theory blows apart and it finds in some quarters a new enthusiasm. Jürgen Habermas, a 'second generation' member of the Frankfurt School, writes of the convergence of politics and deviance in the new protest movement which 'brings to light the cryptopolitical substance of derivative psychic disturbances'.[67] Habermas captures the mood, and the new directness, perfectly even though it still represents for him an imperfect understanding:

I consider the politicisation of private conflicts a singular result of the protest movement. . . . What is peculiar is the short term displacement of the culturally normative border between private and public conflicts. Today, difficulties that a mere two or three years ago would have passed for private matters – for conflicts between students and teachers, workers and employers, or marital partners, for conflicts between individual persons – now claim political significance and ask to be justified in political concepts. Psychology seems to turn into politics – perhaps a reaction to the reality that politics, in so far as it relates to the masses, has long been translated into psychology.

The gentle social control exercised by the mass media makes use of the spectacles of an undermined private sphere in order to make political processes unrecognisable as such. The de-politicised public realm is dominated by the imposed privatism of mass culture. *The personalisation of what is public is thus the cement in the cracks of a relatively well-integrated society,* which forces suspended conflicts into areas of social psychology. There they are absorbed in categories of deviant behavior: as private conflicts, illness, and crime. *These containers now appear to be overflowing.*[68]

DEVIANCE AND POLITICS: A FULCRUM TO MOVE THE EARTH

The emergence of misfit sociology and anti-psychiatry within the political confluence of the 1960s, and in the midst of the 'client rebellion',[69] led to the tabling of a number of awkward questions which group themselves around the central question of the relationship between deviance and politics. Misfit sociology did not know Critical Theory, except in a bowdlerised form. Its response to the correspondence of deviance and politics was, correspondingly, more crude and less indirect.

The problem received a number of formulations. Stanley Cohen posed one of its features particularly well:

There is much talk of alienation, dropping out, disaffiliation and youth on the streets. There is confusion about the line beyond which 'stealing' becomes 'looting', 'hooliganism' becomes 'rioting', 'vandalism' becomes 'sabotage'. When do 'reckless maniacs' become 'freedom fighters'? Are the everyday encounters between the police and urban slum youth throughout the world somehow stripped of their political significance if what is happening is not defined as a 'riot' or 'disturbance'?[70]

This key issue had been raised in a seminal contribution by Horowitz and Liebowitz.[71] There they argued that sociology, social work, law and political science had held to an unnecessarily harsh and artificial distinction between 'deviant' acts and 'political' acts. This distinction is supported by what they call the 'welfare model of social problems,' and by a restricted definition of politics as something confined to the electoral process, the working and maintenance of party political machinery, etc.

This model [the welfare model] has sought to liberalise the visible agencies of social control (the police, judiciary, and welfare agents) by converting them from punitive instruments into rehabilitative instruments . . . [yielding] the conventional tendency to evaluate deviant behaviour in *therapeutic* rather than *political* terms. . . .

Conventional wisdom about deviance is reinforced by the highly formalistic vision of politics held by many social workers and sociological theorists. . . . In its liberal form – the form most readily adopted by social pathologists – the majoritarian formulation of politics prevails. This is a framework limited to political strategies available to majorities or to powerful minorities having access to elite groups. The strategies available to disenfranchised minorities are largely ignored and thus the politics of deviance go unexamined. The behaviour of rule-makers and law enforcers is treated as policy decision rather than as a political phenomenon, while a needlessly severe distinction is made between law and politics.[72]

Horowitz and Liebowitz note that with the emergence of new political groups in the 1960s – Yippies, International Situationists, Zippies ('like Yippies only more fierce' according to Abbie Hoffman), Mad Dog, the Weathermen, Black Power, the Gay Liberation Front – which employed as *political* tactics activities which would formally be defined as deviant (or criminal) and which mix politics with deviant life-style, 'the line between the social deviant and the political marginal is fading. It is rapidly becoming an obsolete distinction'.[73] At this time also, of course, we find the emergence of welfare client groups (or groups of 'potential clients') who pose traditional welfare problems as politics: Claimants' Unions, Gay Liberation, Women's Liberation, Mental Patients' Unions, Child Poverty Action Group, various community and neighbourhood control movements, squatters, Preservation of the Rights of Prisoners (PROP), and in the United States the Mental Patients' Liberation Front and the Insane Liberation Front.[74] Horowitz and Liebowitz write:

The traditional distinction between social problems and the political system is becoming obsolete. Behaviour which in the past was perceived as social deviance is now assuming well-defined ideological and organisational contours; while political marginals are adopting a deviant life style. This merger of social deviance and political marginality creates a new style of politics, based on strategies that are traditionally considered illegitimate. The result of this trend is estimated to be an increase in the use of violence as a political tactic, and the development of a revolutionary potential among the expanding ranks of deviant sub-groups. In the light of such developments, sociology and political science must revise their theoretical formulations to take into account the merger of social deviance and political marginality.[75]

Theoretically, these authors suggest, 'without taking into account the break-down in the distinction between politics and deviance, the meaningfulness of both sociology and political science is seriously compromised'.[76] And commenting on the American race riots of the summer of 1967 they suggest: 'under such circumstances, the established welfare distinction between juvenile delinquency and guerrilla warfare means very little.'[77] From a different perspective J. Edgar Hoover would appear to have spotted something similar when he complained that 'juvenile delinquency' was a term which he found too 'apologetic'; he found the expression 'teenage brigands' preferable.[78]

These considerations, which thrived in the atmosphere of the New Left, constitute quite a sharp break from traditional criminological, psychiatric and social-welfare conceptions of deviance. The labelling perspective had, to a limited extent, already embodied this break and Becker, in *Outsiders*, had drawn attention to the 'political' aspect of deviance:

> The question of what the purpose or goal (function) of a group is, and, consequently, what things will help or hinder the achievement of that purpose, is very often a political question. . . . If this is true, then it is likewise true that the question of what rules are to be enforced, what behaviour regarded as deviant and what people labelled as outsiders must also be regarded as political.[79]

But what emerges in the literature of misfit sociology from the analysis provided by Horowitz and Liebowitz is the imperative that one should understand not only the *labelling process* as a politically derived judgement, but also that *deviant behaviour* itself should be accorded political status. Or, more specifically, that deviance should be grasped as a primitive crypto-political action, in the same way that social bandits in peasant societies, or the machine-smashing of the Luddites, represented a primitive political force. Hobsbawm writes of such 'primitive rebels': 'they are *pre-political* people who have not yet found, or only begun to find, a specific language in which to express their aspirations about the world. Though their movements are thus in many respects blind and groping, by the standards of modern ones, they are neither unimportant nor marginal.'[80]

We choose (or learn) to regard the thefts and murders of Robin Hood not as 'deviant' acts, but as the crypto-political acts of a 'noble robber': in misfit sociology the same intelligibility is to be accorded to the common misfit; this is the culmination of the stance of 'appreciation'. Vandalism, for example, is traditionally conceived of as 'senseless', 'purposeless', 'wanton', 'mindless', 'random', 'arbitrary', and 'motiveless'. Nathan Goldman finds in his research, however, that much youthful vandalism which takes the school as its target is not in the least sense 'arbitrary'. The youth commonly directs his violence against his *own* school. Furthermore, the schools which are more likely to be vandalised, Goldman finds, are those with a rapid staff turnover, low staff morale, low identification between parents, teachers and pupils, obsolete school equipment, and a general atmosphere of insecurity and dissatisfaction.[81] Acts of vandalism are acts of revenge against real, or perceived, injustices. Vandalism in terms of the preceding discussion, is a primitive, inarticulate attempt to 'right' wrongs: in that sense, it is a crypto-political act. Similarly, given the tenuous relationship between secondary education and the life which most working-class youth know they will lead, truanting can be understood as a means by which children comment on their education and 'vote with their feet'.[82] Both vandalism and truanting take on political shape within misfit sociology. A working-class youth who scrawls 'Fuck School . . . Boot Boys Rule' on the school wall may be enjoying a prank, but it is difficult to see his act as 'mindless', 'senseless', or 'motiveless'. Ian Taylor has also provided the case for approaching soccer hooliganism as the soccer fan's attempt to act against certain changes in the football game which follow on its considerable professionalisation and undermine the game's traditional links with working-class culture.[83] One final example will suffice here, and again it is drawn from the mundane criminality of working-class youth. I have elsewhere developed the notion, through a case study of a particular outburst of racial violence in an English town, that one could

conceive of *at least a certain amount* (if not all) of 'paki-
bashing' as primitive political action, given the economic and
employment conditions in some regions and the contingency of
large immigrant populations.[84] The backcloth imagery to 'paki-
bashing' is provided by the idea that 'they come over here and take
our jobs and our women'; violent attacks on Pakistani immigrants
can represent, and can be better understood, as a primitive (and
impotent) means of acting on labour conditions, rather than
thinking, say, in such categories as 'feckless psychopath' or
'unprovoked assault'.[85] A similar conclusion is reached in another
study of racial violence by Bryan Hartley.[86]

What is clear in the accounts which I have given of a 'political
reading' of deviance is that they involve various unspecified shifts
in the meaning of 'political'. It is not enough, however, simply
to say that the notion of politics obtains some fluidity; the precise
nature of this fluidity must be grasped and made intelligible. The
idea of deviance as a crypto-political rebellion emerges as part
of a wider mood of the 1960s which dissolves the firm distinction
of the 'personal' and 'public' spheres. This dissolution creates a
profound loosening of the terms, and provides a great deal of
scope for a free movement of thought. Thus, when Becker writes
of deviance as a 'political' phenomenon, it is clear that he means
little more than 'man-made and negotiable'. Horowitz and
Liebowitz, however, when they confront Howard Becker's statement take it 'as read' that Becker's statement means that 'the
decision to treat deviance as a social problem is itself a political
decision'.[87] And, while it is clear that they are not using 'deviance'
as Becker employs it ('labelled rule-breaking'), there is no
guarantee at all that they use 'political' in the same way. A further
example of the fluidity of the word 'politics' can be taken from
Laing: 'Psychiatry is concerned with politics, with who makes the
law. Who defines the situation. What is in fact the situation. What
is in fact the case, and what is not the case. That is, with ontology.'[88]
Laing's shifting emphasis from politics to *being* captures quite well
the 'personal politics' of the New Left. Fanon wrote, for example,
of the psychology of oppression:

> it is not the soil that is occupied. It is not the ports or the aero-
> dromes. French colonialism has settled itself in the very centre
> of the Algerian individual and has undertaken a sustained work

of clean-up, of expulsion of self, of rationally pursued mutila-
tion.

There is not occupation of the territory on the one hand, and
independence of persons on the other. It is the country as a
whole, its history, its daily pulsation that are contested, dis-
figured, in the hope of a final destruction. Under these conditions, the individual's breathing is an observed, an occupied
breathing. It is a combat breathing.[89]

Fanon's words could stand as a motto for the New Left's view
of the political disfigurement of the human subject. Compare
Nancy Henley's review of the microscopically detailed research
on non-verbal communication and its relationship to political
structure, which she calls 'micropolitical cues':

In front of, and defending, the larger political–economic
structure that determines our lives and defines the context of
human relationship, there is a micropolitical structure that helps
maintain it. The 'trivia' of everyday life – using 'sir' or first
name, touching others, dropping the eyes, smiling, interrupting,
and so on – that characterise these micropolitics are commonly
understood as facilitators of social intercourse, but are not
recognised as defenders of the status quo – of the state, of the
wealthy, of authority, of all those whose power may be
challenged. Nevertheless, these minutiae find their place on a
continuum of social control which extends from internalised
socialisation (the colonisation of the mind) at the one end to
sheer physical force (guns, clubs, incarceration) at the other. . . .

This paper will seek to examine certain nonverbal behaviours,
and some subtle verbal ones, in their social context as a step
toward understanding the myriad faces of power.[90]

The misfit paradigm, in accordance with the spirit of the New
Left, would exclude *nothing* from its political imagination. From
within the collapse of a firm distinction between 'personal' and
'public' domains it promised a politics of the family and child-
rearing, a politics of sexuality, soccer hooliganism, shop-lifting,
pornography, vandalism, play, illegitimacy, madness, and drug
abuse; a 'body politics', a hormonal politics, and a politics of
ecstasy: in the words of Ronald Laing, 'a politics of experience'.

Misfit sociology lives and breathes within a *politicisation of every-day life*. It promised, although it did not secure, a politics of socialisation. In a cautious appraisal of the political implications of the hippies, 'Why All of Us May be Hippies Some Day', Fred Davis pictured them as a pioneer force, 'rehearsing *in vivo* a number of possible cultural solutions to central life problems posed by the emerging society of the future' where 'certain incipient problems of identity, work and leisure . . . loom ominously [in] Western industrial society'.[91] More typically, the social deviant was pictured in a more rebellious light. Returning to him motive and authenticity through the stance of 'appreciation', the misfit emerged as a sort of political hero, kicking through cultural taboos and laying the basis for a new 'freedom'.

In various attempts to 're-write' social deviance politically the idea of the delinquent as an urban bandit inserts itself in the misfit paradigm. As part of the revitalisation of the anarchistic and libertarian impulse in New Left politics this is not surprising. In a 'legal manual', for example, criminal activity is described as follows:

> Most court cases are political cases. Many people get screwed for shoplifting from supermarkets, nicking expensive cars, and other activities designed to transfer the bread from the rich, the banks and the businesses to the dispossessed people of the world. These actions involve the socialist goal of the redistribution of the wealth. The fact that it is illegal is a recommendation of its effectiveness. . . .
>
>   We must reclaim the people's history – of Robin Hood, William Tell, Sabata . . . and all their merry men.[92]

The sentiment also finds a place in more sombre criminology texts: Taylor, Walton and Young write that 'the mass of delinquents are literally involved in the practice of redistributing private property'.[93] The same authors suggest also that Laing's work on schizophrenia carries for them the following implications: 'even in the most extreme cases of verbal disorder where linguistic utterances are hardly possible by the deviant (e.g. schizophrenia), it has been strongly argued by Laing and others that non-communication itself can be understood as political attack upon the double-bind concentration camp of the nuclear family.'[94]

And when *King Mob* magazine turns its critical attention towards social welfare, it asks 'Why do schizophrenia and delinquency have a key role to play in the subversion of the *reasonable* society?':

> Capitalism's most intractable crisis in the advanced industrial states is the crisis of *socialisation*. The attempts to mediate *family* and *school* encounters and aggravates contradictions which must be exploited by an urban youth guerrilla. It must also aim to occupy the hiatus which separates the individual's emergence from the family–school complex and his reintegration into organised society via *forced labour*. The first task is to build up a comprehensive network of Anti-Social Services, designed to combat the system's efforts to conceal its structural weaknesses by means of a unified ideology and practice of welfare.[95]

Deviance, in the most fully developed expressions of the sentiments of the counter-culture, becomes a fulcrum from which to move the dead weight of one-dimensional society. The misfit's delinquencies surface as an inarticulate political consciousness; personal distress turns into the murmurings of personal and crypto-political dissent whether it finds its expression through running away from home, illicit drug use, marital infidelity, truanting, vandalism, thieving, promiscuity, suicide, psychosis, hooliganism, or whatever. By the same measure, those institutions which come face to face with personal distress, and can act to encourage, or discourage, moves toward personal freedom (medicine, welfare, education, the Church) are political institutions and candidates for political analysis and criticism. In Reich's formulation of the matter the family is 'a factory for producing submissive people',[96] and the concept of political domination embraced by the counter-culture engages the mechanism of that blind submission. No longer a marginal conglomerate of paki-bashers, telephone-kiosk wreckers, and feckless psychopaths, the problem of juvenile delinquency was grasped thus: 'The revolt of youth was the first burst of anger at the persistent realities of the new world – the boredom of everyday existence, the *dead life*.'[97]

In a cautious analysis of the political implications of deviance, Paul Rock criticises the 'romanticism which views all criminals as primitive innocents who are engaged in inarticulate political conflict with institutional authority'. He writes:

> If the extravagant romantic is ignored, politicised deviancy may be defined as that activity *which is regarded as expressly political by its participants*. The rule-breaking activity may be shoplifting, arson or violent demonstration. It is the significances that the rule-breaker, and to a lesser extent the rule-enforcer, attach to the behaviour that are important. Otherwise one is forced to resort to fanciful Zen catechism which poses such questions as, 'If the conflict of a thousand American Negroes with the police constitutes a political event, what does a solitary Black delinquent's encounters with the police represent?'[98]

Rock is correct to point to the difficulties and ambiguities introduced into misfit sociology through the fluidity of its sense of politics, but his formulation hardly improves matters: if this 'solitary Black delinquent' understands his police encounters as political, whereas 'a thousand American negroes' do not, what then? Rock's definition reduces politics to a 'meaning': specifically, the meaning which any act has for the actors. It is ironical that he thus becomes contained within the romantic, libertarian, subjectivist politics at which he aims his criticism. *Such is the force of the misfit paradigm, and so extended are its boundaries, that many who believe that they are its critics use tools of criticism which express its core sentiments.*

At the far edges of the 'deviant rebellion' deviance, politically translated, becomes freedom itself. 'Shop-lifting gets you high!'[99] writes Rubin of the Yippies, and in the preface of his book *Do It!* he instructs his readers to 'Read This Book Stoned!', while one of Abbie Hoffman's books is aptly titled *Steal This Book*.[100] As madness constitutes a means of personal and political salvation for Cooper and Laing, a psychic voyage through inner space, so is the liberation of the mind and body through the use of drugs regarded by Leary.[101] Cooper commented once, it will be remembered that meditation was 'armchair madness'.[102] But the voyage to the freedom of inner space and time is one which our culture recognises only as illness; if deviance is a 'freedom' then it is a contained freedom.

In a language which is more moderate, but equally emphatic, Matza and Sykes have argued that delinquency represents the expression of a system of 'subterranean values' in society which co-exist with, and oppose, the values of the work ethic.[103] Emphasising expressivity, excitement, spontaneity, etc., this subterranean world of play, Sykes and Matza propose, is an integral part of the value system of complex, urban-industrial societies; and although it contradicts the dominant ethos of productivity it finds a legitimate expression in leisure values.[104] Delinquency, therefore, represents not so much an opposition to society as an expression of society's contradictions. But within the misfit paradigm this neutral judgement took on a more positive and prescriptive character: deviance *contained* the essence of playful freedom; that freedom could be enjoyed through the exercise of deviant acts. For the 'antinomian'[105] temperament of the counter-culture, deviance was an approach to the 'Buried Temple' of the Romantics.[106]

We can summarise the relationship between politics and the deviant imagination, as it is understood in misfit social thought, in the following terms: it re-asserts, with a novel twist, the relationships between deviance and order, rebelliousness, conformity and reasonableness. In the literature of sociology it has often been noted, flowing from Durkheim,[107] that there is an intimate relationship between deviance and social order. For example, Erikson writes: 'morality and immorality meet at the public scaffold, and it is during this meeting that the line between them is drawn.'[108] Deviance indicates the boundaries of public order. It has also been noted that the control of deviance 'rejuvenates' society. Scott has given a clear account of this:

> To contain and control deviance, and thereby master it, is to supply fresh and dramatic proof of the enormous powers behind the social order. The visible control of deviance is one of the most effective mechanisms by which a social order can tangibly display its potency. The act of harnessing things which are dangerous helps to revitalise the system by demonstrating to those who live within it just how awesome its powers really are.[109]

Scott writes that, 'deviance is an important resource of the group' which must not be annihilated; deviants must be *tamed*, rather than *destroyed*.[110]

Misfit sociology penetrates these relationships between deviance and order, and – if inarticulately – finds that hidden within the images of deviance and its correction are images of freedom and its containment.[111] Men exercise their relationship to certain forms of freedom through their play with the imagery of deviance. In a children's story, for example, a little boy, who has been on a wild rampage wearing his wolf-suit, is sent to bed without any food because he has threatened to eat up his mother. He is very cross, but a magical forest grows in his bedroom and he transports himself on a long journey to a place 'where the wild things are'.[112] And there he is made King of all the Wild Things and enjoys the wildest rumpus imaginable, although he soon gets bored and later finds himself back in his familiar bedroom 'where he found his supper waiting for him . . . and it was still hot'.[113] And in countless crime movies the audience is encouraged, until the final few frames, to identify with the villain: otherwise the movie's plot makes little sense. In those final frames the audience is snatched back into reasonableness and conformity: in the cops-and-robbers game men glimpse a sort of freedom outside the law, and then taste its confinement. Thus, the deviant imagination is set to work as a stabilising force in the one-dimensional world, but, absenting themselves from criminological cops and robbers, misfit sociology and anti-psychiatry suggest that the problem of why the hungry man steals is less worthy of attention than the more remarkable problem that his hungry brother does not.[114] And in this sense, however haphazard its movements, the new misfit social thought returns to deviance theory and welfare practice the vision of cultural criticism.

THE SMELL OF THEORY

We must confront the fact honestly: an analysis which rests its credibility with the 'New Left' and the 'counter-culture' risks its credibility. The counter-culture was prone to silliness and full-blown lunacy, and perhaps because of its more embarrassing aspects it is easy to forget it as a passing whim or a fashion. The French have a nice phrase which sums up this degeneration: *la drugstorisation de Marcuse*. And when on *New Morning* the prophet Bob Dylan sang, 'Build me a cabin in Utah/ Marry me a wife and catch rainbow trout/ Have a bunch of kids who call me pa'/ That must be what it's all about', the rural commune had become indistinguishable from a mentholated cigarette advertisement.[115]

Correspondingly, there is a fragmentation of the misfit paradigm. Paul Rock has even suggested that 'when the last of the dissertations which were fathered during this period are published, the sociology of deviance will fade'.[116] There is a tendency, Adorno wrote in a letter to Walter Benjamin, for 'the recent past always [to present] itself as though it has been destroyed by catastrophes'.[117] This sense of catastrophe is very strong in misfit sociology and anti-psychiatry where the smell of the hunt (for something which was never made fully articulate, but which attracted its supporters) finally evaporates. What is replacing the misfit paradigm is a new, and explicitly political, critique of criminology.

The new critics of the misfit paradigm propose various modifications of the same argument: namely, that its 'radical' promise is an illusion. Liazos, Platt and Thio all argue that misfit sociology's preoccupation with 'nuts, sluts and preverts [sic]' (Liazos) or 'trivia and politically irresponsible hipsterism' (Platt) deflects from the study of the powerful, and from the power of the State which frames what is right and who has the right to say what is right.[118] It is here, they argue, that the grounds of a rigorously political criminology should be laid. Another strand of criticism – represented by Gouldner, Mankoff, Akers, Schervish and Walton – suggests that misfit sociology (and in particular its labelling theory component) depicts the deviant as essentially passive, an innocent who is shanghaied into a deviant career by the clumsy stigmatisation of the social-control apparatus.[119] What is missing in the misfit paradigm, some of them argue, is any sense that deviants might have a just cause for deviation in an unequal, class society. Whatever the differences between these positions, they represent (and reflect) a hardening in political attitudes away from the 'soft' politics of the 1960s.

The options which are taken up in this revolt against misfit sociology are highly dispersed: towards a preoccupation with the sociology of law and law-making (always an alternative within the sentiments of the labelling perspective); towards a continuing preoccupation with the *theoretical* problem of deviance as an aspect of the sociological 'problem of order'; towards different variants of a harder Marxism. David Matza has indicated that he will write no more books on deviance;[120] there are also those who vacate the field of action-research altogether and fly into theoretical whimsy.

I will not deal here with any of the detail of these various shifts. My comments will be brief, and will be directed to the two most cogent criticisms of misfit sociology represented on the one hand by Gouldner, and on the other hand by Taylor, Walton and Young. The main thrust of the latter argument is that the 'societal reaction perspective' in the final analysis ignores power, interest, and social structure in its approach to deviance. Also, quite fundamentally, *it does not offer any theory of 'primary deviation'*; primary deviation is 'polygenetic' and, as Lemert puts it, can arise from 'a wide variety of social, cultural and psychological contexts'.[121] This is an important insight (anticipated by Mankoff and Akers) for it allows the nature of labelling theory to be seen in a clearer light. If the labelling perspective does not provide a theory of how deviation arises, then it can *only* be understood as a critique of labelling agents; that is as a critique of welfare institutions. Taylor, Walton and Young do not develop these points, but their work constitutes a thoroughgoing de-mystification of an area of misfit sociology which had become extremely foggy: compare, for example, Becker's consternation that anyone could imagine that he was offering a theory of deviant aetiology and Matza's confession that he had simply not bothered to say that his book *Delinquency and Drift* was an attack on the juvenile court system because he considered it so obvious that it would be 'an insult to the reader'.[122] In this light Brian Munday's reading of the misfit paradigm looks not nearly so wrong-headed and 'paranoid'.[123]

In his analysis of the political deviancy of the Weathermen, Paul Walton shows how labelling theory, because of its neglect of 'primary deviation' (i.e. why people choose to do it) simply cannot handle, or explain, the Weatherman phenomenon. Ironically, given labelling theory's political undertones, the sharpest expression of its theoretical difficulties comes in relation to political deviation. Walton suggests that the same problems exist for labelling theory in relation to other types of deviation, 'even if it is most openly recognisable only in political deviancy'.[124] Labelling theory's dual incapacity to pay attention to *primary commitment* to deviant action (e.g. 'why men rob banks') and to give insufficient weight to the element of *power* in the creation of deviance (e.g. 'if there were no private property there could be no concept of theft') condemns it for Walton as a fully social theory of deviance: he writes that, 'labelling theory, which appeared to so many of us to offer a radical promise, seems to fall short' and it is 'as profoundly un-radical as its predecessors'.[125]

These criticisms draw much of their authority from Gouldner's earlier work. Gouldner, it will be remembered, charges misfit sociology with a refusal to engage in 'erect partisanship'. Goffman's work is described as having a 'rebel vision' which 'some among the rebellious young' embrace, but in the final analysis it is a cool-out and a deflection from what would properly constitute 'rebel criticism':

> The dramaturgical model allows us to bear our defeats and losses, because it implies that they are not 'for real' . . . winning and losing become of lesser moment. It is only the game that counts. . . . The dramaturgical model invites us to carve a slice out of time, history and society. . . . Rather than offering a world view, the new model offers us 'a *piece* of the action'.[126]

There is, however, an alternative reading of the ideology embodied in Goffman's writings. In *Asylums*, a key work in the misfit paradigm, a hidden motif is that society itself is a 'total institution', a mental hospital, a prison, a concentration camp. Men are 'inmates' of this society; they have only the remnants of an identity, and they suffer from the invasion of their speech, dress, and manners. Goffman talks of the 'presentation of self in every-day life': in Goffman's world men present only limited aspects of themselves to public view; they guard themselves against the threat of further invasion. Here are men who are colonised, but their guards pose as 'helpers' – as 'nurses', 'psychiatrists' and 'aides' – and with a liberal 'repressive tolerance' they define protest against confinement as sickness. In the oppressive ambit of this 'total society' men have their realities defined for them, and then re-defined; their personal histories are public knowledge; their past is distorted to fit the official construction of reality and the only 'reality' is a discourse which takes place within high walls; on the 'better wards' the physical restraint of locked doors is replaced with drugs and with compliance predicated on a hopeful return to the 'good life': the bars of Bedlam, as Laing expresses it, are placed *inside* the patient.[127] Goffman begins his description of 'The Underlife of a Public Institution', we should remind ourselves, *with a discussion of the social bond*.[128]

Goffman's almost poetic metaphor of the total institution, however, is not one of total gloom. There is a place for optimism: inmates can, and do, fight back. Such devices as 'removal activities'[129] and other guerrilla tactics ensure that the struggle for human freedom and personal dignity goes on. The total institution may be a 'dead sea', but it is 'a kind of dead sea in which little islands of vivid, encapturing activity appear'.[130] Goffman does not appear ashamed of his metaphorical use of the prison camp and the mental hospital to bring home the realities of the 'social bond': the individual in 'civil society', he writes, simply has a 'more available' repertoire of removal activities through which he might 'crawl into some protected place where he can indulge in commercialised fantasy'.[131] Even fantasy is commercialised and cannot be a purely personal matter in the total society. If removal activities appear to get out of hand, 'become too engrossing or too continuous' controls reassert themselves: in the guards' eyes 'the institution, not some other kind of social entity . . . must possess the inmate'.[132]

At other points in Goffman's work what are officially categorised as 'symptoms' become tactics which salvage identity in the world of the total society, and constitute primitive, pre-political acts of rebellion and insurgency against the ruling order. The inmate cannot take away his guardian's power-invested right to say what is right, but he can steal the key to his moral authority:

In mental hospitals, one of the most dramatic instances of establishment alienation is provided by the patient who is appropriately oriented in the situation in all visible ways while calmly doing a single thing that sets him quite outside the present reality. . . . I have observed an otherwise well-demeaned (albeit mute) youth walking down the ward halls with a reasonably thoughtful look on his face and two pipes in his mouth; another conducting himself with similar nicety while chewing toothpaste; . . . another with a ball of paper screwed into his right eye as a monocle; another, with a foot-long strip of woven newspaper dangling from his pocket. One patient would graciously accept tobacco for his pipe and then pop the offering into his mouth . . . another would quietly enter the cafeteria and eat his meals peacefully, departing when told to, and manage all his compliant behaviour with a dinner-roll balanced on his head . . . these proclamations were made with a sly look on the patient's face, so that it appeared that he was more than ordinarily aware of the implications of his acts and was performing them with these implications in mind. . . .

This situational self-sabotage often seems to represent one statement in an equation of defence. It seems that the patient sometimes feels that life on the ward is so degrading, so unjust, and so inhuman that the only self-respecting response is to treat ward life as if it were contemptibly beyond reality and beyond seriousness. . . . In short, the patient may pointedly act crazy . . . to make it clear to all decent people that he is obviously sane.[133]

If we make the imaginative effort to understand Goffman's *Asylums*, and all the associated work, as politics – as we must within the convergences of the misfit paradigm – then if it is the politics of a one-dimensional world it is also clearly a politics of optimism which puts social structure up for grabs. Goffman's mental patients flap at powerful institutions, and they appear to vanish. Similarly, in Garfinkel's work social structures almost seem to fall down of their own accord; and, in the famous Thomas Theorem (which informs so much of misfit sociology) 'if men define situations as real, then they are real in their consequences'. Misfit sociology's politics does not file complaints with the domestic bursar, it 'Faces Down the Man'. Not surprisingly, 'some among the rebellious young' respond to it or are 'turned on' by it.

This is a reading of Goffman which places his thought firmly in the world. It relates to Goffman's *Asylums* not only as a theoretical piece on 'the nature of the social bond' and not only as an ethnographic field-study of a mental hospital, but also as something written (and read) as a response to the problems of men living together in urban-industrial society. Something other than 'theory' or 'research', that is, something which gives a voice to contemporary sentiments of alienation, manipulation and conformity; it reads Goffman as a literary response to new and developing experiences of men in relation to problems of deviance and order in a society of high complexity. Alan Dawe, Richard Sennett and John O'Neill are three other writers who have read and recognised in Goffman's work a response to (and a record of) what they identify as violence and terror in the world, the crisis of the modern city and the problems of the modern self in complex organisations.[134] It is this kind of reading, which anchors the social practice of theory-construction and theory-reception firmly in the social world that it tries to articulate, which allows a full appreciation of the 'radicalism' of misfit sociology. But none of the new critics of the misfit paradigm makes this appreciative effort and their criticisms, and the ways in which they attempt to take hold of what misfit sociology offers, are as a consequence flawed and one-sided.

This is not to say that the criticisms of Gouldner and others are not important. Particularly, Paul Walton's critique, developed in collaboration with Taylor and Young, makes available a theoretical analysis of the labelling perspective which enables a decisive distinction to be drawn between its own flawed theory and the radical 'feel' and 'smell' of that theory. But that is only one side of the matter: the new political criminology relates to the misfit paradigm *only* in terms of its internal theoretical calculations. And, even then, the criticism only addresses itself to an element of the whole paradigm (that is, to labelling theory) thus isolating the parts from the surrounding whole, which is not true to the actual nature of the misfit paradigm. Taylor, Walton and Young recognise this problem in so far as they write that their job in criticising labelling theory is, as they put it, 'doubly difficult', for the labelling perspective 'encompasses a variety of theorists who, although they share many assumptions, hold to these with differing degrees of subtlety and sophistication'.[135] And this is precisely the problem, for attention only to the manifest theoretical rationality misses the imaginative core which binds together these theoretical fragments. What seems to be necessary to secure a hold on the various traces left by misfit social thought is to listen to it as a movement of imaginative discourse, particularly of the political imagination. Doing this entails a certain relationship between writer, text and reader which is put very well by Herman Hesse in a preface to *Steppenwolf*:

Poetic writing can be understood and misunderstood in many ways. In most cases the author is not the right authority to decide on where the reader ceases to understand and misunderstanding begins. Many an author has found readers to whom his work seemed more lucid than it was to himself. Moreover, misunderstandings may be fruitful under certain circumstances. . . . I neither can nor intend to tell my readers how they ought to understand my tale. May everyone find in it what strikes a chord in him and is of some use to him![136]

It would be difficult to claim exemption wholeheartedly for social-scientific literature from this kind of consideration. Equally, there are obviously risks here, and this position should not be confused with mere sloppiness or with an anti-intellectualism which turns the relationship between author, text and interpretation into a market bazaar where readers purchase what they like when they like. If anything the stand which I am advocating in relation to the misfit paradigm is very close to Gouldner's expressed intentions of building a 'reflexive' sociology. This would be a social science which understands itself, Gouldner states, in a peculiar manner: not only *theoretically* but also *sentimentally*. Gouldner writes that he is attempting 'to illuminate the manner in which theory-products and theory-performances are generated and received', built on a vital assumption 'that sociologists are fundamentally like other men'.[137] Such a reflection, he argues, cannot attend solely to 'rational and cognitive forces' in the social practice of theory-construction and social action.[138] Louis Chevalier states a similar position when he writes that literary testimony 'must be heard aright, not for what it purports to say, but for what it cannot help saying',[139] given the social world in which its author lives as a man. However, Gouldner's appreciation of the misfit paradigm seems to fall short of his own prescriptions, largely, one suspects, because its subjectivism is anathema to him. Thus, the sentiments of the misfit paradigm are not allowed to speak on their own behalf in Gouldner's critiques, and their sound, and their passion, is always muffled by Gouldner-the-interpreter. In short, Gouldner has a pre-defined view of what misfit sociology signifies, and pre-definition is a bad ground on which to build reflexivity.

In establishing the links between misfit social thought and the world to which it is a response I wish to suggest more than a 'sociology of knowledge' of the misfit sociologies and anti-psychiatry. Particularly, it is desirable to say something of the residues and problems which they place before practitioners, researchers and theorists in the field of deviance, and also something of the way in which these are come to terms with. The first problem, and the most obvious, is the profound *subjectivism* of misfit social thought's practical and political implications. It is again a meeting point with the counter-culture where what was often at stake was a *redefinition* of the world, and a reversal of power-invested beliefs about deviance and normality: gay is good, black is beautiful, 'a pig for president', deviance is the norm, madness is hyper-sanity. It often involved 'counter-stigmatisation' of the good, the clean, and the healthy. David Cooper, for example, writes: 'narcissism and homosexuality are no more diseases or fixated states of development than are phenomena such as holding down a steady job, duly providing for one's family, or, in general, being a pillar of society.'[140] Here the deviant imagination sets itself up as critic of society, and its tactic is to struggle over the meaning and sense of *words* which commonly invalidate and discredit human action in deviance theories. The relationship between language and action is complex. Anselm Strauss suggests that 'contention for terminological prizes is not mere squabbling over words for words are mandates for action',[141] and in this he is surely right. But misfit social thought, which is extremely antagon-istic to traditional modes of deviance-control, does not get that mandate for action and its break from traditional conceptions of deviance remains a break in thought and language. But, more significantly, its own ideological underpinnings lead it to imagine that all that needs to be done is to re-write the world, in one's head as it were. This sentiment is found everywhere, reaching the most popular and vulgarised expressions of the misfit paradigm, and rational sentimentality should not stand in the way of our searching these depths to uncover the really quite drastic subjectivism which they reveal. For example, peddling his own version of 'labelling theory' Timothy Leary pushes it to the limits of its own subjectivism. He re-labels (re-writes) history, and turned on his lathe the 'social problem' of alcoholism among Red Indians is transformed into 'chemical warfare': 'The destruction

of the American Indian culture was not accomplished by physical
force. The deliberate strategy was pharmacological. The specific
tactical weapon was alcohol.'[142]

Leary's interpretation of history is always *pharmacological*.
Jack Douglas, a social theorist of high repute, prefers to anchor
his to *pluralism* and *phenomenology*. But the effect is much the
same since both are governed by subjectivism. Leary sees the
phenomenon of western man taking to chemicals (drugs) as a sign
of social change, and he recommends social change through a
'chemical revolution'. Douglas sees massively centralised technology leading to 'pluralism', and he recommends new forms of
pluralism as an avenue to 'new forms of freedom'.[143] But Douglas's
phenomenological conception of history is no less fanciful than
Leary's, so that he is able to write a short history of the American
black population without paying any attention to the fact of
slavery.[144] Douglas's *American Social Order*, it should be added,
is probably the most sophisticated sociological contribution of the
American 'radical right'. In this book he takes phenomenology to
the White House as the solution to the problems of both sociology
and the United States; in it he proposes a means by which 'to meet
the even greater challenge of wisely constructing our everyday
lives'.[145]

Another sociologist who has approached this problem of
creating a 'new' sociology which is more relevant to the 'new'
life is T. R. Young. In his book *New Sources of Self* (described
on its dust cover as 'a book for today's student demanding more
than "establishment" sociology') Young puts Mead, Cooley,
Goffman, Laing and others to work as the theorists who make
'the new life' possible. He turns his attention to new styles of
living (communes, and so on), to encounter groups, the construction of 'retirement communities' for the old, and to how new
belief systems will establish themselves in what he calls the *neo-
gemeinschaft* of the 'freak community' of the future society. Once
more one is confronted with a deep subjectivism. The fact that
astrological beliefs are possibly false, writes Young, 'is irrelevant
to the sociologist. If people organise their behaviour in terms of
the Zodiac signs, there is sociological interest':

For many people the *sign* under which they are born becomes
a self-fulfilling prophecy in just the same symbolic interactionist

way that masculinity or ethnicity becomes a self-fulfilling prophecy. . . . Because there is structure there, one can organise self from Zodiac. Because astrology is institutionalised [in the freak community] it will survive just as the Marine Corps and the Catholic Church survive in that they are institutionalised.[146]

Some of these issues which Young raises are quite intriguing, but their unmistakable subjectivism sinks the ship: history, class, economy, technology ruled by the Zodiac. Nor, Young writes, should one ignore 'witchcraft, palmistry, numerology, and hand-writing analysis'.[147] And they are not ignored in the misfit sociologies of the 1960s. For example, the popular anthropological ethnography of Carlos Castaneda resonates with the spirit of the deviant imagination and is flavoured with a little of Garfinkel's tutorship.[148] Castaneda journeys to the desert to meet an old Indian, don Juan, who teaches him some of the skills of Yaqui sorcery; his books have been described as an allegory of the meeting of the young and old generations.[149] Apart from all the necessary trappings which secure counter-cultural popularity – psychotropic drugs, mysticism and Red Indian 'cool' – don Juan offers a mechanism by which to 'stop the world'. The reality of the world that we know, don Juan teaches, is only a *description* of the world. It is a description learned from childhood; when a child has accomplished this learning he has become a *member* of the taken-for-granted social world.[150] By learning the discipline of an alternative unitary world-view – a 'separate reality' – which defies the descriptions of the taken-for-granted world, the practising sorcerer can 'stop the world' and free himself from the sorcery of his socialised imagination. It is a revaluation without revolution, the hall-mark of radical subjectivism: the world could be different, we are told, but first you must 'see' and not 'look'. And in the same way that don Juan, and his sinister colleague don Genaro, spirit away motor cars in the Mexican desert, so Goffman's asylum inmates spirit away the power of institutions by means of situational improprieties.

I have demonstrated a measure of the utter subjectivism of the misfit paradigm, and it is this subjectivism from which the new political criminology recoils almost in horror. And here we can say that these critics of the misfit paradigm have got one thing quite right: misfit social thought does not take account of the realities of power and social structure in its appreciation of deviant conduct to the extent that it pretends. The misfit sociologists sometimes write as if men made history (and their lives) under conditions entirely of their own choosing: as if there was no such thing as 'economy', 'power' or 'social stratification'. Russell Jacoby has written of this tendency as a 'reduction of oppression to a whim of the individual. Alienation becomes a headache and oppression annoyance. "I'm oppressed", announces someone, and that's that'.[151]

What the new moves against the misfit paradigm do to some extent is theoretically to redress the balance of this subjectivist emphasis. Nevertheless, the sheer depth of the subjectivism which they oppose turns reappraisal into flight, and a trouble with all these critiques is that they fall into an old trap which is the tension between man-as-creator and man-as-constrained. *Objectivity* and *subjectivity* are approached by those who now reject the misfit paradigm as if they constitute an either/or choice. Abstractly, that is, 'subjectivity' is ditched for 'objectivity'.

Misfit social thought glimpses the complex mediations between deviant conduct, reasonableness, welfare practices and ideologies, and politics. It is perhaps only the shadow of a knowledge which it can hardly articulate, but it engages the convergences (and tensions) of the personal and the political. Its theoretical critics do not so much surpass this as forget it. What these different theoretical moves do in their different ways is turn their backs on the questions raised by the misfit sociologies and anti-psychiatry. Imperatives such as 'This is politically irresponsible hipsterism' or 'You are only dealing with nuts, sluts and perverts' sound too much like slogans for one to miss the fact that they *are* slogans. And they are slogans thrown up by the still mysterious process which 'hardens' politics in the 1970s just as it 'softened' them in the 1960s: 'thinking falls under the spell of fashion: change without change'.[152] With one voice the new political criminologies urge: 'There is not enough *power* and *social structure* in the analysis', but they forget that men also have a psychology, motives and impulses, and this theoretical critique thus unwittingly perpetuates what the resurrected voice of the deviant imagination had cried out against: the petrification of the human subject, both in theory and in social practice.

There is room for quite sharp disagreement here with the new political criminology. Particularly this disagreement takes shape against its complete neglect of psychoanalysis. This theoretical forgetfulness finds its reflection in the way in which the counter-cultural dressing of the misfit sociologies' radicalism is pushed to one side as a passing whim: as if it were something *other* people were doing at the time, people (that is) who were not in the 'data sample'. There is no attempt to understand theoretically the relationships between deviance, human impulse and techno-logical and political domination – only Freud's psychoanalysis approaches the critical edge of eros and civilisation.

I choose psychoanalysis here as an example of psychology because that, it seems to me, is where the proper direction lies. But it only represents a preference and there is not the space to argue the matter out. Nevertheless, no matter which specific psychological model one takes, the political critique of misfit social thought leaves issues of psychology and social psychology to common-sense judgement. True, the misfit paradigm only had a psychology of sorts because of its implicit links with anti-psychiatry, symbolic interactionism and the counter-culture – its psychology needs, as it were, to be 'read in' – but its critique neither has one nor implies one. Cardboard, wooden figures exercise something called 'choice' in the face of something called 'restraints' and that is all: just as the extreme moments of the counter-culture swallowed up politics in the 'personal', the move against misfit sociology threatens to swallow up the person in the 'political'. But not quite: Gouldner writes of an 'unemployed self', an area within the individual subject which defiantly, doggedly, has no wish to enter the social contract of labour – an area of social reality which asserts that utility and work 'is nothing less than a waste of life'.[153] And Taylor, Walton and Young in their embrace of one of the many faces of Marx state that their theory needs a 'social psychology of consciousness'[154] which does not neglect the indivi-dual subject, and they pin their banner to something called 'human diversity'.[155] But one must risk being unfair to the critics of the misfit paradigm in order to make the point: namely, that human subjectivity is tied abstractly, as an afterthought, to theoretical analysis. People called deviants began to speak out in the 1960s, and they found a voice in the discourse between social scientists and welfare professionals in the misfit paradigm. But now misfit social thought appears to turn its back on itself.

I have spent some time mapping out the theoretical problems and residues which misfit social thought deposits. What these theoretical difficulties should not be allowed to conceal, however, is a second cluster of deeper and more human troubles. Misfit sociology and anti-psychiatry return deviance to the realm of moral discourse; that is as discourse in the fully human, fully social man-made world. In reified technical discourse the relationship between the social scientist (or the social practitioner) and deviant conduct is pickled and fossilised in abstract formulae which place a comforting shield between 'that disorderliness out there' and the life which professionals (as men and women) lead. In dereified moral discourse that shield is taken away and deviance is recognised fully as part of the man-made world in which men (not unlike you and me) live. It poses in a very sharp form a life problem which is the difficult problem of how to live and conduct oneself properly in a human world. Ernest Becker puts the problem which this stance tables particularly well when he writes that choosing between different theories of human ills is not only a *professional* decision, but also a choice for 'the kind of world one is going to wake up in, the kinds of human beings that one will have to come across in the street'.[156]

The 'radical' sociologies of the 1960s shared here a common preoccupation which was to close the gap between the professional-as-professional and the professional-as-citizen. Jack Douglas, for example, remarks that a consequence of his own sociology is that '*we discover everyday life*. We no longer simply live everyday life independently of our sociological enterprise'.[157] Stanley Cohen argued that a responsibility of the social scientist was to make his definitions of reality 'not only intelligible, consistent and aesthetically satisfactory, but also human'.[158] T. R. Young reflected another attempt to close these gaps and, for this reason, he wished to defend Goffman and Garfinkel against the criticisms of Alvin Gouldner because this work 'has helped us to sustain an underlife in western sociology and survive'.[159] Gouldner himself, of course, wanted to make these connections between life and work in his own 'reflexive' sociology.[160]

The misfit paradigm seemed to make this difficult task of the connections in one's own life that much easier. But it also posed clearly the problems involved. If deviance was to be seen as a moral, social condition then it posed the problem of the relationship between *collective* human practice to change those conditions and *individual* practice in one's own (professional) life. However, again, it also seemed to resolve it, allowing easy connections between what feels right and what is right. The personal and the political joined in some sort of way, and men could meet themselves in their various roles in that conjunction. And crucial to the understanding of the human qualitiees of this paradigm is that it contains and reflects a great deal of hopefulness, particularly in some complex sentiments about the redeemability of the human subject and the human condition.

A further problem for any appreciation of deviant conduct is how to connect a concrete understanding of deviance as authentic human conduct of men attempting to live *this* life under *these* specific conditions with an abstract understanding of it as a waste-product from the good society (or the bad society). Theoretically one might express this tension as the relationship between voluntaristic theories (stressing purposive human action) and structural-deterministic theories (stressing constrained human responses). We have already seen how the new criminologies hang on the hinge of this theoretical dilemma. As a *lived experience* the same tension lies between concretely attempting to aid *this particular* deviant and abstractly criticising (or theorising) on 'the human condition'. And the problem here is how to live with this tension without slipping into tinkering with the individual lives of individual misfits on the one hand, or into equally abstract theoretical or political sloganeering on the other. Because it refuses wholeheartedly to go one way or the other misfit sociology frames that difficult human problem, perhaps one of the most difficult human problems. And it also seems to resolve it and make the proper connections.

In summary, this movement of thought in the 1960s had millenarial qualities. That fact should not be dodged; nor should it become an excuse to forget the implications of misfit social thought and get on with more 'serious' and 'realistic' matters. Millenarial movements are not only difficult to appreciate, it is also difficult to live with the gulf between the human possibilities which they open up and the facts of the world as lived. The sentiments which they embody are for this reason frail, and the sentiments of misfit social thought are such frail sentiments – frail, that is, in the sense of their understanding of the relationship between theory and practice; frail in the sense of their relationship to the organisational embodiment of welfare practices; frail in relation to the massive undertaking against the powerful common-sense view of deviance which misfit social thought implies. And they are frail in the sense that their own compassion for the deviant subject contradicts so much of what is taken for granted as compassionate in welfare theories and welfare practices. The human value of humane welfare provisions cannot be questioned with an easy conscience; no more easily than its opposite – a critical judgement of the sham humanity which lies behind so much liberal deviance-control – can be denied. So much of the futile tension (and creativity) in the field of deviance research and practice is informed by these human problems which contemporary social theories of deviance and deviance-control have thrown into a fresh antagonism. Eric Hobsbawm expresses the nature of these problems precisely when, writing generally of the difficult nature of utopian and millenarial beliefs, he describes their qualities which resist easy articulation, their refusal to tinker in this world when the possibilities of a better world lie exposed, and the manner in which they pose some exceptionally hard lessons :

> Without wishing to make it appear more sensible and less extraordinary than it often is, it is advisable . . . to appreciate the logic, and even the realism – if the word can be used in this context – which moves them, for revolutionary movements are difficult to understand otherwise. It is their peculiarity that those who cannot see what all the bother is about are disabled from saying anything of great value about them, whereas those who do . . . cannot often speak in terms intelligible to the rest. It is especially difficult, but necessary, to understand that utopianism, or 'impossibilism' which the most primitive revolutionaries share with all but the most sophisticated, and which makes even very modern ones feel a sense of almost physical pain at the realisation that the coming of Socialism will not eliminate *all* grief and sadness, unhappy love-affairs or mourning, and will not solve or make soluble *all* problems.[161]

These remarks stand whether it was socialism, some version of a liberal democratic state or the Heavenly City of pluralism which writers in the misfit paradigm embraced as the solution to the deviant question. Hobsbawm's comment raises one of the most serious human dilemmas of social theory and social practice, and it captures perfectly the human problem of misfit sociology and anti-psychiatry: how to phrase those unequal equations between hopes and realities, theory and practice, life and work, individual practice and collective practice, this world and that world?

The dilemmas of modern deviance theories and modern social-welfare practice are run through with such ambiguities. And it is not enough to tie a knot around these two halves and call their relationship 'dialectical': 'dialectic' then becomes nothing more than a tired, over-used word. One must not be afraid to say, even publicly, even by way of a conclusion, that some problems are terribly awkward.

PART II
THE IDEOLOGY OF
WELFARE

' . . . certain waste products of social life do not return into the circulating currents, but are carried off by underground channels . . . the [social] liver, separating certain waste products from the blood, throws them into the intestine as bile.'

Herbert Spencer

'The caseworker hopes that he is, in some small way, an instrument of Divine Providence.'

Felix P. Biestek

The first part of this book describes how new approaches to deviance – anti-psychiatry and 'radical' deviance theories – throw their weight against traditional viewpoints. In the traditional view, the social system is regarded as being unquestionably rational, and nonconformity is hence judged to be irrational. Traditional criminology and psychiatry, therefore, is in one sense not interested in deviant conduct: it only wishes to see deviance scrubbed out. The new misfit social thought, on the other hand, is intrigued by deviant conduct and it overturns the unequal contest between the rational social scientist and the irrational misfit, joining sides with the misfit and lending him an ear and a voice.

These shifts in social thought gain their popularity at the point of a specific crisis in the development of urban civilisation. They are thrown up at a time when the rationality of the social system is placed in question in the following terms: it is asked whether everyday life in the modern world is a truly satisfying life, and rational conformity is itself condemned on many sides as an unnecessary burden on men. This constitutes a crisis in culture, which is opposed by the 'counter-culture', and misfit social thought thus expresses the wish of men to be free of the domination of a social order which is itself judged to be irrational. Deviants, who have departed from rational conformity to an irrational system, can therefore appear to be cultural critics, or even heroes. In its more extravagant moments misfit social thought proposes an inversion of the liberal–utilitarian welfare state's attempts to curb deviance with compassion: deviants will rule the world. In its more measured judgements it appeals for the creation of a society which will not punish and criminalise human diversity. In its frequent flirtation with a cheaper form of romanticism it simply admires the misfit's 'get up and go', in a manner not unlike the thrilling stories told about the adventures of highwaymen. But wherever one looks, and however it is phrased, the misfit's conduct is described as an attempt at a rational solution to the problems of an irrational world.

The question is therefore posed, although sometimes in a roundabout way, as to whether the care and control of deviants is all that it appears to be. Is the welfare state a culmination of human freedom and an expression of human compassion? Or is social welfare simply an enormous confidence trick which in fact restricts the freedom of human expression? Does the welfare state help to bring about social equality? Or is the work of the 'people-professions' a means of disguising social inequality? Are misfits people who fall to one side, and who are unable to take their place in the good life, because they do not have 'what it takes'? Or are they people who are pushed to one side, because they are people for whom there is no place?

The criticisms of misfit social thought do not, by and large, come from within the welfare professions. They are the work of academic sociologists and rebel psychoanalysts such as Laing and Szasz. The professional and semi-professional world of social welfare is at once intrigued and repelled by these political interrogations of its good intentions – intrigued because the welfare professions view themselves in some ways as the champions of the poor; repelled because it is a troubling business to reflect on the moral and political implications of what is 'self-evidently' good work which advances the principles of tolerance and compassion towards the unfortunate and underprivileged class of misfits. Political and moral controversy also cramps the professional's style, and he will often excuse himself from engaging in this controversy on the grounds that he is 'a professional' – a neutral, technical specialist whose job is to get on with the job in hand. The welfare professions are even capable of turning their pseudo-psychiatric guns against their critics – judging the critics to be 'immature' people who have 'problems with authority', and dismissing the criticisms themselves as a passing adolescent whim.

These criticisms of the welfare state, however, amount to more than a conspiracy by a few radical intellectuals to make the field of welfare and deviance appear to be more political than it is. The second part of this book makes it clear that the explosion of politics into criminology, psychiatry and social work is nothing new. The welfare professions cannot dodge these thorny issues: their profession is one which is dominated by the political questions of the deviant imagination, and although these questions are often highly disguised it is possible, by cracking the codes of the welfare state, to unearth the buried ideology of welfare. Thus Part II begins with a brief, and admittedly schematic, account of the rash of political controversy which has broken out in contemporary social work. This is followed by an historical exploration which goes to the roots of the welfare state. It describes how the origins of the welfare field, and the social practice of deviance-control, find their place in the political order as a response to the problem of creating a stable pool of factory labour in an unequal society.

5

THE AMBIGUOUS POLITICS
OF SOCIAL WORK

Misfit social thought poses the questions of deviance and politics; social work more sharply than any other sector of the welfare apparatus faces these questions in its practice. The question, primarily, is what is the deviant imagination – an expression of an authentic, possibly rebellious human spirit; or a waste product of society to be processed and re-cycled, or neutralised so that it causes the minimum of fuss?

An underlying premise of ths book is that the 'space' in thought and action which is called 'deviance' is a unitary space of social practice, and that although it is fragmented – into research, theory-construction, social work, the police, psychiatry, social-security systems, medicine, etc. – it is only to be grasped properly as a unitary whole. But it is in social work, for various reasons, that the question of the deviant imagination poses itself in its most visible form, and in this chapter I explore something of the contemporary predicament of social work. Very loosely, it is possible to say that social work is faced with the problem of whether it is an agency which enlarges human freedom or restricts it, and whether it is relevant to the problems which it confronts or irrelevant. And although these are issues which have taken a novel, contemporary form they should not be thought of as new. In the 1930s, for example, Bertha Reynolds wrote about the troubling questions which faced social work then (and now): 'Doing case work seems to some like setting out deck chairs for the comfort of a few passengers when everyone on board a sinking ship should be manning the life boats.'[1] In recent years this kind of question has been posed once more in social work: but social work has seemed unable to relate to the dilemma as anything more than a private worry in the minds of some professionals. What is necessary is to begin to raise these questions to a level of theoretical appreciation so that they are no longer simply troubling professional nightmares: this chapter starts, therefore, with an account of the nature of professional sleep.

PROFESSIONAL CULTURE: FROZEN IMAGES

Men look out on the world with eyes, and professional men (and women) look out on the world with professional eyes. But professional eyes do not see the distortions in the world which this particular kind of vision produces. Wittgenstein expresses this problem of vision philosophically when he writes that, 'But really you do *not* see the eye . . . . And nothing *in the visual field* allows you to infer that it is seen by an eye'.[2] And in the same way the professional eye does not recognise itself in its operations; the modes of thought and action which characterise any particular professional activity are not observable from *within* professional culture. There is even a sense in which professional vision can be thought to miss the point of its own enquiries altogether, for, as Alfred Schütz observes, one of the functions of culture is 'to eliminate troublesome enquiries by offering ready-made directions for use, to replace truth hard to obtain by offering comfortable truisms, and to substitute the self-explanatory for the questionable'.[3] Thus in a professional culture a profession renders the world less awkward. And in its professional culture a profession also obliterates the traces of its own activity: from within professional culture the professional sees the world, or so he thinks, *as it is*.

The shared understandings and beliefs of an occupation – its 'collective representation' of reality – are rarely, if at all, made articulate, even though they sometimes approach the status of a world-view. Recruits to a profession are socialised into this shared view of the world – which can differ sharply from lay conceptions of world and from other professional world-views – by a number of subtle (and not so subtle) means. Everett Hughes has suggested that professional socialisation puts the subject into a kind of professional daze: in the extreme case, he writes, entry into a profession is like 'a passing through the mirror so that one looks out on the world from behind it . . . [creating] a sense of seeing the world in reverse'.[4] Without doubt Hughes overstates the case for the completeness of the transition from layman to professional: professionals are also men (or women) who live in a more-or-less common world. Nevertheless, the professionally socialised subject goes about his (or her) business in a more-or-less routine fashion which embodies certain assumptions about himself, his occupational group and the world at large, and these assumptions are not open to reflection. The French talk about a *déformation professionnelle*: a deformation of the self which can affect not only attitudes and beliefs, but can even reach to the character structure.

Professional ideology, then, is more extensive than any official creed or code which the profession puts on display. This does not, however, imply a professional conspiracy against the laity: as Wittgenstein's puzzle suggests, it is, at least in part, a result of the difficulties of articulating the function of the eye from the standpoint of the eye. As we have seen, it is the dissection of professional gaze in the misfit paradigm which provides a key point of antagonism between the radicalism of misfit sociology and the welfare professions.[5]

The central problem of social work's current predicament is its own character: what *is* social work? This problem can be approached through social work's representation of itself to itself and by teasing out the contradictions in its professional codes and culture.[6] For these codes give a guarded literacy to the collective experience of social workers, and although social work contains a highly diverse body of activities it is not difficult to identify its 'mainstream' culture and ideology. Social work emphatically embraces *human subjectivity* and regards itself as a carrier of the humane tradition of compassion: it also sometimes behaves as if it were the only carrier of that tradition, and critics have taken social work to task for this.[7] In its professional slogans social work appeals to an attempt to 'start where the client is' and not where the organisational-bureaucratic machinery of the welfare state might wish him to be for the sake of administrative convenience. It expresses through its ideology the desire to treat its clientele as 'individuals' and to pay attention to their individual 'rights' and 'needs'. It advocates a 'non-judgemental' attitude towards the client: it 'accepts' him, whatever his deviations or shortcomings, as an individual of 'full dignity and worth'. It urges that client-misfits be approached through a warm, concerned and compassionate personal relationship which does not treat them as objects, or as cyphers, but which even contains a degree of 'controlled emotional involvement' on the part of the social worker. Entering the client's life empathetically, it holds to a principle of 'client self-determination': that is 'the practical recognition of the right and need of clients to freedom in making their own choices and decisions in the casework process'.[8] Clients, the culture says emphatically, are *not* to be coerced.

This side of professional culture is fairly well articulated. Most commentators agree, however, that social work has some sort of dual commitment both to 'society' as well as 'the individual'. But just what kind of place this abstract 'individual' has in this reified 'society' is not at all clear. And, crucially, the precise character of social work's 'obligations', 'commitment' and 'accountability' to society – that is, the nature of its own location in the structures of power, interest and politics – is very poorly articulated within the professional culture. This provides for a considerable degree of instability and uncertainty within professional culture.[9] One of the yields of this false division of 'individual' and 'society' (false because just *who are* these individuals who live apart from society?) is that social work finds it very difficult to think or act on the question of its politics. As C. Wright Mills puts it, social workers 'have an occupationally trained incapacity to rise above a series of "cases"'.[10] It is this impotence in the face of social structure and politics which has haunted social work's liberal championing and defence of the 'needs' of the abstract 'individual'.

Let us pose the problem in the highly abstract form which it finds in social-work ideology: on the one hand a free, autonomous human spirit; on the other the binding obligations of civil society. This rupture in the fabric of social work's 'collective representation' of itself, its clientele and its place in the world reflects the ambiguous relationship of social work to social structure: on the one hand, it provides an expression of the liberal, humane impulse towards the 'good society'; on the other, the control of the useless, expendable waste products of the 'goods society'. In another (directly related) form this rupture expresses itself in the way in which social work perpetually dithers about whether it represents the *technical* business of deviance-control, or some kind of *artistic* enterprise built on faith. But although the contradictions of its professional culture embody the ambiguities of social work, in its collective representation the profession has been forgetful of its place in the world: as Ruth Smalley has argued, the wider programmes of 'social reform' and 'social improvement' of which social work is only one element have been ignored at the expense of developing technique, and specifically psychothera-peutic technique.[11] Social-work thinking and action thus fell under the spell of what has been called the 'psychiatric deluge'[12], and there the tension between waste-product and civil-right dissolves: the client becomes a *potentially* willing subject of Leviathan, *a spirited machine* which has lost its way in the social world; the professional emerges as a *technician of faith*. Ambiguity asserts itself at every point in professional culture: Halmos, for example, points to a 'double vision' at the heart of the 'faith of the counsellors' in that clients *at one and the same time* are held to mean what they say, but not to know what they mean.[13] Timms points out that social workers hold to voluntaristic beliefs that men can change themselves while embracing psychological theories 'which would appear to place severe limitations on the capacity of individuals to change'.[14] What is at issue is whether client-misfits are, like other men, willing members of a man-made world.

These ambiguities mirror social work's ambiguous relationship to social and political structure, and the question of whether social work represents a personal counselling service for active, free-willed human agents or a mopping-up operation for society's 'dregs'. One should also recognise that in its attempt to bridge these ambiguities social work (and social workers) bear a heavy weight of political and cultural strain. The 'psychiatric deluge' dissolves this strain and the psycho-analytical model of social work welds 'waste product' and 'citizen' into a unitary object: the client who protests at the inadequacies of social welfare provision is a 'hard-to-reach' client who suffers from a shortage in 'reality testing'; the social worker who complains about the same in-adequacies in his own work organisation has 'problems with authority' and is thought to be professionally (or personally) 'immature'.[15] Moral and political ambiguities and antagonisms are thus dissolved in a solution of psychological explanation.

It is not easy to differentiate the events which placed this emphasis in professional culture (which had frozen out its place in social structure) under scrutiny. It is, in any case, the totality which must be grasped. For example, although social work has got to do with much more than poverty, the 'rediscovery' of poverty in the 1960s undermined the easy complacency in social work which held that welfare clients' problems had intrapsychic roots and that material hardships (housing, unemployment, debt) were only superficial 'presenting problems'.[16] Equally, the fitful emergence of client organisations which were more militant in their demands (claimant organisations, tenant movements, the Child Poverty Action Group) placed social-work culture under strain. A significant, but largely ignored, development in social policy also altered dramatically the professional structure of social work: namely, the full emergence in the 1960s of *professional* social work into public welfare agencies. Prior to this, professionally trained social-work elites had their major bases of operation in child psychiatric clinics, hospital social-work departments and privately sponsored family-welfare agencies: the emphasis of standard casework texts reflects this focus of interest; we can also note in passing the belief (which seems to have evaporated) that 'psychiatric social work' was the proper way (and the best way) to do all social work. The rapid growth of social-work training schemes in the 1960s, however, prepared a new professional cadre which signalled a much more intimate (and direct) relationship between social work and political structure, both at a local and national level. One can only guess at the effects of this merger between social work and the State: the shifts in professional consciousness which might result from a broadening and a deepening of social work's recruitment base; or the effects produced by professionally socialised subjects being confronted less with 'esoteric', quasi-psychiatric family problems and increasingly with 'mundane' welfare matters such as rents, evictions and poverty. Within the 1960s, however, by whatever means the changing structure of the welfare state both in Britain and in the United States caused professional social work to reflect on itself, creating a crisis in the profession.[17]

The professional culture of social work had stabilised itself prior to these developments around a picture of the world seen through psychodynamics. The professional 'faith' of the counsellors, which Paul Halmos had carefully depicted, had belonged to this period and had rested on the grounds of a particular set of working conditions, a particular relationship between social work and the apparatus of government, and a particular kind of political ideology which itself rested on the possibilities of limitless economic growth.[18] When those *highly specific* conditions changed, so the faith of the counsellors entered a period of convulsion. In particular, the forgotten questions of power, social structure and social class posed themselves. Social work had entered its radical hour.

However, the debt of the stable professional culture had to be paid, and the problems of the relationship between social work and the State, which had been put to sleep within professional consciousness, re-asserted itself in a series of frozen images: social control *or* social change; therapy *or* reform; adaptation *or* self-actualisation; casework *or* revolution; the adjustment of the individual to society *or* a change in society to meet the individual's needs; welfare intervention focused on the 'individual' *or* on the 'environment'. And so with the emergence of the 'radical question' in social work the ambiguous, badly phrased problem of social work's politics does not, somehow, come to an end; it merely takes a new turn.

'RADICALISM' IN SOCIAL-WORK CULTURE

The professional culture of 'mainstream' social work has a frozen, timeless quality. The 'principles' and 'values' of social work are established by snatching the thought and action of other generations of social workers – Octavia Hill, Mary Richmond, Virginia Robinson, Charlotte Towle – out of their historical and cultural contexts: in this professional imagination social work administers to a cluster of eternal 'common human needs'.[19] Correspondingly, there is what is very probably a mythical history of social work – which is also part of its professional folk-lore – in which social work is depicted as unambiguously apolitical throughout the 'psychiatric deluge' until the abrupt radical politicisation of the 1960s. In a brief study of British social work in the inter-war years Ray Lees has punctured this history: social work, he argues, also contained in these years a concern 'with wider social influences and with the need for social reform'.[20] But the (unwritten) history of radicalism is fitful and discontinuous, and what also needs to be said is that the politics of social work in the years which Lees describes was largely 'bread and butter' politics which concerned itself with poverty: it did not mount a criticism of welfare *as such*, but simply urged more of it. The radicalisation of the 1960s posed different questions: the value of social work itself was interrogated and even condemned as irrelevant. In particular, casework – the dominant method in social work – was criticised sharply as an attempt to 'cool-out' the anger of clients, an anger which it was imagined was directed at a welfare state which did not deliver the goods of material prosperity.

Although it is by no means clear that the 'radicalisation of social work' found a firm base in social-work practice, it deposits troublesome questions in the professional consciousness. The main thrust of the radical critique of social work was that it was a method through which to control the poor, the oppressed, the disaffected and the useless. Social workers were depicted as 'social policemen' or 'social tranquillisers'.[21] In the magazine *Case Con* (a magazine 'for revolutionary social work') the social worker was pictured in a harsh caricature as 'King Konn', the grinning compère of a T.V. quiz programme, humiliating contestants (problem families, inadequates) as they compete for prizes (welfare benefits): the rules of the social-work game were that 'contestants' must discuss their problems without using the words 'housing', 'money', or 'protest'.[22] In his scathing 'Fat Cat Sociology' speech to the American Sociological Association Martin Nicolaus addressed these remarks to the Secretary of Health, Education and Welfare:

> The Secretary of HEW is a military officer in the domestic front of the war against the people . . . . In charge of what is called Health, Education and Welfare . . . the department of which the man is head is more accurately described as the agency which watches over the inequitable distribution of preventable disease, over the funding of domestic propaganda and indoctrination, and over the preservation of a cheap and docile labor force to keep everybody else's wages down. He is Secretary of Disease, Propaganda, and Scabbing.[23]

In another political cartoon of the period two 'slum kids' hold a conversation: 'We've got rats', says one; the other replies: 'Shit man – we've got social workers.'

The tone of the critique appeals to, and reflects, the disillusionment of a generation of professionals who had been raised to affluence. 'Radical social work' emerges at the time of other professional rumblings: 'radical lawyers'; 'radical psychologists'; 'radical therapists'; 'radical architects'. 'Radical social work' indicates a mood of professional malcontents; it hardly addresses itself to the problems of welfare. If mainstream social work had made a fetish out of technique, then radicalism denied it: there was no more 'technique' to doing social work than knowing how to 'get on with people'. If mainstream social work had emphasised the individual's personal troubles, 'radical social work' pointed to the material problems of whole communities and to socially structured inequalities. It urged a technique of 'advocacy' through which social workers should act as partisans who struggle *alongside* clients, rather than confronting them as professionals.[24] 'Radical social work' also embraced community work as a more relevant, and less mystifying, activity. But, ironically, in its move towards social-structural problems and more obviously 'political' solutions to personal problems, 'radical social work' became absent-minded about both personal problems *and* political structure. Personal troubles were lost in that 'radical social work' replaced casework with abstract formulae through which clients could secure their welfare rights: as if the wand of material abundance could wish human subjectivity away. Programmes of advocacy, community action, neighbourhood law schemes, advice centres, and so on, placed the political contexts of social work on the agenda without any consideration of how these same political contexts influence and limit the prospects of a 'radical social work': community work unmoored itself in its mind from political structure, and emerged as a free-floating freedom-fighter.[25] Radicalism gave birth to a parody of abstract professionalism: clients, on the one hand, without a presence *except as defined within a given system of 'rights'*, who met up with professional Robin Hoods who were dislocated from the structure of the welfare state. The ambiguities of the political location of social work simply re-stated themselves. If social workers adopted the role of advocate, for example, as Mungham and Thomas have noted (without grasping the full ambiguity of their remarks): 'it would just be the logical extension and formalisation of a role that is already a part of their work.'[26] But if it is the routine work of social workers which is the object of the radical critique, then a formalisation of that routine simply formalises the political ambiguity of social work: everything has changed, but nothing has moved. The impulse of 'radical social work' stutters to a halt, not only because its abstract political slogans float free from the day-to-day urgencies of welfare recipients, but also because its theory is spasmodic and ignorant. The client in 'radical social work' has become a wooden, dehumanised figure at the bargain basement of a welfare-rights stall. The cult of activism in 'radical social work' rules at the expense of its humanising object. Russell Jacoby's remarks on the fate of the New Left match the fate of radicalism in social work precisely: 'Sustained political and theoretical thought is not simply rejected, but forgotten. The slogans and rhetoric that replace it are necessarily abstract and formal, like the society that tossed them up'.[27] The dehumanisation of the person in the mind of 'radical social work' to some extent anticipates that same development in the latest outgrowths of misfit social thought.[28]

THE DEVIANT IMAGINATION WITHIN SOCIAL WORK

There has been no consistently argued or sustained attempt from within 'mainstream' social work to provide a defence against its radical critics. On the one hand this is an indication of the depth of the contemporary crisis in social welfare. But it also indicates a degree of sympathy *from inside* social work with its radical critics who charge it with being an instrument of social coercion: 'Yes we know . . . but what can we do about it?' Nevertheless, when radical criticism has caused the professional eye to reflect upon itself (if only fitfully) the response has provided different harmonies on the same theme: there are still clients; there are still individual cases of distress; radicalism does not sweep away human misery.[29] But social work does not simply junk radical criticism in order to get on with the job. Social work also asserts its own system of values and priorities in its dogged insistence to do good, and right wrongs, *whatever the over-all character of society*. Perlman, who has provided the most consistent line of defence, thus argues that casework can slice through all this and get rapid help to those in need:

[Man] should not have to wait – suffering, struggling, withering, as the case may be – while the wheels of social justice grind out social change, or, even when reform is swift, until that change makes its way through the labyrinth of policy–programme–process to affect him at weary last.[30]

There is an impatience in social-work thought and action. In its day-to-day activity on behalf of its client-misfits over matters of housing, debts, evictions, the struggle to get through this day to the next; and in its quarrelsome engagements with other professional bodies (doctors, lawyers, teachers) and the powerful agencies of government, mainstream social work takes part in 'moral hustling' which defends the weak and gives them a voice against the powerful. We find echos of social work's day-to-day moral hustle in Hobsbawm's description of the aims of the social bandit and the 'noble robber':

> his object is comparatively modest. He protests not against the fact that peasants are poor and oppressed. He seeks to establish or re-establish justice or 'the old ways', that is to say, fair dealing in a society of oppression. He rights wrongs. . . . The stories told about him record modest triumphs: a widow's farm saved . . . an imprisoned man set free. . . . At most – and the case is rare enough – he may . . . order bailiffs to give bread to their labourers, to permit the poor to glean, or he may distribute salt free, i.e. to cancel taxes. . . . He is an individual who refuses to bend his back, that is all. . . . They cannot abolish oppression. But they do prove that justice is possible, that poor men need not be humble, helpless and meek.[31]

The 'inside codes' of social work's occupational culture – those codes which are unwritten (or only half-written) – are filled with this rebellious spirit. A study of 'industrial deviance' in social work demonstrates a wide-spread acceptance of rule-bending and rule-breaking among social workers 'as part of the job'. Violations of parole conditions and probation orders are ignored; 'blind eyes' are turned towards welfare recipients who bend and break the rules of social-security benefit schemes.[32] An important source of this professional deviance (if that is what it is) lies in the occupational socialisation of recruits. In education programmes they are introduced to the critical concepts of social science and to a 'professional vision' of an alternative system of welfare which transcends the shortcomings of the welfare state. Faced with the realities of their working conditions, and their function within the welfare state, this industrial deviance sometimes becomes the only means by which social workers are able to exercise a measure of control over their work and realise the objectives (on behalf of their clients) which conform to the standards of the 'professional vision' of welfare. It is, therefore, industrial deviance which helps them to secure the objectives for which they are led to believe they are trained and paid.

It is possible to say, then, that the social-work sector of the welfare state is an improver and a fighting betterer – even if, to use an expression of Gouldner's, it fights largely on counter-punching.[33] Another key notion in social work's 'inside codes' is that of 'caring': there is much talk of a 'caring' person, a 'caring' community, a 'caring' attitude, a 'caring' profession, a 'caring' (or careless) society; and social work sees itself as more 'caring' than the careless world at large. As a profession (or semi-profession) it holds great hopes for itself; that it might ease, and finally bring to an end, the extrusion of misfits, thus transforming, once and for all, waste-products into citizens. In the 1930s Bertha Reynolds described social work as the ' "personnel department" of the community of the future', while more recently Olive Stevenson has written that 'those who commit themselves to social work contribute, in my view, to the *sensitization* of our society'.[34] In the same vein Paul Halmos has argued that the counselling ideology of the personal service professions is a potent agent of social change, one which brings about a 'moral reformation' of political and industrial leaders.[35] Carol Meyer's equally grandiose proposition is that 'the primary purpose of social work practice is to individualise people in the mass urban society', and Harriett Bartlett suggests that social work might yet develop 'a kind of service not yet perceived or offered in Western civilisation'.[36] However, the moral calculus of the welfare state is more complex than these ambitious and hopeful promises, and the hope of the social worker's theory seminar easily turns into a cynical, even despairing, practice.[37] In one ambitious attempt to locate the ideology of the personal service professions in the political structure of urban-industrial society, Maurice North argues that the social worker's belief in the innate dignity and worth of their deviant clientele comes to grief in the world of action:

the social milieu in which they work has been but slightly affected by their faith. The surrounding social structures utilise their ideological actions but only as palliatives. The brute fact is that the society for which the social worker operates does not subscribe to his beliefs in the worth and significance of the individual and in his rights against the majority.[38]

North's account of the 'secular priests' of modern society – social workers, psychotherapists, and so on – centres on the function which their 'psychotherapeutic ideology' serves in relation to political and social change. Some embrace this 'counselling ideology' as the true index of a caring society; others criticise it for deflecting men from political goals, and obscuring the politics of deviance-control. North's conclusions are remarkable for the way in which they express the full ambiguity of the professional creed of social work :

> The meaninglessness of work, the fatuity of leisure, endemic violence and crime, acquisitive and competitive relationships engendered by the industrialised society can be rendered less noxious by psychotherapy. . . . The psychotherapeutic ideology provides the only path to personal salvation. That it is apolitical, anti-radical, and supports the status quo is not important when compared with its positive contributions to human well-being. . . . The inestimable service that the psychotherapeutic ideology supplies is that it gives the individual the feeling that somebody cares – even if it is not true.[39]

However, North's conclusions are not an *analysis* of social welfare; they are a *symptom* of its predicament.

Social work registers the contemporary dislocation of the welfare state in an acute form because, although it operates within a welfare ideology which prescribes that the useless will be returned to utility, its professional culture also respects the authenticity of the misfit. In sympathy with the underdog, social work 'knows' that deviants are not waste-products, but that they are wasted human potential. Social-work theory and practice strive to give the deviant a voice; the most recent expression of this is to be found in the modish studies of client perceptions of social welfare services.[40] The voice of the deviant imagination even speaks from within social workers themselves: in a study of the motivations of recruits to social work, I found that the dominant impulse which brought them into the job was a rebellion against a life which they feared, otherwise, would waste their own human selves; they were runaways from commercialism, the 'rat race' and what they described as 'boredom'.[41] But ambiguity quickly re-asserts itself: the irony of their position was that they were returning their misfit-clients to the good life from which they were themselves in flight.

PERSON AND POLITICS IN SOCIAL WORK

Social work grasps the problem of the deviant imagination (and is grasped by it) in its own specific manner. Superficially at least, its relationship to the deviant question appears to be quite different from that of the social sciences. But it is not, somehow, cut off from the social practice of theory-production and research by a wall of professional culture. And although it is concerned much more with care and correction than with understanding, social work's professional culture is itself, as I have shown, a response to the problems of the deviant imagination and its ambiguities: the two-sided character of the deviant imagination (waste product/ authentic conduct) impresses itself on the practice and ideology of social work, just as it inserts itself in the practice and ideology of theory-construction. There are, of course, difficulties and obstacles in communication between the social scientist and the social worker. But that is not the point. I have elaborated some aspects of the professional culture of social work and how the world 'looks' differently from behind it, but it is the same world as that approached by the social scientist and it is grasped in the same categories. Deviance theory and social work, from their different vantage points, act on a given space of culture known as 'deviance'. And in recent years both the theory of deviance and social welfare have gone through a period of convulsion in which, particularly, the question of how politics inserts itself in this space has been posed.

In misfit social thought this has presented itself, in a large measure, through a dissolution of the firm boundaries of the 'personal' and the 'political'. Social work's own radical hour, however, takes a different direction. There radicals criticise social work for paying too much attention to the personal sphere and urge it in the direction of politics: for example, they urge community-action tactics instead of casework with individuals and families. Those who wish to defend the traditional orientation of social work, on the other hand, argue that the personal sphere does not go away, in spite of political critiques. The argument becomes, almost, the personal *versus* the political.

This badly phrased argument, which is still dictated by the crude opposition of the abstract 'individual' versus the reified 'society', does not only betray the intellectual and imaginative weaknesses of the field of social work – weaknesses which it would be hard to deny. It also states a truth about the radical critics of social work: very often, invariably, their criticisms are mounted at a level far removed from the actual practice and experiences of contemporary social welfare. Radical thought (which seems quite unable to find its radical *praxis*) advocates various kinds of moves towards a political understanding of social work, but it rarely backs these up with any real appreciation of how these prescriptions connect up with the day-to-day practice of social workers and the organisational conditions of social welfare. So that Ray Lees, for example, is able to conduct what passes for a survey of the field of 'politics and social work' without ever tying his analysis to case-study: that is, without mentioning the *work-unit* of the social worker.[42] In an earlier piece Lees writes that: 'The interesting thing to me about some of the recent developments among those who are concerned with helping the under-privileged at a face to face level is the new stress on collective action, *what is in effect their entry into political activity*.'[43] Here is a very clear instance of that formal definition of what politics is which keeps 'politics' and 'welfare matters' firmly separated. The assumption is that what social workers *were* doing with individuals and families had nothing to do with politics: their turn to community work, and so on, thus becomes an 'entry into' politics.

In one sense these weaknesses have the effect of making political criticism almost unintelligible to practising social workers since it does not connect up with their working lives. In another, more fundamental, sense it can be seen that this problem flows from the theoretical assumption that personal problems do not have anything to do with politics. This is a fatal assumption in any attempt to grasp the nature of the politics of social work. A scheme which perpetuates that strict theoretical and ideological division between the individual and society, and the personal and the political will neither be able to understand the politics of social work, nor direct its practice, since social work operates at the intersection of what is 'personal' and what is 'political'.

Perhaps the most significant feature of social work's newly found radicalism is that it is in some ways divorced from the more general movements of politics in the period of its growth: that is during the 1960s. It does not, for example, meet (and confront and take hold of) what the 'soft politics' of the 'New Left' reached for: an understanding of the politics of everyday life and the mediations of family, work, school, welfare state. The relationship between social work's sphere of interest and that of modern feminism, for example, should not go unmentioned. The tactic of the 'consciousness raising group' in the feminist movement, to take the most obvious point of intersection, employs methods and techniques not unlike casework and social group work in a way which understands some of the political ramifications of personal distress, and tries to join up 'therapy' with 'politics'.[44] There are similar developments in the emerging homosexual movement.[45] Some feminists are now arguing that social work is in fact an activity which has a real unity of interest with traditional women's work: as Myra Garrett describes it, 'the unending, unspecific task of helping, nurturing, caring, educating, supporting'.[46] The implication is that the feminist understanding of the political aspects of family life and child-rearing can aid the political understanding of social work. But the fact is that although so many social workers are women there is an absence of any strong modern feminist interest or influence in social work, which is perhaps surprising. As a whole, in fact, social work's radicalism has ignored the programme of the New Left; and the personal, disorganised, inarticulate, small-scale troubles of clients are left disconnected (in theory and in practice) from the large-scale, public, organised, collective, articulate issues which are thought to constitute politics. It is the failure to recognise the interconnections between these two areas which establishes the awkward problem of the person in social work's politics.

In C. Wright Mills's *The Sociological Imagination* we find a clear expression of an alternative stance which provides the foundations for a secure appreciation of social work's politics:

> Do not allow public issues as they are officially formulated, or troubles as they are privately felt, to determine the problems that you take up for study. . . . Know that many personal troubles cannot be solved merely as troubles, but must be understood in terms of public issues – and in terms of the problems of history-making. Know that the human meaning of public issues must be revealed by relating them to personal troubles – and to the problems of the individual life. Know that the problems of social science, when adequately formulated, must include both troubles and issues, both biography and history, and the range of their intricate relations.[47]

The phrase has an easy ring to it: 'the range of their intricate relations'. But it is not an easy matter to formulate that range, although it is there that the politics of social work are to be found. The vision of the New Left was a more recent encounter with the problem which re-opened some of the issues. It is, however, an irony of the uneven development of history that at the time when the Left was rediscovering psycho-analysis, social work was busy forgetting it.

6

THE HISTORICAL OBJECT OF DEVIANCE: KING MOB

In traditional social thought and social practice deviance has placed itself outside politics, secured in a neat division between 'welfare matters' on one side, and 'political science' on the other. It is a state of affairs which David Matza found 'hardly believable': that one could conceive of the regulation of disorderly behaviour and crime independent of the workings of the state.[1]

The 1960s announced a partial surrender of these firm boundaries. The misfit paradigm exploited a number of the thinning spots in this division of politics and welfare and argued the essentially moral and political character of deviance-control. Anti-psychiatry pointed to the need for an engagement with the political undergirdings of psychiatry and the ideology of humane, liberal social-welfare programmes. Social work itself underwent a crisis of some magnitude. The glitter to this abrupt shift in social thought was provided by the counter-culture and the re-discovery of the Frankfurt School: in the 'personal politics' of the New Left the control and counter-control of human experience and sensibility became *the* most significant political act. The benign face of social welfare emerged as a candidate for political dissection: it was seen, that is, as a political agent. Within the convergences of the misfit paradigm the personnel of the welfare apparatus become the 'brain police'.

The political alternatives embodied within this perspective were never altogether clear: a characteristic of this convergence is that it throws together in a political soup snatches of Marx, a romantic mysticism, some shreds of democratic pluralism, and a politically untutored wish to better the condition of all people, everywhere. Notably absent from the politics of the confluence of the misfit paradigm was any concern with piecemeal social engineering. It was, and is, a utopian movement of thought: the power to *imagine* an alternative way of life was its political engine; the deviant imagination, which 'takes the law into its own hands', was an inspiration which had stepped outside one-dimensionality.

A characteristic of subjectivist politics is to imagine that there is a richer human sensibility to be found on the edges of society. A very short list of precedents in this tradition would include beats and bohemians; Norman Mailer's hip 'White Negro' together with the 'natural rhythm' of the 'real' negro;[2] visionaries and lunatics whose madness goes close to genius, and whose simplicity approaches innocence; Red Indians, Eastern mystics, and the 'proles' of *Nineteen Eighty-Four*: here, the message of subjectivist politics runs, are the truly creative, sensitive, human people; here are men whose minds are not fettered by the constraints of reasonableness. The tradition, which is quite powerful in western thought, says little more than that: commonly, in subjectivist politics, inspiration from the edges of social order is held as a charm against the drudgery of the day. In the theoretical vocabulary of the New Left, however, the deviant imagination is given a more vigorous political articulation, and misfit sociology imagines that it has political heroes for its research data.

But 'deviance' is an object with a dual character. On the other side of its 'inspirational' qualities is a darker face: contemporarily viewed as a conglomerate of oddballs, misfits and inadequates, at earlier times in history one would have talked of the 'submerged tenth' of the population, the 'residuum', or the 'dangerous classes'.

These two faces of 'deviance' are not at all separate. They intermingle and leave traces of themselves in each other. When Timothy Leary, self-acclaimed high priest of the underground imagination of the counter-culture, reflected on early experiments on the quasi-therapeutic use of the drug LSD with 'the most dangerous uncontrolled criminals',[3] he formulated his notion of the freedom of the deviant imagination in the following terms. (It should be held in mind that Leary is in dialogue with critics who suggested that while disciplined minds [Huxley is the prototype] might find the drug-effects illuminating, undisciplined minds would burn out in total chaos, 'like a zoo with all the cages open'.) I have retained Leary's emphasis:

AND THEIR MINDS DID INDEED OPEN LIKE ZOOZ [*sic*] WITH ALL THE CAGES OPEN – AND THIS BECAME THE METAPHOR OF OUR JOURNEY. <u>OPEN THE CAGE DOORS!</u> LET THE WILD ANIMALS BE FREE! WHEN THE DOMESTICATED DISCOVER THEIR WILD NATURE THE RESULT IS CHAOS ONLY TO THE ZOO-KEEPER JAILER WITH HIS BRASS RING OF KEYS. WHEN THE CAGE DOORS OPEN NATURE RULES.[4]

Leary's metaphor has a history: we read that during the Gordon Riots of 1780 rumours circulated London 'that lions had been let loose from the Tower and that lunatics were to be released from Bedlam'.[5] The earliest form in fact in which the space of 'deviance' announced itself was that of the 'city mob'. To put that another way: the forms, categories and images which are brought to bear in the modern social thought and practice which fixes its gaze on 'deviance' were born out of the confrontation with the dangerous energies of King Mob. And, as I will show, these categories have not changed, although they have rearranged themselves across history in different points of emphasis. The following sections set out to illuminate some aspects of the intimate connections between the origins of the field of deviance and the emergent politics of industrialism and the city. It is the necessary historical spade-work to attempts to fix the uncontrolled politics of deviance and welfare.

A SPACE OF KNOWLEDGE

Michel Foucault has argued that between the beginning of the nineteenth century and the end of the eighteenth a mutation took place, by which thought entered a new dimension from which it has yet to emerge. There had been earlier ruptures in thought to which he draws attention, but his focus (and ours) is on the transformation into the modern age. The character of these ruptures and discontinuities in thought is so massive, so total, that it is as if men had left the darkness of earlier times and could now name the world as it really is: 'One has the impression that . . . someone has at last taken on the task of stating something that had been visible from the beginning of time, but had remained mute before a sort of invincible distraction of men's eyes.'[6]

Foucault, who is engaged on a project of such breadth that we

cannot hope to even indicate its scope here, is concerned to unravel some of the aspects of these ruptures in thought, which offer
clues to the nature of thought itself, and he has traced them
through the development of medicine and psychiatry,[7] as well as
in the study of life, labour and language.[8] Foucault is also concerned to emphasise the way in which these ruptures signify the
historical limits of thought. Thus, the break at the end of the
eighteenth century, which announces the end of the Classical Age,
means that while we can trace some of the present-day notions of
psychiatry and medicine back to early nineteenth-century psychiatric
and medical ideas, 'if we try to trace the development of psychopathology beyond the nineteenth century, we soon lose our way'.[9]
And the reason that we lose our way, or 'the path becomes
confused', is not because these earlier medical notions are more
remote, but because before the rupture men saw the world through
a different 'grid of knowledge'. They therefore *saw* the world
differently in quite a radical sense. The extent of our rootedness in
this grid, space, or episteme is such that the descriptions offered to
us by nineteenth-century medicine of tissues, membranes, and so
on, describe to us (through the same grid) 'the shape of things
as they really are'; whereas the descriptions offered to us by
medicine in the Classical Age we can only recognise as fantasy.[10]

An 'episteme', then, we can describe as a formation of knowledge
in the broadest sense. It is a 'space of knowledge', a space within
which thought can take place: thought is limited to that space.
It cannot escape it, and it cannot engage in controversy with
thought from an earlier space: the ruptures which Foucault has
set out to trace mark off the limits of discourse. Indeed, we have
no wish to engage in controversy, for example, with eighteenth-
century medicine, other than to abuse it as 'pre-scientific': it has
nothing to tell us, because it does not *see* things 'properly'.

Foucault argues that the themes, disputes, preferences of
opinion, and controversies (represented by individual books,
oeuvres, texts) which populate an episteme are simply the marks
– one might almost say the scratches – which men make on (and
within) the space which is available for knowledge and thought.
In order to grasp Foucault's point, that is, one must adopt a
position of extreme humility in relation to the thought of one's
own age. Foucault distinguishes a *'history of opinions'* – that is,
a history 'of the choices operated according to individuals, en-

vironments, social groups' – from what he calls an '*archaeology of knowledge*':

> If one wishes to undertake an archaeological analysis of knowledge itself, it is not these celebrated controversies that ought to be used as the guidelines and articulation of such a project. One must reconstitute the general system of thought whose network . . . renders an interplay of simultaneous and apparently contradictory opinions possible. It is this network that defines the conditions *that make a controversy or problem possible* . . . .[11]

The themes, disputes and controversies between rival schools of thought in the field of deviance are, in the same way, superficially in mutual conflict: there is little give and take, for example, between a constitutional–genetic theory of deviance and a socio-cultural one. But these rivalries are only possible to the extent that there is a 'space of knowledge' available for them to take place within. This space, which gradually unravels itself as modern welfare theory, becomes available at the precise moment of the rupture which precipitates thought into the Modern Age. At this precise point – not before, and not later – the modern controversies announce themselves.[12] There was crime, deviance and madness before this point, of course, but it is then that men begin to relate to it, and see it, in a different way. Social thought and social practice undergo a convulsion, and out of it emerge the institutions of the police, the penal system, psychiatry, education, and welfare; and also new conceptions of life, family and work. Within these institutional embodiments of the new episteme its themes, disputes and controversies are unwrapped: the field of deviance, that is, emerges not as a conglomeration of separate theories and practices, but as a unitary space within which these theories and practices have dominion; the arguments of the following sections will make this clear.

The reasons for this brief digression into Foucault's project of an archaeology of knowledge must be spelled out: I do not intend to offer an archaeology of the knowledge of deviance, or anything approaching it. Foucault's ideas are important here because this chapter takes as its object something larger than any single text.

Foucault's work, also, can stand as a corrective to those histories of criminology, psychiatry, deviance theory, and social-welfare ideas which trace specific ideas and concepts to 'founding fathers'. There are controversies and disputes in the field of deviance, to be sure, and at particular points in time certain individuals give a particular perspective a particularly sharp formulation. But, when we look more closely at the matter, we find that these various notions were already in the air in one form or another: 'founding fathers' gather together threads already available in the 'space' of knowledge. The brief history of a sector of welfare ideology offered by Leon Radzinowicz's *Ideology and Crime* is an example of a 'founding fathers' history which nevertheless recognises that its subject 'was forged during that memorable turning point in human affairs, the eighteenth century, and tempered in the fires of more than one revolution'.[13] 'One is reminded again', writes Radzinowicz, 'of the saying . . . there is nothing new but what has been forgotten.'[14] But that too is easily forgotten in the rapid pace of publications and research which are hawked around as 'revolutions' in thought and practice; revolutions in thought, we should remind ourselves, cannot be bought at the cash-and-carry.

What follows, then, is not an archaeology of the field of deviance. It does not measure up to the task of delineating the transition into a modern conception of deviance. What it does is point to the unnerving constancies between our thought and the primitive, 'pre-scientific' thought of reformers, investigators, and even scribblers in the nineteenth century. By then the space of knowledge which we call deviance had already become available for disputes and preoccupations which, while they might be expressed in a different language, are clearly recognisable as our own.

IMAGES OF THE NINETEENTH CENTURY MISFIT

The nineteenth century did not speak of 'deviance'. It spoke of 'paupers', the 'dangerous classes', the 'perishing classes', 'vagabonds', and 'nomads'. Which is not to say that it did not know deviance: in what follows I outline how the major themes of modern deviance theory were fully available within the nineteenth century's consciousness.

To begin with the 'labelling' or 'societal reaction' perspective;

something very modern, announced – I think – by Edwin Lemert in 1951 and reaching a peak in its popularity in the 1960s. Taylor, Walton and Young draw attention to a comment by Marx in 1859 where he notes that rises in crime can be attributed to changes in the definition and structure of law, and that 'law itself may not only punish crime, but also improvise it'.[15] They describe Marx's statement as 'a qualified, "social reaction" position', and elsewhere Ian Taylor has written that Marx's view was 'an emphasis that was lost . . . throughout the following century'.[16] The stated implication is that Marx was 'ahead of his time . . . in this respect'.[17] In fact, Marx was not alone in his expression of a viewpoint which we now call the 'labelling perspective'. The different strands of the social reaction viewpoint were common currency in the nineteenth century.

Alexander Thomson, for example, in 1853 commented on the social-psychological implications of labelling and the stigma of the convicted criminal – the 'plague spot' as he called it.[18] Both Thomson and C. J. C. Talbot (Viscount Ingestre) – and they were not alone – argued the case for providing magistrates with powers such that they could avoid the stigmatisation and criminalisation of 'neglected juveniles' who commit delinquencies.[19] The alternative to sentencing which they suggested involved the provision of various kinds of industrial training schools, the forerunners in the United Kingdom of Approved Schools, now called euphemistically 'Community Homes'. Talbot wrote of the dangers of sending 'a poor little boy . . . to gaol, making a martyr of him, and stamping him as a vagabond at once'.[20] Both Thomson and Talbot were arguing in this context for a change in the notion of law so that penal action would improvise less crime and criminalise fewer categories of disorderly conduct. We also find concern expressed about the effects of 'labelling' in the report of a Select Committee on Prison Discipline in 1850: committed for 'perhaps . . . a very trifling offence . . . [such as] sleeping under a hayrick or for bathing', wayward youngsters might be 'branded as prison birds' and 'trained to prison life'.[21] Commenting on this report May has written that the committee recognised that: 'Children treated as adult criminals reacted accordingly. "Branded as prison birds", they played their role for the admiration of their peers; for a boy once labelled as a criminal "regards himself as belonging to the criminal class" .'[22] Certainly in a stumbling fashion the committee tried to formulate for itself how a person might come to regard himself as a criminal, acquiring 'a criminal status'; and they wondered whether 'the mere fact of being taken before a magistrate [might] . . . place that child in the criminal class'.[23] But one should be careful not to claim too much for the sociological perspicacity of nineteenth-century reformers: they were, without any doubt, *not* symbolic interactionists, whereas May's choice of words implies that they might have been. Nevertheless, there is a persistence in the sentiments: as Schur puts it, one hundred and twenty years later, in his policy of 'radical non-intervention': 'leave the kids alone wherever possible'.

Henry Mayhew was also alive to the labelling influence: philanthropic actions, he wrote, which denied the self-will of deviant actors produced 'philanthropic serfs' through a *villeinage of benevolence*'.[24] The 1841 *Report . . . on the Training of Pauper Children* had its own view of the 'secondary deviation' produced by societal reaction. It warned of the dangers of institutionalisation, 'crushing the free spirit of the child . . . who when he grows up will return . . . to the chain which so long has bound him, and which use will have made him *a kind of second nature*'.[25] Of course, notions of the 'demoralisation' and 'pauperisation' of the poor by 'societal reaction' have a long history in the nineteenth century; and just as the labelling perspective often goes close to suggesting that there is no such thing as 'deviance',[26] so 'pauperisation' theories easily forgot that there was any such thing as poverty.

We can take one final example of the labelling perspective in the nineteenth century which anticipates Marx by thirty years. Edwin Chadwick, in 1829 in an article in the *London Review*, commented on the rise in crime: criminal statistics, he argued, were not a reliable guide to the incidence of crime since they reflected, and were created, by the activities of law-enforcements agencies. Criminal statistics, in more modern language, reflected organisational routines and these routines contained variations in the implementation of law (and police vigilance) at different times and in different districts.[27] The nineteenth century understood quite well how the State 'improvised' crime.

A second major theme of modern deviance theory stresses the importance of genetic and constitutional factors. The nineteenth century could not do a chromosome count, but it could count heads. Historians of crime and social problems have tended to

see Lombroso's work as the primary source of an interest in the
deviant's constitutional make-up. Lombroso identified various
physical stigmata – 'the flattened nose, the scanty beard, the lop-
sided skull', etc.[28] – as features of his atavistic criminal. For many
years before Lombroso various notions of semi-scientific craniology
and phrenology had been in circulation,[29] but his work is generally
regarded as the first serious and systematic approach to the subject.
But Lombroso's discovery – which he described as a 'flash of
inspiration' – was not a reserved scientific territory; it grew out
of a much more commonplace set of attitudes about misfits and
the 'dangerous classes'. Henry Mayhew, for example, had identified
the wandering tribes of the street-folk as a race apart from normal,
settled citizens; they were to be distinguished by their 'high cheek-
bones and protruding jaws'.[30] A history of deviance theory
encounters difficulties if it insists on being a history of founding
fathers and their influence which directs the course of events.
Mayhew, the journalist, we can be sure, was not influenced by
Lombroso the scientist: he was writing twenty-five years before
him.

Mayhew was not alone in identifying the dangerous and
criminal classes as a *race* of nomads, savages and barbarians.
Beames, in his book *The Rookeries of London*, proposed as one
possible cause of lawlessness (Beames, like many of his and our
contemporaries, had a 'multi-factorial' theory) that it was
behaviour which fulfilled 'a hereditary curse'.[31] Chevalier also
reports how in the early nineteenth century Gall and Lavater
'found no difficulty discovering wolf-men and lion-men among
their clientele' of convicts.[32] He also comments on the way in which
within bourgeois opinion the dangerous classes and labouring
classes were pictured as ugly, deformed creatures. Chevalier
argues that these characterisations of physical appearances became
weapons in a struggle between classes.[33]

The idea of a relationship, then, between deviance, criminality,
or whatever it might be called, and a constitutional predisposition
which stamped the lower classes with physical stigmata was
available in popular belief and opinion long before Lombroso's
flash of inspiration. Theories of the constitutional nature of
criminality and deviance dwell within, and express, these popular
notions. Chevalier reaches much the same conclusion: theory and
contemporary opinion ran along the same tracks; 'the theories were

not transformed into popular beliefs, but rather reinforced beliefs held previously'.[34] Furthermore, it is not enough, writes Chevalier, simply to note that 'the Paris working class was ugly in most of the contemporary documents';[35] what must also be grasped is that the physical appearance of the labouring classes was equated with that of the 'dangerous classes'. This convergence in nineteenth-century opinion of the 'dangerous classes' and the working class as a whole is of crucial significance, as we shall see.

Another common theme among nineteenth-century writers who looked at the field of deviance was that of socialisation and subculture: the question, as Henry Mayhew puts it, of how men are *bred* to the streets.[36] This is such a common perspective that examples can be taken almost at random. Beames, again, talks about dangerous elements of the population being produced 'through perverse adherence to the errors or traditions of their fathers'.[37] In a sort of nineteenth-century social-problems reader entitled *Meliora, or Better Times to Come* John Leigh was only one of the authors to allude to 'a large proportion of the youthful population of the community in regular training for crime'.[38] The *Report . . . on the Training of Pauper Children*, concerned with the methods and effectiveness of training schools and apprenticeships, takes it for granted that the task of producing an efficient artisan with good working habits was that of 'removing the consequences of a descent from vicious parentage or the effects of pauper nurture'.[39] To the Victorian gaze the troublesome behaviour of the dangerous classes appeared almost like a trade which was learned as a child in the streets, the 'flash-houses', and the densely populated rookeries; that is, in the ghetto.

At the same time (and even coincidentally) any deviation by the poor from the behaviour of the middle classes or the 'respectable' workman was equalled to savage bestiality. One must not expect too much consistency from nineteenth-century writings on the poor, the oppressed, and the criminal. Indeed, these inconsistencies are quite vital if one attempts to understand the origins of modern deviance-control: particularly as they relate to how the problem of the 'dangerous classes' was understood. Henry Mayhew, for example, at times provides a sensitive account – one might say even an 'appreciative' account – of the subcultural value system of the London street-folk – their work organisation, sexual habits, family organisation, and slang.[40] But he also implies that this is an expression of a nomadic, racial constitution. While noting the similarities with some twentieth-century accounts of 'lower class culture' and the 'culture of poverty' Mayhew can speak for himself:

> The nomad . . . is distinguished from the civilised man by his repugnance to regular and continuous labour – by his want of providence in laying up a store for the future – by his inability to perceive consequences ever so slightly removed from immediate apprehension – by his passion for stupefying herbs and roots . . . and for intoxicating fermented liquors . . . by an immoderate love of gaming . . . by his love of libidinous dances . . . by his delight in warfare and all perilous sports – by his desire for vengeance – by the looseness of his notions as to property – by the absence of chastity among his women, and his disregard for female honour . . . his rude idea of a Creator, and utter absence of all appreciation of the mercy of the Divine Spirit.[41]

As Eileen Yeo notes, 'Mayhew was no relativist'.[42] And yet that is only part of the truth. Cultural relativism – one of the hall-marks of the misfit paradigm – tends to be regarded as a very recent innovation in approaching the deviant question. Ideas of 'community control', 'neighbourhood control', or the control of drug problems by utilising the know-how of drug subcultures[43] have a very modern ring to them. The constancy of the 'space' of deviance, however, can again be measured against the fact that the 'relativist' approach is already available in popular consciousness in the nineteenth century and Mayhew, predictably, is the person to give it voice. The following excerpt from an address to parolees ('ticket-of-leave men') shows yet another face of Henry Mayhew – Mayhew the relativist:

> as a class you are distinguished mainly by your love of a roving life, and . . . at the bottom of all your criminal practices lies your indisposition to follow any settled occupation. . . . I am satisfied that if anything effectual is to be done in the way of reforming you, Society must work in consonance and not in antagonism with your nature. In this connexion it appears to me that the great outlet for you is street trading, where you are allowed to roam at will unchafed by restraints not congenial

to your habits and feelings. . . . It strikes me that a number of poor men's markets might be established very advantageously . . .[44]

Perhaps more than any other writer of his time Mayhew voices the ambiguities of the deviant question. His work was not firmly anchored to any coherent political tradition, and 'he showed sympathy for an almost bewildering variety of agencies and reforms'.[45] Although a furious classifier, theorisation was not his strength: with all the agility of a story-teller, and under the pressure of a journalist's deadlines, Mayhew's accounts of the urban poor shift and float within a number of conflicting theories of the causes of their condition. In one moment of bold classification he distinguishes three categories: 'Those who are *bred* to the streets . . . those who *take* to the streets . . . [and] those who are *driven* to the streets.'[46] But his classifications (of which this is only one) do not constrict his narrative of the London poor and the London oddballs of the nineteenth century. Gertrude Himmelfarb, for example, has indicated some of the ways in which Mayhew's accounts fluctuate between various causal theories of the habits of the poor from page to page, paragraph to paragraph, and even sentence by sentence.[47]

The inconsistency of nineteenth-century writings on 'deviance' betrays more than a naïveté of social-scientific consciousness, or a simple lack of empirical evidence. These inconsistencies, interchangeable conceptions of deviance, and battles between rival schools of thought remain with us to the present day: they indicate something quite fundamental to the nature of the deviant imagination and the origins of deviance-control in the convulsions of the Industrial Revolution. They are ambiguities which now, of course, are institutionalised (and obscured) in vast bodies of research and literature. Fundamentally, they are expressions of the relationship between crime and poverty, deviance and class membership, and the relationship of the 'dangerous classes' to the labouring population as a whole. The issue is the relationship of deviance to society.

LABOURING CLASSES OR DANGEROUS CLASSES?

The poor and their customs seemed as strange to the bourgeois inhabitants of the early industrial cities as they must appear to us today. And they were strangers to the middle classes in more ways than one. The alienation found expression even in the geography of the cities. Engels, for example, in his *Condition of the Working Class in England* describes how one courtyard in a poor district of Manchester was 'so shut off, so secluded' that he did not discover it until an extension to the Leeds railway demolished the surrounding courts and alleyways and exposed it to view.[48] Beames describes a similar occasion in London where it was the construction of New Oxford Street which made certain parts of the rookeries (the ghettos) accessible; Beames also describes the rookeries as *Alsatias*, even though that ancient right of criminal sanctuary had been removed one hundred and eighty years before him.[49] And it would appear that the word 'rookery' and the use of the word 'warren' to describe a tangled nest of poor dwellings entered the English language during this period. In an earlier usage 'warren' meant 'brothel': the word 'rookery' signified a crammed, non-conjugal gathering of birds; 'warren' carried with it a sense of sleazy, indiscriminate breeding.[50] Tennyson employed the image to its full effect, connecting its different (but joined) meanings: 'And the crowded couch of incest in the warrens of the poor.'

This oppressed population were also strangers in their habits, not only because their customs were alien to middle-class morality, but also because middle-class moral codes were alien to the poor. Ingestre, for example, recounts the 'fearful' statistics found in a report by the chaplain of Preston Jail in 1850:

> out of 1656 males . . . it is a fact that 674 were unable to read in the slightest degree; 977 did not know the reigning sovereign's name: 646 were ignorant of the Saviour's name, and unable to repeat a word of prayer; and though such was the case, 713 of them were well acquainted with the exciting adventures of Turpin and Jack Sheppard; knew that they were famous robbers and housebreakers; admired them as friends of the poor . . .[51]

Engels recites a number of identical reports from other districts of England: Wolverhampton, Birmingham, Lancashire, Sheffield, and the potteries.[52] Here was a truly 'vicious' and 'dangerous' class who stood as an emblem of the confusion of capitalism in a period of rapid growth and change.

The bourgeois inhabitants of early industrial cities are sometimes thought to have overstated the conditions of the poor, and even to have mistaken their identity. No attempt to rescue the reputation of Henry Mayhew, for example, as a serious social investigator[53] should shy away from the fact that when he fixed his attention on the poor he spent a considerable effort recording the habits of the rag-pickers, bone-grubbers, pure-finders, and other wretched exotica of the streets, rather than attending to the more ordinary poverty of the artisan.[54] This is neither a fault, nor simply an obsession on Mayhew's part: it is an expression of his Age, and it is a preoccupation which reaches further than London. In his study of Charles Baudelaire, for whom the rag-picker also exercised an ineluctable charm, Walter Benjamin writes:

> When the new industrial processes had given refuse a certain value, ragpickers appeared in the cities in large numbers. They worked for middlemen and constituted a sort of cottage industry located in the streets. The ragpicker fascinated his epoch. The eyes of the first investigators of pauperism were fixed on him with the mute question as to where the limit of human misery lay.[55]

Modern social historians, however, are frequently perturbed by the way in which the Victorians made the mistake of confusing the conditions and life-style of the working class as a whole with those of the most submerged sections of the population; confusing, that is, the 'provident' workman of the 'labouring classes' with the 'dangerous classes', the street-folk, and the 'criminal classes'. What is the nature of this 'mistake'?

Himmelfarb has commented on this confusion in Mayhew's *London Labour and the London Poor* where the title itself is a carrier of the ambiguity: 'Were the two categories "Labour" and "Poor" ' she asks, 'meant to be conjunctive or disjunctive?'[56] And Himmelfarb interrogates the relationship between Mayhew's assertion that he is providing 'a cyclopaedia of the industry, the want, and the vice of the great Metropolis . . . the first attempt to publish the history of a people'[57] and the actual substance of the four-volume work; the first three parts concerning 'The

London Street Folk, comprising Street Sellers, Street Buyers, Street Finders, Street Performers, etc.',[58] and the final volume concerning itself with 'Those That Will Not Work . . . Prostitutes, Thieves, Swindlers, Beggars'.[59] Himmelfarb writes: 'What is important is not so much the confusion itself as its significance, the reasons why so many people found it possible to identify the Street Folk with the Labouring Poor, why even those who were aware of the distinction tended to ignore it at crucial moments.'[60]

Through this confusion, she suggests, Mayhew did not create a *novel* image of the poor; what his work did was to 'reflect, disseminate, and perpetuate a not uncommon image'.[61] Given the nature of the ambiguity, Mayhew's choice of the occupation of the costermongers for the first study of the first volume of *London Labour* could hardly be more apt: his study of 'those street-sellers attending the London "green" and "fish markets" '[62] describes an ominous group of men and women who are *half* hard-working street-sellers, and *half* dangerous gang of vagabonds who would 'upon the least disturbance . . . seize and disable their policemen'.[63] Mayhew also found in his enquiries into the politics of the costermongers that, 'they are nearly all Chartists. . . . Some of them, I learned, could not understand why Chartist leaders exhorted them to peace and quietness, when they might as well fight it out with the police at once'. 'I am assured', he wrote, 'that in case of a political riot every "coster" would seize his policeman.'[64]

Thus the picturesque vagabond and the labouring man merge, and this, Himmelfarb argues, 'reflects something in the times, something in the subject, which permits the confusion'.[65] That 'something' – which Himmelfarb points at, but does not name – is a central feature of the emergence of the notion of 'deviance' which associates criminality and improvidence with the growth (and squalor) of industry and the city; and, more specifically, the fear of pandemonium and political insurrection.

The same convergences occupy much of the work of Louis Chevalier, who carefully traces the emergence of the *social* theme in nineteenth-century literature on crime. Earlier literature depicted the criminal as someone truly exceptional and picturesque in a monstrous sort of way; gradually – and sometimes dramatically – he emerges as a man of the masses, and crime unfolds as an everyday feature of city life. In the work of Balzac, for example, Chevalier notes the confusion of 'personal adventure . . . [and] collective destiny' and the difficulty of saying 'what is crime and what revolt, what savage and what social' :

> criminality was now described, though incidentally and often irrespective of the tone of the rest of the book, as no longer merely an appanage of those giants of crime to whom Balzac devoted his main attention, but an emanation from the popular masses as a whole; not something exceptional, but something ordinary and genuinely social. . . . Thus Vautrin suddenly assumes destinies that are not his own; he is an exceptional criminal, but also an 'embodiment of the people in revolt against the laws', a people which is not simply the people of crime.[66]

In his analysis of the writings of Balzac, Hugo, Sue, Janin, Mercier, and social theorists of the time, Chevalier shows how the literary testimony of the early nineteenth century must be heard 'not for what it purports to say but for what it cannot help saying' : so that the convergence of criminality and the commonplace, 'the transformation of the theme of crime into a social theme'[67] presses itself into the writings of the period, *even against the will of the author*. But also, economic crises, political crises, epidemics, and the ravages of hard winters were 'everywhere presented as the same abnormal phenomenon, leading to the same abnormal results, unanimously described as manifestations of criminality'.[68] Deviance and politics are firmly welded in nineteenth-century opinion; in the dangerous classes there is an echo of King Mob.

In her essay 'The Culture of Poverty' Gertrude Himmelfarb finally back-tracks on her suggestion that 'something' in the times lent itself to the confusion of the labouring poor and the dangerous inhabitants of the rookeries. She writes that reformers of the time were over-zealous and unable to resist the dramatic instances of poverty, squalor and improvidence represented by the most submerged sections of the population.[69] First, to view this argument in its most favourable light, it explains very little: the question of why the Victorians persistently made this confusion is reduced to an error of judgement which is corrected as the historical circumstances which precipitated the 'error' change and fade away. To put the matter bluntly, it depicts history as it is read in books written in *our* time, and not as it is made by men living in their time. Secondly, to challenge Himmelfarb's argument more directly: it is simply wrong. There is an established connection, 'in both fact and opinion' as Chevalier puts it,[70] between the commonplace, everyday, ordinary population and the alarming, dangerous and abnormal circumstances of city life which is reflected, as we have already seen, even in how the physical appearance of the labouring population is represented in nineteenth-century thought.[71]

G. M. Young once said that if one wishes to characterise an age, it is always a good rule to ask, 'What were the people most afraid of?'[72] For nineteenth-century Europe the short answer to that question is provided by Charles Kingsley: 'Look at France and see!'; or by Ashley who complained in his diary that 'revolutions go off like pop-guns!'[73] Nineteenth-century thought returned, time and again, to the spectre of the French Revolution and the desperate energies of the mob.

In Britain, E. P. Thompson writes, 'the eighteenth and early nineteenth century are punctuated by riot' and the causes of mob riot were numerous.[74] The city mob was a complex phenomenon which we cannot unravel here,[75] and my argument in this chapter to this point should warn against any easy judgement as to whether the mob was peopled by 'respectable' or 'criminal' elements. It often contained both, and always it was motored by an immediacy which aimed to settle scores with the rich – if only for the day. The fear of the mob was a powerful undercurrent even until the closing years of the century. As late as February 1886 London placed itself on a state of alert to meet revolutionary mob violence: the city, writes Gareth Stedman Jones, 'was visited by something akin to the *grande peur*',[76] and the tension reached another climax in the autumn of the following year. The tenacity of mob fear can be measured by the fact that simply counted in years – admittedly not the best guide to history – the 1880s were as distant from the French Revolution as they are from our own time.

In this chapter I will make one major claim: the space of knowledge which we call deviance opened at the time of mob fear; and traces of this fear are sedimented in our conception of deviance. Further, I will argue that the origins of deviance-control and welfare are unambiguously political. In order to support this claim it is necessary to enter fully into the spirit of the time at which the institutions of deviance-control announced themselves, for we read history through a gauze of twentieth-century experience. Without this effort it is easy to dismiss the nineteenth century as alarmist and naive. Writing of nineteenth-century Paris Chevalier puts the matter this way: 'The appearances have vanished, together with beliefs which we no longer find intelligible, old fevers and revolutions which no longer alarm us, the colours of the sky, the sounds, the forms of a Paris we can barely imagine.'[77] One vital image which we have lost, but which is found everywhere in nineteenth-century thinking on social problems, is that of the sewer.

IMMORTAL SEWERAGE

The people who came to London expecting to find the streets paved with gold found it otherwise:

> It is enough to accept the broad outline, as many authorities have handed it down to us. The streets were noisome in every respect; stench, ordure, germs, decomposing bodies of animals, malarial pests, slime and vomit – with such candidates as these, it is impossible to draw up an order of offensive magnitude. If things were bad in the daytime, they were worse at night.[78]

Pat Rogers here is describing the city of the eighteenth century. Things got no better with the passing of time; Victorian cities 'were full of stinks'.[79] We can quote an excerpt from Mayhew's celebrated visit to the people of Jacob's Island, London, 1849:

> The striking peculiarity of Jacob's Island consists in the wooden galleries and sleeping-rooms at the back of the houses which overhang the dark ditch that stagnates beside them. . . .
> As I passed along the reeking banks of the sewer, the sun shone upon a narrow slip of water. In the bright light it appeared the colour of strong green tea, and positively looked as solid as black marble in the shadow, – indeed, it was more like watery mud than muddy water; and YET I WAS ASSURED THIS WAS

THE ONLY WATER THE WRETCHED INHABITANTS HAD
TO DRINK.

. . . I saw drains and sewers emptying their filthy contents
into it; I SAW A WHOLE TIER OF DOORLESS PRIVIES
IN THE OPEN ROAD, COMMON TO MEN AND WOMEN,
BUILT OVER IT; I heard bucket after bucket of filth splash
into it; and the limbs of the vagrant boys bathing in it seemed,
by pure force of contrast, white as Parian marble.

. . . as I stood doubting the fearful statement, I beheld a
little child . . . lower a tin can with a rope, to fill a large bucket
that stood beside her . . . . In this the inhabitants put the mucky
liquid to stand, so that they may, after it has rested for a day or
two, skim the fluid from the solid particles of filth, pollution,
and disease which have sunk below.

As the little thing dangled her tin cup . . . a bucket of night-
soil was poured from the next gallery.

. . . I asked if they *really* did drink the water?

The answer was, 'They were obliged to drink the ditch . . . .'
But have you spoken to your landlord about having it laid on
for you?' 'Yes, sir; and he says he'll do it, and do it – but we know
him better than to believe him.'[80]

The problem was, of course, eventually to go underground: the
vast 'hidden network of pipes and drains and sewers', writes Asa
Briggs, 'was one of the biggest technical and social achievements of
the [Victorian] age, a sanitary "system" more comprehensive than
the transport system'.[81]

Sewage and drains were guiding metaphors for those who
depicted the deviants of this time.[82] 'Foul wretches' and 'moral filth'
lay heaped in 'stagnant pools' about the streets. When they moved,
they were seen to 'ooze' in a great 'tide'. The population was 'slime'
which gathered in ghettos which were described as 'poisoned wells',
'canker-worms', 'sinks of iniquity', and 'plague-spots'. Their
houses were described as 'cess-pits'; and their way of life was a
'moral miasma', for it was essentially a *moral* condition which was
captured in these lurid images. The city 'reeked' of vice; the 'scum'
and the 'dregs' of society was a 'moral *debris*' and 'residuum': the
words 'pustule', 'fever', and 'wart' came readily to hand when
describing the moral condition of the labouring and dangerous
classes. Popular belief had it that prostitutes and criminals lived in

the sewers, or used them as a means of escape from the police; but whether this belief referred to the subterranean sewers or the houses built over open ditches is not clear. Even more terrifying stories surrounded the sewers: scavengers reported to Mayhew that a race of wild hogs inhabited some sections of the sewers of London;[83] and Hugo writes of Paris that 'people talked of it as of that monstrous cesspool of Thebes, in which centipedes fifteen feet long swarmed'.[84]

Back on the surface, the cloacal imagery of the social investigators pursued the social 'offal' and 'moral refuse'. Mayhew reserved for the costermongers the tag, 'a vast dungheap of ignorance'.[85] And the Reverend Sidney Godolphin Osborne, from whom I have borrowed the heading of this section, provided a delightful Christian image, rich in its ambiguity, when he wrote of 'the "sewerage immortal" of our land'.[86] In search of what he calls 'moral sewerage', Osborne made visits by night to the apartments of the Glasgow poor, and his account of the night's business wallows in excremental metaphor:

> What a gully-hole is to those that are interested in ordinary sewerage matters, the doors of such places as these are, to any who wish to study immortal refuse, the draining of civilisation, the lowest stratum of human existence.
> . . . this was one of the deep dirt-pools of social life, in which accumulated filth lay, for its season, quiet and inoffensive; stir it, and I have no doubt that it would have been most offensive. . . .[87]

There is an impressive correspondence between the way in which the Victorians describe the physical and moral characteristics of the labouring population. Himmelfarb supplies a brief comment on this, writing of 'a curious and disturbing correspondence between the "sanitary condition" described by Chadwick and the human condition described by Mayhew'. The word 'residuum' referred both 'to the offal, excrement and waste which constituted the sanitary problem, and . . . to the lowest strata of society that constituted the social and political problem'. In Mayhew's work, she writes, 'the two usages . . . dramatically, tragically merge'.[88] Chevalier handles the same convergence in a more imagistic manner: 'in 1833, Regey's murder of Ramus, the cashier's messenger, whose body was found beside the Seine at the outlet of the sewer in the rue de la

Huchette was the first instance of the conjunction of sewer and crime, the two by-products of urban life ...'.[89]

Another writer to have noticed the sewer metaphor is May, who reckons that it is simply a question of writers who adopted 'the rhetoric of public health reformers', which is to miss the point.[90] It is easy nowadays to underestimate the power of the sewerage image for the nineteenth century with its ability to connect the physical and moral characteristics of the poor, and of the city itself. There are a number of themes here: first, the way in which the growth and waste of industry is captured by the cloacal metaphor. De Tocqueville employed it after a visit to Manchester: 'From this foul drain the greatest stream of human industry flows out to fertilise the whole world. From this filthy sewer pure gold flows. Here humanity attains its most complete development and its most brutish, here civilisation works its miracles and civilised man is turned almost into a savage.'[91]

Rogers approaches the same question from a different angle. Through a study of eighteenth-century Augustan writings and a sociology of London of the time, he penetrates the recurrent image of the Fleet Ditch (an open sewer) in these writings: 'The confluence of all that is most physically oppressive and fetid reveals the modern capital in its full glory.'[92] That the sewer is also a great leveller is indicated by one of Mayhew's informants who had recently been employed making the drains of Buckingham Palace 'decent': he comments that 'I was hardly ever in such a set of stinks'.[93] Chevalier also describes how sewers contained 'a record of the material and moral consequences of the city's growth'.[94] But the last word here belongs to Victor Hugo, in whose *Les Miserables* the book dedicated to the Paris sewer is titled '*L'Intestin de Leviathan*' ('The Bowels of Leviathan'):

The drain is the conscience of the city. Everything converges and is confronted there. . . . All the uncleanness of civilisation, when no longer of service, fall into this trench of truth. . . . This random mixture is a confession. There no false appearance or plastering is possible; filth takes off its shirt. . . . The effigy on the double sou grows frankly verdigrised; the saliva of Caiaphas meets the vomit of Falstaff; the louis d'or which comes from the gambling hell jostles against the nail whence hangs the end of the suicide's rope; a livid foetus rolls by

wrapped in spangles which danced at the opera last Shrove
Tuesday. . . . It is more than fraternity; it is the extremest
familiarity. All that was painted is bedaubed. The last veil is
torn away. A sewer is a cynic. It tells everything.[95]

The sewer speaks to the nineteenth century about its dangerous
moral and material condition. This is the dominant theme of the
sewer metaphor and around it a number of subsidiary themes group
themselves. A common image of the poor, for example, was that
they were licentious and enjoyed a sexual freedom (and a sexual
corruption) not available to the middle classes: the sewer con-
veniently describes a concealed, and occasionally overflowing,
nastiness.[96] Pat Rogers also shows how the location of the sewers
links them directly in public opinion to the dangerous parts of
London. His study of how early London's moral geography is
reflected in Alexander Pope's *Dunciad* reaches the conclusion that
The Dunciad anticipates the social disorder of the Gordon Riots by
acting poetically on 'events . . . already immanent in history'.[97]
Radzinowicz's *History of Criminal Law* agrees that there were
already rumblings in the early eighteenth century of the shape of
things to come – only to reach fruition later – 'to penalise certain
habits of the lower classes'.[98] Radzinowicz captures the passion of
the time, writing of 'the existence in London of a vast and unruly
mob, always ready to take advantage of any incident to create
disorder and endanger public safety'.[99] The picture is undoubtedly
overdrawn as fact, but it stands as opinion. And like the mob, the
sewer on occasion erupts, flows into the streets, and reminds the
city of its dangerous refuse: particularly the unemployable human
refuse of an unpredictable economic system. The sewer and the
'dangerous classes' also find direct (and geographical) links in
Rogers' study with the 'underworld', crime and punishment, hell,
the mob, fire, fever, a perceived decline in cultural values, and
sexuality.[100] The final theme which finds its expression in the image
of the sewer is that of *contagion and contamination*; a political
contamination, that is, over and above a simple health hazard. For
the sewer is, above all else, a political image in the nineteenth
century. The fear expressed here is the ever-present fear of *the
contamination of the respectable labouring classes by the dangerous
classes*, and the possibility that economic fluctuations, hard winters,
or epidemics might throw large numbers of 'honest folk' into their

'dangerous' ranks.[101] Beames, in his study of the rookeries, describes these ghettos as 'canker-worms' and 'plague-spots', and he warns that a plague more dreadful than cholera will sweep London if they are not re-ordered. He leaves no room for doubting the function of 'public health rhetoric' in nineteenth-century thought. Taking time off (in a book about housing policy) for a forty-page account of the history of revolution in Europe, Beames writes: 'Rookeries are among the seeds of Revolution . . . they poison the minds of the working classes against the powers that be, and thus lead to convulsions.'[102] He points to 'the French Rookeries, hot-beds of insurrection' and asks, 'we have termed our Rookeries plague-spots; are they not indeed such?'[103] Biological and body metaphors are commonplace in social thought – both before and after the nineteenth century. But the image of the sewer in nine-teenth-century thinking holds a privileged place as a rich metaphor of political unrest, fear, and control: we can pursue it further through the work of the great pioneer of sanitary reform, Edwin Chadwick.

But first, a note about the *psychoanalytical* interpretation of the early nineteenth-century excremental preoccupation. Given Freud's equation between money and faeces, and between hoarding and sphincter-control, the emergence of anal preoccupations at a time of early capital accumulation is an easy psychoanalytical target: money is, in Norman O. Brown's memorable phrase, 'filthy lucre'.[104] The relationship has been explored in a number of ways.[105]

Richard Schoenwald has taken the psycho-analytical argument in its obvious direction by providing what he calls a 'psychological dimension' to the sanitation movement of the nineteenth century.[106] At the psychological level, he argues, the control of insanitary wastes involves the crucial task of training urban man to be orderly and regular in his habits. The sanitary demands on city dwellers cause them to 'become conscious of having a self which needed and repaid watching and regulating'. The secret task of 'Chadwick and his snooping cohorts', writes Schoenwald, was to produce persons 'more productive and more disciplined than the insides of any creatures known to history'.[107] Sanitation extended social control into the most intimate aspects of living, involving massive instinc-tual enclosure and, eventually, self-control:

Today the man who asserts most imperiously that his home is

his castle can only do so by forgetting that his throne is plugged into a network of municipally maintained means for removing, forever, products of his own royal self.

. . . Beneath every city Chadwick foresaw a network of pipes so fully branched that no man could declare himself free of its tentacles. Sewers below, and the water closet above: no exemption for rank, sex, age, all conforming and all performing with discipline, not once a year or once a month, but several times each day.[108]

Schoenwald's explorations of these circumstances take him towards a psychoanalysis of the characters of Edwin Chadwick and Herbert Spencer.[109] And it is urged on by the fact that these two men saw intimate connections between excrement and money and explored means of turning human refuse into money: quite simply, they asked, why import guano for fertiliser when we throw human guano into the rivers? Flinn writes, for example, that 'to Chadwick the emptying of sewers into rivers anywhere seemed like pouring away liquid gold'.[110] The re-cycling of sewage was not an uncommon preoccupation of the time: Victor Hugo complained that Paris threw twenty-five million francs of 'golden dung' into the sea each year; Mayhew, who undertook painful calculations of the volume and mass of sewage produced by London, agreed.[111] The equation of excrement and money in the dawn of the high era of capitalism is, then, a give-away for psychoanalytical interpretation.

An account of the origins of the sanitary movement would have been incomplete without a brief mention of its psychoanalysis. But it would require a lengthy excursion into the difficulties involved in the psychoanalytical interpretation of history in order to reach a sound judgement of its contribution: is this the point, for example, at which the preoccupations of the Frankfurt School join up with the origins of deviance-control? This can only be deposited as a question; there is, in any case, a much more direct and obvious line of argument, for Chadwick's *Report on the Sanitary Conditions of the Labouring Population of Great Britain* of 1842 provides an explicit account of the intimate relationship between the various dimensions of public health, housing, morality, criminality, deviance-control, sexuality, and politics. It is through Chadwick's work that we can penetrate the hidden agenda of the origins of the field of deviance. And, to agree with the most superficial of Schoenwald's observations, this hidden agenda concerns the creation of a stable working population within the rising domination of a factory system of labour.

NEW-FANGLED MEN: THEN AND NOW

The 1841 *Report . . . on the Training of Pauper Children* provides an obliging inroad. The report opens on a strange note. Its official subject is that of the pauper child, but this appears only to offer a disguise for its real object, which is the moral condition of the whole population. The first chapter of the report offers evidence collected by Chadwick on the good effects on the work habits of the labouring population produced by 'education suited to the wants of that class'.[112] We learn, for example, that compared with other European labourers and American labourers, English workmen are 'the most disorderly, debauched and unruly and least respectable and trustworthy of any nation'; they are 'dissipated . . . discontented . . . the greatest drunkards'.[113] The significance of this warning can be measured in the much more substantial body of the *Report on the Sanitary Conditions* of 1842. The main substance of the report concerns drains, but hidden away within it is an insistent political message which returns us to the relationship between the labouring classes and their 'dangerous' brothers and the intersections of the sewer and the mob. Repeatedly Chadwick leaves the thoroughfare of sanitation reform and turns his eye to people-control.

Chadwick is very keen on people being watched, and Schoenwald has made psychoanalytical capital out of this.[114] More directly, however, Chadwick sets out evidence on the structure of factories which allow close supervision, inspection and observation, and which yield 'moral advantages of high value'.[115] He remarks on the improved work habits produced under certain factory conditions – 'more energy and better labour' – and the effective control of drunkenness.[116] This is followed by advice on the structure of wage-payments so as to influence, and reduce, intemperance, recklessness, temptation, and 'ill-spending',[117] but not a word about drains.

At another point Chadwick turns from the socialising influence of the factory towards the question of workmen's housing, advocating the separation of families: 'until a degree of education of the lower classes is attained, which is hopeless for the present generation at least, it is desirable to avoid any arrangement which brings *families* into close contact with each other'.[118] Common bakehouses, wash-houses, and common water pumps lead to disorder: Chadwick advocates separate dwellings or walls between the houses which are 'very thick'.[119] Still on the subject of housing Chadwick recommends that employers build houses for their workmen in 'proximity to the employer or the employer's family'.[120] He writes that 'in the present state of the habits of the people' this is 'at a cost beyond any return . . . in the shape of rent'.[121] Nevertheless, properly undertaken, such projects yield a remuneration 'in money and money's worth', the benefit being 'in motives to neatness and cleanliness by their being known [to the employer] and under observation'.[122] The conduct of life in 'by-lanes and out-of-the-way places' is 'below those exposed to observation'; and the employer also secures advantages in terms of the risk of the non-payment of rent and the opportunity to control disturbances and evict tenants of poor character and conduct.[123] In contrast, Chadwick cautions, in out-of-the-way alleys and courts in Manchester 'the whole population of a street have risen' to resist police attempts to enforce evictions; housing in the view of the employer reduces these and other problems of the 'vicious workman'.[124] The 'slavery of existing habits of labourers' which requires alteration by the structural arrangements of housing and factories includes the most intimate: the sense of smell, for example. The labourer, Chadwick writes, 'appears to be insensible to anything but changes of temperature, and there is scarcely any stench which is not endured to avoid slight cold'.[125]

Chadwick also wished to meddle in the entertainments of the labouring classes, replacing 'the debauchery and demoralisation promoted by a fair' with 'a regulated and rational and beneficial entertainment' of, for example, a ploughing match.[126] This concern with the entertainments of working men was not only Chadwick's. It seems quaint, old-fashioned, and amusing, for example, to find Viscount Ingestre describing music halls as one of the five major causes of crime and moral degradation.[127] It would be amusing, that is, if one forgot the modern preoccupation with 'rock festivals' and the effects of television violence. In 1853 Ingestre argued that 'Cheap Theatres, Balls and Concerts' led directly (via drink) to pauperism as the working man was 'sucked into the deadly whirlpool' which ended in 'lunacy, disease, premature death, pauperism, prostitution, and various crimes'.[128] At a later date, when medical psychiatry had secured a stronger foothold in the space of deviance, Jane Addams quotes 'an eminent alienist' who had encountered a number of young patients 'whose emotional natures had been so over-wrought by the crude appeal [of the theatres] . . . that they have become victims of hallucinations and mental disorder'.[129] The 'House of Dreams', which is how Addams described cheap theatres, encouraged other forms of unrest.[130]

Just as Ingestre found little difficulty in linking booze to politics and an assault on Chartism, whose notion of 'Universal Suffrage', he wrote, 'appears to be fallacious',[131] Chadwick's political interests are never far from the centre of his concern with the amusements of the labouring classes. In his *Report on the Sanitary Conditions* he has things to say about the provision of public parks and amenities, and he quotes with approval the actions of Sir Charles Shaw, Chief Commissioner of Police in Manchester. Faced with the difficult problem of a public holiday in celebration of the Queen's marriage, when Chartists had called a meeting 'for getting up what was called a demonstration of the working classes which greatly alarmed the municipal magistrates', the police commissioner had recommended that the botanical gardens, museum and zoo should be 'thrown open to the working classes at the hour they were urgently invited to attend the Chartist meeting'.[132] There were worries about this arrangement, but 'the mayor undertook to be personally answerable for any damage that occurred from throwing open the gardens and institutions to the classes *who had never before entered them*'.[133] The conclusion of the affair was that the workpeople 'were highly pleased', the Chartist meeting 'entirely failed', and 'scarcely 5s worth of damage' was done in the gardens and the zoo.[134] Chadwick writes that, 'I have been informed of other instances of similar effects produced by the spread of temperate pleasures on ordinary occasions, and their rivalry to habits of drunkenness and gross excitement, whether mental or sensual'.[135]

The provision of parks and play-spaces – provided always, of course, that they are not 'out of sight'[136] – is also congenial to the industrious moral health of children. The absence of adequate play-spaces has the undesirable effect of bringing together children of the lower classes with those of the middle classes and is a causative factor, Chadwick writes, in the creation of youthful unrest and juvenile delinquency. The inadequate provision of play-spaces contaminates reasonableness with dangerous elements and 'force all into one company to the detriment of the better children. . . . There appeared several cases of children of honest and industrious parents, who had been entrapped by boys of bad character.'[137]

Chadwick's *Report on the Sanitary Conditons of the Labouring Population* is focused on the intersections of physical and moral health, 'the coincidence of pestilence and moral disorder'.[138] Physical improvements in housing, ventilation, factory conditions, sanitation, the reduction of overcrowding, etc., provide what he calls 'the architectural barriers or protections of decency and propriety'.[139] Without the removal of 'the physical barriers to improvement . . . moral agencies have but a remote chance of success',[140] and the labouring population living under such physical conditions remain 'prone to passionate excitement, and . . . apt instruments for political discontents'.[141] It is not, however, as some vulgar critics of welfare imply, simply that social welfare is seen as a sop' to the working class. Chadwick's advocacy of sanitation is more directly political than that and is intimately linked with the creation and consolidation of stable work habits and skills,[142] the containment of the influence of trade unions ('the folly as well as the injustice of their trade unions'),[143] the incidence of strikes,[144] 'meetings held by torchlight' and 'the anarchical fallacies which appeared to sway those wild and really dangerous assemblages'.[145] Chadwick's work hints at the intersection of biology and politics:

The facts indicated will suffice to show the importance of the moral and political considerations, viz., that the noxious physical agencies depress the health and bodily condition of the population, and act as obstacles to education and to moral culture; *that in abridging the duration of the adult life of the working classes they check the growth of productive skill, and abridge the amount of social experience and steady moral habits* in the community: *that they substitute for a population that accumulates and preserves instruction and is steadily progressive, a population that is young, inexperienced, ignorant, credulous, irritable, passionate, and dangerous. . . .*[146]

There is a recognition here that premature mortality rates

constitute not only a health hazard, but also a political hazard: 'The disappearance by premature deaths of the heads of families and the older workmen . . . must to some extent involve the necessity of supplying the lapse of staid influence amidst a young population by one description or another of precautionary force.'[147] The mobs of Bethnal Green, Bristol and Manchester, Chadwick reminds his readers, were always youthful: 'the great havoc . . . was committed by mere boys.'[148]

'One of the most deceptive myths of Victorianism', writes Richter, 'has been the alleged orderliness of its society, the peaceful apathy of its people.'[149] Persistently, the question of political unrest and the 'vicious habits' of the labouring population inserts itself in Chadwick's proposed sanitary measures: commentators who have seen his work as a simple question of public-health reform have read his work with one eye closed. Specifically, Chadwick's programme is attuned to what Schoenwald has called 'the training of urban man'; but what is at issue is the regimentation of disciplined work habits and reasonable political attitudes among labouring men, and not just a regimentation of their bowels.

Asa Briggs, for example, writes of 'novel modifications in the worker's way of life' which were necessitated by the rise of capitalism.[150] These modifications took a number of forms: 'new disciplines, new incentives, and *a new human nature* upon which these incentives could bite effectively'.[151] The rise of the factory system, for example, could not tolerate the attitudes of the casual labourer who might work a while to earn some money, and then rest a while to enjoy his earnings. McKendrick, drawing attention to this aspect of the development of a factory system of employment, suggests that 'to change such habits was not easy: nor was it always pleasant'.[152]

Even the structure of time itself underwent a profound mutation. Briggs describes how 'time, which had acquired a new significance for the employer, had to acquire a new significance for the employee too'.[153] This was a period in history which insisted on a revolution in the whole conception of life-style: 'If the new industrial workers . . . had to develop a new attitude towards work', writes Briggs, 'they also had to develop a new attitude towards leisure and home life.'[154] One can even say, with Smelser, that the modern conception of the family (so central to welfare ideologies) was *created* within these new conditions of factory employment.[155] As Karl Marx put it, industrial capitalism produced 'new fangled men . . . as much the invention of modern times as machinery itself'.[156]

The emergence of the new-fangled man – what costs were involved in the process, what was achieved and what was lost – is the personal dimension of industrial domination. And it is here that the field of deviance finds its historical object. It is a largely unwritten history, although it finds some articulation in the 'history from below' written by Rudé, Lefebvre, Hobsbawm and Thompson: a history which is written from 'below' in the sense that it is written from the point of view of the people, and not from 'above' in the committee room, Parliament or from the elevated perspective of rulers.[157] If we over-draw the picture (and this is over-drawn) it is the history of the enclosure of a rural peasantry in a factory system. It makes its presence felt in the late eighteenth and early nineteenth centuries (in France and Britain) through various experiences: machine-smashing; riot against the price of food and the enclosure of the land; the 'hippie' philosophy of Owenism, which aimed to 'simply *by-pass* the property-rights and power of the rich';[158] various messianic cults; and the periodic outbursts of property-destruction by a 'mob' which sometimes transforms into a 'revolutionary crowd'. It is a difficult area of human experience and it is easy to romanticise what is imagined as the lost bliss of rural simplicity. In *The Country and the City* Raymond Williams has supplied the best corrective to this romanticism.[159] And Edward Thompson also warns that what needs to be said

> is not that one way of life is better than the other, but that this is a place of the most far-reaching conflict; that the historical record is not a simple one of neutral and inevitable technological change, but also one of exploitation and of resistance to exploitation; and that values tend to be lost as well as gained.[160]

While it is not difficult to romanticise the shift – in the sense of stressing what is lost – it is equally easy to take this far-reaching transition for granted and to imagine that once completed its work is finally accomplished; that new-fangled men have entered the world of reasonableness for once and for all. And it is Thompson again who hints at the possibility that the regimentation of work habits is only a tentative solution to the conflicting interest of industrial capitalism:

by the division of labour; the supervision of labour; fines; bells and clocks; money incentives; preachings and schoolings; the suppression of fairs and sports – new labour habits were formed, and a new time-discipline was imposed. It sometimes took several generations . . . and we may doubt how far it was ever fully accomplished. . . .[161]

Certainly, with what has been called the second industrial revolution – the emergence of 'post-industrial society' – the work ethic develops cracks and in some sectors of the industrial world time-clocked efficiency begins to lose the meaning which it had acquired in the first industrial revolution. Under these conditions the nineteenth century speaks to us with a surprising directness from a time when the politics of deviance-control were less disguised than they are in contemporary social thought. There the concerns of work, life, deviance, reasonableness and politics were recognisable as the same thing: particularly, politics and deviance had not yet separated in social thought and social practice.

I have already remarked, in an earlier chaper, on the analogy which Bastide has drawn between the social concerns and social movements of the first and second industrial revolutions: Bastide sees the two periods as a striking parallel.[162] Equally, the similarities between Robert Owen's utopianism of the 1820s and the counter-cultural revolt of the 1960s challenge the historical imagination to arrive at a breath-taking, but far too easy, historical synthesis of the psychological dimension of urban-industrialism. The plain fact of the matter is, however, that there are no available tools for the historical comparison of psychological mood.[163] The question must be left: open, embarrassing in its simplicity, tantalising. It is the same problem which causes George Rudé, historian of the 'pre-industrial' crowd and city mob, to reach for safe ground when, having pointed to how the Negro rebellion in the United States' northern cities in the 1960s has 'a distinct flavour of the "pre-industrial" riot' he writes: 'But why this should be so . . . I prefer to leave to my readers to work out for themselves.'[164]

Setting aside the question – however crucial – of the dynamism of these coincidences, issues of work, life and leisure (which had been temporarily displaced from thought) have again posed themselves as serious questions as some of the new-fangled men recognise work as less than life itself. As part of this more general convolution, we find the emergence of different (and more direct) forms of action by clients of welfare organisations, who have been called the new 'paupetariat'.[165] And with the rise of misfit social thought the deviant imagination poses its question once more in the world of politics.

In his outstanding study of social problems and economic conditions in Victorian London Gareth Stedman Jones has argued that the last decade of the nineteenth century (and in particular the great dock strike of 1889) forced an abrupt shift in how the question of the deviant outcasts of London were perceived:

> Once disentangled [in middle-class opinion] from the respectable working class, the residuum could not on its own overturn London. Once detailed social investigation and the activity of the strikers themselves had established a clear distinction between the 'legitimate' claims of labour and the ugly symptoms of 'social disease', fears of revolution could be turned aside. The casual residuum was no longer a political threat – only a social problem.[166]

However, history is neither written that quickly nor that finally. It is true that the politics of deviance becomes hidden within the idea of a de-politicised welfare system and buried under what Horowitz and Liebowitz call the 'welfare model' of social problems.[167] I wish to suggest, however, that there is a hidden, forgotten tradition of the mob which still poses its question in the theory and practice of deviance-control and welfare.

The idea of the mob is something which in our day we find it difficult to relate to: it is strange, distant, almost prehistoric. The word 'mob' itself is reserved for things which happen abroad, for occasions when strikers organise effective mass picketing, or for when soccer fans invade a football pitch. It is not a 'modern' word, although in some British cities it retains a marginal (and significant) contemporary use for describing neighbourhood gangs of youths: for example, the 'Mile End Road Mob', the 'Finchley Mob' or the 'Mob from Highbury' in London.[168] Rudé writes that there are two traditions of scholarship which relate to the mob, either 'admiringly as "le peuple", or, slightingly, as "la canaille" '.[169] That is, either the people (in the sense of the masses) or the rabble. Commonly the mob is understood by historians either as motiveless, or as a bunch of riff-raff who rioted for the fun of it, the gin and the pickings. Dorothy Marshall comments, for example, that in the Gordon Riots of 1780 the vicious temperament of the 'dregs' 'no doubt loved destruction for its own sake'.[170] Her remarks would not appear out of place among many contemporary comments on contemporary deviant activities.

Rudé's work particularly, however, shows the complexity of the actual motives of the mob – in so far as they can be de-coded from historical records – and the rich variety of the 'faces in the crowd'.[171] And in this 'history from below' we can recognise similarities between the motives of contemporary deviants and the hapless discontents of the 'pre-industrial' crowd; we can recognise them, that is, when the deviant is given a voice in the subterranean traditions of the misfit paradigm. Both misfit social thought and a 'history from below' drive for the same results: they search for the motives, meanings and realities of phenomena where previously the 'misfit' and the 'mob' had been buried in silence beneath an assumption that here was only behaviour which was senseless. In the depoliticised 'welfare model' of social problems the idea that *there might actually be someone there* in the deviant class who is saying something (to us, for example) is denied; nor is it something one looks for in the mob. It is as if those things existed outside and apart from society. And it is fitting that the same questions (perhaps the most important questions) are addressed to contemporary social welfare by a voice speaking from outside the 'First World', by Paulo Freire from the 'Third World' where the mob still has an unambiguous political domain. Freire is writing about literacy programmes in Latin America, and as so often when looking at the Third World from the 'First' it is as though one were looking at one's own past through a historical mirror as the Third World grapples with the industrial domination which ours has accomplished. There now (as here in the nineteenth century) social reformers seem bent on 'saving' deviants and paupers from something: a tradition which is preserved in modern welfare ideology. Freire is asking what 'deviants' are being *saved to*, and how it comes about that deviants are somehow thought not to have a place (and hence a voice) in the world in which other men live:

Educators would be benevolent counsellors, scouring the outskirts of the city for the stubborn illiterates, runaways from the good life, to restore them to the foresaken bosom of happiness by giving them the gift of the word.

In the light of such a concept – unfortunately, all too widespread – literacy programmes can never be efforts toward freedom; they will never question the very reality which deprives men of the right to speak up – not only illiterates, but all those who are treated as objects in a dependent relationship. These men, illiterate or not, are, in fact, not marginal . . . to the structure, but oppressed men within it. Alienated men, they cannot overcome their dependency by 'incorporation' into the very structure responsible for their dependency. There is no other road to humanisation – theirs as well as everyone else's – but authentic transformation of the dehumanising structure.[172]

SOCIOLOGICAL PASTORAL

If the political element has gone underground in dominant theories of deviance, its lyrical counterpart, which equally firmly ties the fields of deviance and welfare to the city, factory and industrialism, has not: always close to the surface in traditional theories of misfits and welfare is the theme of a sociological pastoral. Sociological pastoral takes a number of forms, but each of them agrees that the deviant question is resolved only in the *gemeinschaft* where men are (allegedly) tolerant of diversity. The complexity of urban life is contrasted with the simplicity of a community of persons who are in some kind of harmony: to put words of contemporary liberalism around this, a community of participation, sharing, plural tolerance, etc. In this *gemeinschaft*-like community (which is part of social science's memory) it seems as if social order gets along without skills, control or know-how. Raymond Williams notes the same recurring deception in *literary* pastoral where fields and crops grow (as it were) by themselves, vegetables come automatically out of the ground and land (equally automatically) on the dinner plate, and all this against a scenic backcloth in which Nature gets on with the business (unaided by men's labour) of delivering up her providence: the pastoralist 'looks out over the fields . . . and sees, not work, but a land yielding of itself'.[1] Farm labourers have a place in this pastoral landscape only to the extent that they position themselves aesthetically against the line of hill, vale, tree and brook. But in his book *The Country and the City* Williams reminds us again and again that the threat of eviction, enclosure and the 'improvement' and 'settlement' of the country by the city rich was always lurking behind this pastoral tradition: 'It is not easy to forget that Sidney's *Arcadia*, which gives a continuing title to English neo-pastoral, was written in a park which had been made by enclosing a whole village and evicting the tenants.'[2] It is not easy to forget, that is, once it has been pointed out to you. Pastoral is not about the countryside or simplicity, but about *a comparison* between simplicity and complexity, field and factory, country and city; a comparison which bridges the decisive historical transition of industrial capitalism. This chapter sketches the broad outline of pastoral in social thought with an eye to the trap which sociological pastoral falls into if it forgets that it has to do with that transition; it owes a great deal to the way in which Raymond Williams uncovers the cheat in literary pastoral.

SOME NEW VERSIONS OF PASTORAL

As it is conventionally understood pastoral contrasts the corruption of manners in the sovereign's court with the graceful innocence of nymphs and shepherds. However, in the transforming experiences of the Industrial Revolution pastoral adopts new forms, which provide a critical comment on the arrival of the modern city, the factory system and a money economy.

As a commentator on the emerging city, Georg Simmel made many intriguing observations on 'the psychological conditions which the metropolis creates'. He wrote of 'the rapid crowding of changing images, the sharp discontinuity in the grasp of a single glance, and the unexpectedness of onrushing impressions. . . . With each crossing of the street, with the tempo and multiplicity of economic, occupational and social life, the city sets up a deep contrast with small town and rural life'.[3] For the men who lived through these transforming experiences the city had a frightening face, and when we turn to both literary and sociological testimony of the period we find that even in the time of the most forward-looking and rapid expansion of the high era of capitalism writers warned of the dehumanising, and politically explosive, advancement of the factory system, and could not resist a nostalgic, backward glance to what was being lost.[4] And they were able to see, perhaps more clearly than we can see now, something of what was involved. Certainly, they commented on some of the disturbing qualities of urban life which we would now probably disregard as commonplace. Simmel, for example, drew attention to the influence of the new systems of transport on relationships between people:

Social life in the large city as compared with the towns shows a great preponderance of occasions to *see* rather than *hear* people. . . . Before the appearance of omnibuses, railroads and streetcars in the nineteenth century, men were not in a situation where for periods of minutes or hours they could or must look at each other without talking to one another. Modern social life increases . . . the role of mere visual impression . . . and must place social attitudes and feelings upon an entirely changed basis. The greater perplexity which characterises the person who only sees, as contrasted with one who only hears, brings us to the problems of the emotions of modern life: the lack of orientation in the collective life, the sense of utter lonesomeness, and the feeling that the individual is surrounded on all sides by closed doors.[5]

Another apect of this transition which held the attention was the pressure to conformity. Education in this emerging social system was, according to Charles Dickens, a process of 'murdering the innocents': in *Hard Times* children had hard *facts* (and nothing more) ground into them by the suitably named schoolteacher, Mr M'Choakumchild, and his utilitarian patron, Mr Gradgrind.[6] Max Weber also wrote that 'the individual is shorn of his natural rhythm as determined by the structure of his organism',[7] and he warned against the growth of organisations in which man 'cannot squirm out of the apparatus in which he is harnessed' and where 'he is only a single cog in an evermoving mechanism which prescribes to him an essentially fixed route of march'.[8] This was not a development which Weber viewed favourably, although he was pessimistic about the final outcome: 'the idea of eliminating these organisations' he wrote 'becomes more and more utopian.'[9] Max Weber saw an 'iron cage' surrounding men which would produce 'a mechanised petrification, embellished with a sort of convulsive self-importance'.[10]

But if these changes were seen as overwhelming, they were also in some ways precarious: Simmel wrote that in the typical metropolis relationships and affairs 'are so varied and complex that without the strictest punctuality in promises and services the whole structure would break down into inextricable chaos'.[11] 'If all clocks and watches in Berlin would suddenly go wrong in different ways, even if only by one hour, all economic life and communication in the city would be disrupted for a long time.'[12]

The new metropolis was unimaginable, Simmel argued, without the collection of life 'into a stable and impersonal time schedule' so that eventually 'punctuality, calculability, exactness are forced upon life', connecting 'its money economy and intellectualistic character' with 'the exclusion of those irrational, instinctive, sovereign traits and impulses which aim at determining the mode of life from within, instead of receiving the general and precisely schematised form of life from without'.[13]

In *Hard Times*, just as facts dominated the philosophy of the classroom, they reached into the structures of housing, architecture and personality. 'Coketown' (which is apparently based on Preston in Lancashire) was, thus, itself 'a triumph of fact':

> It was a town of red brick, or of brick that would have been red if the smoke and ashes had allowed it; but, as matters stood it was a town of unnatural red and black like the painted face of a savage. . . . It contained several large streets all very like one another, and many small streets still more like one another, inhabited by people equally like one another, who all went in and out at the same hours, with the same sound upon the same pavements, to do the same work, and to whom every day was the same as yesterday and tomorrow, and every year the counterpart of the last and the next.
>   . . . You saw nothing in Coketown but was was severely workful.[14]

It was in this area of Lancashire, we should remind ourselves, that in the late 1760s working men had marched, rioted and pulled down houses in protest against the spinning jenny, and – at least in some traditional accounts – had driven its inventor Hargreaves out of the county; and the history of the area had been punctuated by riot, strike and violence against the encroaching factory system, through to (and beyond) the great loom-breaking of 1826.[15] *Hard Times* was published in 1854, but when Dickens compared the hard, factual, workmanlike aspect of Coketown with another way of life he did not turn to that historical transition; what he did was turn to a romantic, 'pre-industrial' mentality which he saw in wanderers, horse-breakers and circus people: 'there was a remarkable gentleness and childishness about these people, a special inaptitude for any kind of sharp practice, and an untiring readiness to help and pity one another.'[16]

Dickens, however, had a more fully rounded grasp of the new transformation than his denunciation of Coketown suggests: he understood it also as an enlarger as well as a flattener of men. For the rich variety of contacts in the town as opposed to the country was also part of this transformation of consciousness. Raymond Williams draws attention to how Dickens understood these transitions 'as at once the exciting and threatening consequence of a new mobility, as not only an alien and indifferent system but as the unknown, perhaps unknowable, sum of so many lives, jostling, colliding, disrupting, adjusting, recognising, settling, moving again to new spaces. Dickens went to the centre, the dynamic centre, of this transforming social experience.'[17] Edward Baines, in his admittedly eulogistic account of the *History of the Cotton Manufacture in Great Britain*, captures this spirit quite well, for although he warns of the dangers of large towns where 'there is much greater activity, both in the principles of good and evil . . . than in the country' he contrasts the advantages of the city with the common enough notion of rural idiocy:

> The opportunities of associating with each other, the facilities of obtaining books and newspapers, and the discussions in their unions, combinations, and clubs, stimulate and sharpen the intellects of the working classes in towns; whilst the solitary labourer in husbandry too often grows up in stupid ignorance and inertness.[18]

It was (and is) a vital and confusing transformation which set men in new relationships with each other, and changed the power-invested conceptions of normality and conformity. It was not only, for example, the 'anonymity . . . unmerciful matter-of-factness; and the intellectually calculating economic egoisms' or the 'blasé attitude' which made city folk 'appear to be cold and heartless' which caught Simmel's attention.[19] He also understood that in the small town the tight, coherent, close community 'cannot allow the individual freedom and unique inner and outer development'.[20] Whereas in the more diversified social organisation of the metropolis 'inner unity loosens . . . [and] the individual also gains a specific individuality to which the division of labour in the enlarged group gives both occasion and necessity'.[21] Simmel captured the full ambiguity of the historical transition as we can see in the following section of his essay 'The Metropolis and Mental Life' :

> The individual is reduced to a negligible quantity, perhaps less in his consciousness than in his practice and in the totality of his obscure emotional states that are derived from this practice. The individual has become a mere cog in an enormous organisation of things and powers which tear from his hands all progress, spirituality and value in order to transform them from their subjective form into the form of a purely objective life. . . . Here in buildings and educational institutions, in the wonders and comforts of space-conquering technology, in the formations of community life, and in the visible institutions of the state, is offered such an overwhelming fullness of crystallised and impersonalised spirit that the personality, so to speak, cannot maintain itself under its impact. On the one hand, life is made infinitely easy for the personality in that stimulations, interests, uses of time and consciousness are offered to it from all sides. They carry the person as if in a stream, and one needs hardly to swim for oneself. On the other hand, however, life is composed more and more of these impersonal contents and offerings which tend to displace the genuine personal colorations and incomparabilities. This results in the individual's summoning the utmost in uniqueness and particularization, in order to preseve his most personal core. He has to exaggerate this personal element in order to remain audible even to himself.[22]

Simmel's report on the city is under no illusions that the psychology of the metropolis is geared and driven by the objectifying spirit of money relations: his report is an account of the corruption of manners at court which push men towards faceless exaggeration and display. One of the responses to these overwhelming experiences was a withdrawal into private, family retreats. Peter Schmitt, for example, draws attention to how the middle classes began to gather themselves together in the home where they also surrounded themselves with symbols of the lost countryside. For as men settled in the city the country made its way into the interior of the home in the form of tokens of 'wild nature' – 'the lilypads and morning glories of Tiffany art glass and the nature themes woven in oriental carpets . . . the twining vines of *Art Nouveau* graced lampshades and picture frames, paper weights and candle sticks, silverware and bookplates, inkstands and hair brushes'.[23] Schmitt writes that in the United States by the 1890s Arcadian essays in newspapers and magazines – which signified a move 'back to nature' and not 'back to the land' – were well-established, and 'the pursuit of country happiness was a recognised part of the city dweller's dream life'.[24] Walter Benjamin also draws attention to these developments, but more significantly to the retreat from the world into the home and into family life, so that for the bourgeois citizen 'his drawing-room was a box in the world-theatre'.[25] And with this retreat into an ideology of familism the family increasingly came to be understood as the source (and place of resolution) of human troubles, finding its most contemporary development in the ideology of 'family therapy' which cuts off human difficulties in living finally, and totally, from the world.[26] The career of concepts such as 'anomie' and 'alienation' – originally conceived of as criticisms of dislocations in *social* structure – follow the same course as they become increasingly understood as *personal* headaches and hang-ups.[27] For example, Robert Nisbet (who should know better) writes that 'by alienation I mean *a state of mind* that can find a social order remote, incomprehensible, or fraudulent; beyond real hope or desire; inviting apathy, boredom, or even hostility'.[28] Thus what was a reorganisation of the social world, and all that it implied, comes to be understood as a purely private matter: Nisbet's words voice the confusion, but forget what it is a confusion of.

Another aspect of this baffling confusion is that new styles of heroism emerge with the industrial city. Both Raymond Williams and Walter Benjamin comment, for example, on the emergence of the detective novel at a point in history where a man can lose himself (or be lost) in the city crowd.[29] For Williams, Sherlock Holmes thus represents a 'pure intelligence penetrating the obscurity which baffled ordinary men'; the urban detective 'begins to emerge as a significant and ratifying figure: the man who can find his way through the fog, who can penetrate the intricacies of the streets'.[30] One should not, in short, underestimate the enormity of this transition – not only in purely economic terms, or in terms of scale – but also in its intimate detail, which impresses itself on social life and social thought up to the present day. 'In the image of a dense black cloud hanging over the city' which Dickens used so often, Williams writes that he (Dickens) is describing 'the human moral consequences of an indifferent and "unnatural" society. It is an image to which he often returns: the obscurity, the darkness, the fog that keep us from seeing each other clearly and from seeing the relation between ourselves and our actions, ourselves and others.'[31] It is in areas of human experience such as these that we find the roots of sociological pastoral.

As the city enters a new crisis, which some commentators feel might be its last death throes, updated versions of pastoral assert themselves in social thought. We can point, particularly, to the modern sociological pastoral of Erving Goffman. His work is preoccupied with face-to-face interaction, etiquette and manners, and holding a mirror to city life he shows the corruption of its community: men at court wear masks, engage in deceptions and then learn the tricks of 'impression management'. In Goffman's world we find men cultivating the art of concealment and the art of the impostor: we find wiseguys, go-betweens and various attempts to create 'a desirable impression'.[32] At certain points persons who are in fact 'non-persons' become a crucial part of social exchange:[33] the absence of community is so total in the world as Goffman describes it that it has become the essence of social life itself. Goffman describes servants who sneer and gossip about their masters, things happen behind people's backs, and people exchange secret signals and are afraid of being spied upon.[34] Knowing looks are swapped, and through guarded and ambiguous disclosures about themselves men put out feelers for each other as they engage in double-talk: life might even best be understood as a gamble or a con-game.[35] Brittan writes of how 'for Goffman, identity seems to have evolved into a mask . . . façade . . . charade' and that his world is full of 'everyday hypocrisy and lying'.[36] Life is also transformed into a constant attempt to avoid blunders: bumping into people in the streets, breaking wind in public, or in *Relations in Public*, his latest, terror-struck work, being knifed in the back.[37]

Goffman's jaundiced appraisal of urban living has marked affinities with the commentaries made on sharp practices in court by the rural swain in the traditions of literary pastoral. However, Goffman is no rural swain: his sociological work is characterised by the same guarded, elusive and ambiguous self-disclosures which he describes in the lives and works of other men. Thus the possibilities of controversy about his sociology are considerable, and Stanford Lyman has raised the important question of whether or not we really understand him.[38] Since there is no *obvious* moral or political direction in Goffman's sociology, we must accordingly ask whether it is right to claim his work as sociological pastoral. There is, for example, a sense in which Goffman might be thought to be celebrating the complexity of the city and the fun and games which men have juggling their many masks and roles. Also in his early study of country life in the Shetland Isles we find Goffman's subjects equal to all the tricks of city folk: and that amounts to a sort of anti-pastoral. And a further complicating factor in his sociology is its satirical quality: the sheer volume of work (regulating eye contact, posture, body position, space usage, and so on) involved in 'impression management' sometimes turns Goffman's account into a lampoon of civil conduct. However, all this is still well within the contours of pastoral: in his study of pastoral poetry Laurence Lerner claims that 'when the pastoralist goes to court he automatically becomes a satirist'.[39] Goffman's sociological pastoral operates at these many different levels, and more.

Lyman describes Goffman's latest work as a 'prophecy of doom'.[40] The key to this assertion is that as the crisis of the American city intensifies, as it becomes possible that 'the streets [will be] redefined as naturally precarious places . . . [where] a high level of risk becomes routine',[41] Goffman's sociology stops being funny and falls into despair. His work may not come clean in professing to an Arcadian vision, but Goffman is by no means a fully integrated courtier. In *Relations in Public* Goffman ends on a forlorn note: the city, he seems to be saying, is becoming a place where you dare not look another human being directly in the eye for fear of betrayal.[42] 'This "vision"', Richard Sennett writes, 'is Goffman's report on us.'[43] If that is so, then it is also a report which is external, barren and amoral: what the connection is between the critical attention which he pays to the corruption of city manners and the vaguely hopeful, insurrectionary underlife of *Asylums* which I described in an earlier chapter,[44] for example, Goffman does not even bother to say.

Richard Sennett's own work is itself an interesting example of the updated pastoral theme in social thought. Noting the tendency for social theorists and welfare theorists to see the city as a dis-organising influence in men's lives, Sennett reverses the argument and provides a celebration of the diversity – the 'multiple contact points' – which the city offers.[45] In the old cities, Sennett argues, where men were thrown together with people from a different class and background, there were opportunities for constructing a rich and diverse life and personal identity. The modern city, by contrast, is characterised by deep social divisions – the poor ghetto on the one hand, and the middle-class suburb on the other – and rooted within this suburbanised city it what Sennett calls the myth of a 'purified community' where happiness is thought to be found in everyone being the same. The 'purified community', Sennett's argument continues, is associated with a 'purified identity' (which is intolerant of diversity) and an 'intense' family life (which is inward-looking and can only tolerate sameness). The result of living in the 'purified community' of the modern city is to stamp adults with a sort of adolescent intolerance of diversity which also makes people afraid of social change.[46] It produces 'this society of fear, this society willing to be dull and sterile in order that it not be confused or overwhelmed . . . and the family becomes a place of refuge in which the parents try to shield their children, and them-selves, from the city'.[47] Sennett proposes that the 'anarchy' of the city should be put to good use to break down these cages of 'purified identities' and 'purified communities', and he hopes that 'by provid-ing a wide network of social contact that the people of a city must use in order to survive, the polarisation of intimacy in the home circle and the impersonal functional tasks in the world beyond might be erased'.[48] He writes: 'a disordered city that forced men to deal with each other would work to tone down feelings of shame about status and helplessness in the face of large bureau-cracies. Participation of this sort could mute in affluent workers that sad desire for repressive law and order.'[49]

There is a refreshing, imaginative quality in Sennett's attempt to grapple with the problems of urban living, especially as they relate to the criminalisation of diverse styles of life. But there is also an unmistakable (albeit somewhat inverted) pastoral quality in his work as it stands. What Sennett hopes to do is to locate some 'good' aspects of city life historically, but although it runs against his expressed intentions he seems to do no more than render a vision of an Arcadian metropolis, a Golden Age of city life. We know, for example, that in the days when cities were (according to him) more diversified, men of the time were already regretting the city. Lerner puts this aspect of pastoral rather well when he writes: 'The Golden Age, where pastoral takes place, is not the same as the Good Old Days. For the Golden Age lies outside history: it is a dream, based on childhood, perhaps. . . . [The] Good Old Days claim to have existed, even at a particular time. The time is often hard to locate. . . . As like as not, it is a time when men were already lamenting the good old days.'[50]

Another version of pastoral which emerges in the face of this new crisis is 'labelling theory', which implies that social control leads to, and creates, deviance. No matter how it is phrased the labelling perspective thus appeals to a form of natural social harmony and simplicity, and its sentiments are critical of a bungling social-control apparatus which upsets that assumed natural harmony. As Jock Young has put the matter, it appeals to 'the image of a naturally good man – whose goodness would be expressed more extensively were it not for the interference of "civilised" society'.[51] Thus according to Schur, it will be remembered, the solution to delinquency is to 'leave the kids alone'. And in Laing's anti-psychiatry, which frequently dabbles with the sentiments of the labelling perspective, schizophrenia is thought to be possibly the result of the psychiatrist's own activities. Laing writes: 'I am unhappy about using the term schizophrenia at all. But it would be somewhat whimsical to eliminate it from my vocabulary, since it is on the lips of so many.'[52] Nevertheless, he goes on to propose a hypothesis that 'the behaviour most typically regarded as hard-core schizophrenia [is] iatrogenic': the doctor's behaviour, 'this set of ascriptions to a person, and this induction into the role of schizo-phrenic, themselves generate much of the behaviour that is classified as "symptomatology" of schizophrenia'.[53]

In another of their core sentiments the misfit paradigm and anti-psychiatry (which intersect once more in their pastoral attitude) suggest that deviance might even provide *a solution* to the problems of the domination of factory and city. As Eric Wolf has written, the occasional rural revolt of the peasant can seem to be 'an incarnation of the life-force, barring the onward march of the machine with cross-bow and bamboo spikes'.[54] Equally, from within the contours of a modern sociological pastoral, deviance – and particularly the expressive (non-utilitarian) deviance with which misfit social thought preoccupies itself, a deviance which breaks from the prescribed conformity of city and factory – quite easily comes to appear as a leap even into Arcadia. But those who criticise and condemn the new approaches to deviance for their romanticism forget that this romantic attitude continues, rather than shatters, one of the major ideological traditions of social thought and social practice in the field of deviance and welfare. Therefore, an understanding of the sociological pastoral in misfit sociology and anti-psychiatry should become a point from which to begin to understand the pastoral appeal in even the most traditional welfare theories, rather than dismissing misfit social thought's own Arcadian impulse as an aberration.

CORRECTIONAL ARCADIAS

The hero of Nathaniel West's novel *Miss Lonelyhearts* is one of those social-worker–journalists who write advice columns in newspapers and magazines. Miss Lonelyhearts (who is a man) carries the burden, therefore, of many distressing personal and social questions which begin, for him, 'Dear Miss Lonelyhearts . . .'. But he has problems of his own: to put the matter simply, life is closing in on the social worker's ability to answer questions – both inner and outer. His girl friend Betty tries her hand at advice-giving: 'She told him about her childhood on a farm and of her love for animals, about country sounds and country smells and how fresh and clean everything in the country is. She said that he ought to live there and that if he did, he would find that all his troubles were city troubles.' [55] Nathaniel West's device – which in this instance fails – is not only one which finds a literary expression. Although from its beginnings the field of deviance and welfare was shaped by the urgent requirements of industrial domination, its ideology also contains the opposite: social welfare repeatedly celebrates, and appeals to, the values of the small town, village, kinship group, community and neighbourhood. The city, on the other hand, is criticised as artificial and corrupt, and it is described as the nursery of crime, madness and deviance. From the start the fiercest antagonism exists – although largely unrecognised – between utilitarian measures to press the casual labourer, the wanderer and the dislocated agrarian worker into the service of the factory system and what Anthony Platt describes as a 'nostalgic allusion to the stability and intimacy of a pre-industrial way of life'.[56] This is expressed through various notions of correctional arcadias. For example, Frederic August Demetz proposed as a motto for his reformatory school at Mettray in the 1840s 'The moralisation of youth by the cultivation of the soil'.[57] And Cyril Burt in *The Young Delinquent* writes that 'time after time, a holiday in the country has proved a successful cure for crime'. He goes on later:

> By choice these impressionable young people seek surroundings full of strong, diversified, and personal stimuli. They are born inhabitants of Vanity Fair. In the life of the city and its streets, with its ever-changing sights and sounds, its eventful whirl and motion, its rich variety of people and crowds, its spectacular shop-windows and endless amusements – there is the favoured haunt of the lover of excitement; there he can be giddy all day long. No environment could be more unsuitable. If he is to gain and preserve his balance, a level life, a steady stage, a quiet background for his everyday existence, are essential. The most stable surroundings, both physical and social, are the best for the unstable child. Intense, sudden, and desultory distractions should be avoided or withdrawn. A pastoral life, with its relative uniformity and monotony, its orderly procession of seasons, its natural and impersonal interests, makes an excellent school of repose.[58]

It was (and is) a common, and paradoxical, belief among reformers in the child-welfare movement that in order to train delinquent youth to the civil habits of city life they must be returned to the country:

> away from evil associations and temptations, away from the moral and physical filth and contagion, out of the gaslight and sewer gas; away out in to the woods and fields free from temptation and contagion; out into the sunlight and the starlight and the pure, sweet air of the meadows. . . .[59]

What is described here, of course, is not *real* country life, but Arcadia: the image of a Golden Age – both of society and, perhaps, childhood – which embodies a picture of pastoral simplicity. I have already described some of the versions of sociological pastoral and it is not restricted to correctional arcadias and cottage homes for troublesome city youth. Robert Nisbet authoritatively identifies 'the rediscovery of community . . . [as] unquestionably the most distinctive development in nineteenth-century social thought': 'The most fundamental and far-reaching of sociology's unit-ideas is community. . . . [It is] a development that extends well beyond sociological theory . . . [and] it is hard to think of any other idea that so clearly separates the social thought of the nineteenth century from that of the preceding age, the Age of Reason.'[60] Nisbet writes of a relationship between revolutionary turmoil in Europe 'and the emergence of those concepts which were from the outset the distinctive subject matter of sociology', for 'it was precisely those areas of human association most severely treated by the Revolution [in France particularly] which became conceptually important in sociology'.[61] Nisbet is arguing here, that is, that sociological thought is to be understood as a conservative reaction to that period in history, leading among other things to a preoccupation with the idea of 'community'. He defines the use of 'community' in sociology in the following terms:

> The word, as we find it in much nineteenth- and twentieth-century thought encompasses all forms of relationship which are characterised by a high degree of personal intimacy, emotional depth, moral commitment, social cohesion, and continuity in time. Community is founded on man conceived in his wholeness rather than in one or another of the roles, taken separately, that he may hold in a social order . . . . Community is a fusion of feeling and thought, of tradition and commitment, of membership and volition.[62]

Sociologists would appear to be under some obligation, however, to interrogate this concept of community and to ask where, and when, and how it has existed or might exist. But it goes without saying in the traditions of sociological pastoral that it is enough to say that 'community' is in these terms everything that the city is not. And elsewhere Nisbet has recited the familiar enough story of 'a continuing weakening of the ties of *Gemeinschaft* – the communal ties of family, guild and village – and a constant maximisation in modern times of the more impersonal, atomistic, and mechanical relationships of . . . *Gesellschaft*'.[63]

We can see again, therefore, how sociological pastoral in its broadest terms finds its roots in a fear among bourgeois intellectuals of the political instability of these new forms of social life which are attendant on the rise of industrial capitalism, involving a harking back to some idea of a pre-industrial intimacy (and charity) between different classes. Norman Dennis is another writer who has pointed to the popularity of the neighbourhood-community idea in social thought, and specifically its function in the mid-nineteenth century as a concept which could be used to legitimate the geographical dispersal of the 'dangerous classes' from the inner city. It was also, Dennis argues, part of the armoury of those reformers who established 'settlements', believing that these would help to dissolve the explosive political force which they saw in a high density of working-class dwellings.[64] We learn from Mrs Barnett, for example, that Hampstead Garden Suburb was understood as a place where 'all classes would live together under the right conditions of beauty and space', and she lays out some of the philosophy of this movement: 'we believe that in cleaner air, with open space near to their doors, with gardens where the family labour would produce vegetables, fruit, and flowers, the people would develop a sense of home life and an interest in nature which forms the best security against temptations.'[65] In her biography of her husband's life and work Mrs Barnett also writes of the establishment of correctional Arcadias, 'two girls' homes, where sixteen girls are received and scolded and loved into training'. This is in 1879:

> we furnished Harrow Cottage, facing the White Stone Pond, Hampstead Heath. There we placed old Nurse and little Fanny who hated noisy, dirty Whitechapel. Between them they trained the girls. . . . Our neighbour Miss Lister housed the pony, who introduced us to the beautiful Hertfordshire country, and the girls to unimagined delights.[66]

In order to introduce the girls to these unimagined delights, however, she writes that 'sometimes the circumstances made it necessary to kidnap a girl, and immediately'. And writing of one such case: 'we gave her shelter, and at 6.30 the next day my husband took her into the country to a place of safety.'[67] Canon Barnett believed, however, that the country could not be a simple cure-all and that even Arcadias required careful management.

Thus he roundly condemned what he called 'monster day-treats' for children: 'the pleasure, such as it is, is that which is given by drink. The children lose their self-control, they shout and scream, they quarrel and fight . . . they ill-treat the donkeys, the frogs, and the crabs, and they return home dishevelled, cross, and ashamed. They do not by their day in the country accumulate memories which will draw them to a country life. . . .' He recommended instead the opportunity in small groups without 'the unwholesome food of pies, cakes, ices, and sweets . . . to wander in the fields and woods, make friends with strange playfellows, obtain excitement by new revelations of country ways, dare the elements, and learn to understand the beasts'.[68]

It is not clear, perhaps, who we are supposed to feel sorry for – the children or the frogs – and the sentiments of Canon Barnett's life and work exemplify one aspect of the Arcadian spirit admirably: when an Arcadian festival of music and dancing gets out of hand, for example, and turns into a romp of 'lawless dancing' and 'noisy horse-play' the answer is to close it down.[69] This caused the 'rough element' to throw stones at Mrs Barnett and her friends, although luckily, she tells us with some satisfaction, she was wearing a good, strong bonnet and the crowd were poor shots.

Octavia Hill is another example of the Arcadian correctionalist who firmly believed that social problems could only be resolved by 'sweet, subtle human sympathy, and power of human love'.[70] She writes, for example, of her attempts to settle a disturbance in a London court which was 'quarrelsome, hot, dirty' and where on warm summer evenings 'the drinking is wildest, the fighting fiercest and the language most violent'.[71] Octavia Hill may even have recognised something of the utopian impossibility of what she was about, or at least the way she was going about it:

Sometimes on such a hot summer evening in such a court where I am trying to calm excited women shouting their execrable language at one another, I have looked up suddenly and seen one of those bright gleams of light the summer sun sends out just before he sets, catching the top of a red chimney-pot, and beautiful there, though too directly above their heads for the crowd below to notice it much. But to me it brings sad thought of the fair and quiet places far away, where it is falling softly on a tree, and a hill, and cloud, and I feel that quiet, that beauty that space, would be more powerful to calm the wild excess about me than all my frantic striving with it.[72]

It is worth noting, here and in other examples of this sentiment, that the sun is shining: the sun is always shining in Arcadia, unlike the countryside where it sometimes rains. Octavia Hill writes of the need for 'places to sit, places to play in, places to stroll in'. 'One of the best things the Institute has done' she writes 'has been to arrange expeditions every Saturday during the summer, to park, or field, or common.' [73] But, again, she recognises that it provides only a momentary retreat from what the problem is really about: 'they sit down on the grass; the baby grabs at the daisies, the tiny children toddle about, or tumble on the soft grass, the mother's arms are rested . . . there the May still grows; there thousands of buttercups cover the slope with gold; there, best of all, as you ascend, the hill lifts you out of London . . . even London is hushed for you for a few minutes.' [74]

If here the Arcadian solution was understood as something which gave just a few moments' rest from the violence of the city, to which it might return you refreshed, it has also sometimes been understood as a more durable solution which could restore deviants and runaways to permanent utility. Jane Addams, for example, writes of the drudgery of factory work and describes the case of a young boy who after having nine jobs in a year finally decides that he has 'had enough'. However, a job is found for him as a telephone lineman: 'climbing telephone poles and handling wires apparently supplied him with the elements of outdoor activity and danger which were necessary to hold his interest, and he became a steady supporter of his family.' [75] Addams wrote (this is in the United States in 1909) that perhaps science had done all that it could for the development of machinery without placing an 'unwarranted strain on the nervous system of the worker'. 'It may be that . . . industrial advance will lie not in the direction of improvement in machinery, but in the recovery and education of the workman. This refusal to apply "the art of life" to industry continually drives out of it many young people.' [76] In her concerns Jane Addams shows an early face of the man-management business and 'personnel management', and in passing we can compare this with the later work on human relations in industry as represented by Elton Mayo.

He was far too hard-headed to fall into arcadian nostalgia and constantly reminds his readers that 'earlier studies tend naturally enough to look back on the life of simpler communities with regret . . . this, however, is a road which we cannot travel in these days; for us there can be no easy return to simplicity . . . the remedy cannot be a return to simple apprenticeship and the primitive establishment'. Nevertheless, he could write that as a consequence of modern factory conditions 'the individual inevitably experiences a sense of void, of emptiness, where his fathers knew the joy of comradeship and security'.[77] What is required is to set this statement alongside the actual history of the transition from a predominantly agrarian economy to industrial capitalism. We need to ask ourselves, just who *were* these factory labourers whose fathers had known such undiluted comradeship and security?

What we see here, even in Mayo, is that common pastoral trick of an idealised rural past which is set against the problems of the present which are then 'understood' as inevitable, and as historical mishap. We find something similar in Jane Addams's own work. She understood the problems of urban youth in part as the product of a dehumanising factory system, and in part as the product of what she thought of as a dislocated peasantry. Significantly, the boy who returns to utility as a telephone lineman was of Swedish extraction, and Addams points to the fact that the parents of troublesome city youth in her day were 'rough-working and hard-playing peasants'.[78] These youth, she writes, were in 'revolt against conformity' and had an overwhelming desire to prove that they could do things 'without being bossed all the time'. However, 'whatever really active pursuits he tries to engage, he is promptly suppressed by the police' and he 'sullenly settles back into inactivity'. 'He thus learns to persuade himself that it is better to do nothing, or, as the psychologist would say, "to inhibit his motor impulses".'[79]

What has happened here in Jane Addams's account is worth noting, for it illustrates quite well how pastoral explanations, which are not anchored to any conception of real history and real economic conditions, can easily forget what they are explanations of. Thus the interpretation of these troubles from which she begins, although it is an admittedly arcadian short-cut to history, is an interpretation based on the dislocations and strains of emergent industrial capitalism as they impress themselves in its labour force; but this has now become lost within, and replaced by, psychological interpretation. Social and economic considerations only remain as a backcloth against which a psychological drama unfolds, a psychological drama which depicts what these human troubles are said to be 'really' about, as we see in the following excerpt which describes the fate of the disillusioned city youth:

> When 'slack times' come, he will be the first workman of least value, and the first to be dismissed, calmly accepting his position in the ranks of the unemployed because it will not be so unlike the many hours of idleness and vacuity to which he was accustomed as a boy. No help having been extended to him in the moment of his first irritable revolt against industry, his whole life has been twisted toward idleness and futility.[80]

Here it is now psychopathology (and not 'slack times') which explains why men are idle and unemployed; as in some pastoral poetry the humanitarian impulse of pastoralist social work of this sort has become blunted: 'it is the care of paupers, not the creation of pauperism, which holds the attention and feeling', writes Williams.[81] The whole tradition has come to rest on an assumption, and it is a ridiculous one, that if all men were psychologically adjusted to industry there would no no 'slack times'.

Mrs Barnett had also encountered, of course, the 'vicious', 'idle' ways of the poor and she too had opinions on the arcadian correction of these habits. Indeed, on training-farms, work camps and labour colonies – of the type which Charles Booth had recommended for the correction of paupers – Mrs Barnett thought she saw miracles: 'We saw their work and wondered, for did we not know these men in East London? Had we not had experience of their lounging ways, their idle habits, their derision of industry. . . . What had worked the miracle? Just the gift of hope, plus enough food, clean air, organised labour – surely the birthrights of every man.' [82] But even Mrs Barnett knew something of the limitations of pastoralism, and although in a reflective passage she can congratulate herself on how she had helped some of the urban poor to find a moment of pastoral harmony, the deeper divisions of social class show through:

> As two little groups of hot happy East London children gathered round the tea-table in my garden on Saturday, July 9th, 1916, their hands full of treasures – for they were a nature-study party

– I contrasted them with gratitude with the thin faces, lawless ways, and animal habits the same sort of small people would have shown in those early rambles forty years ago. But the pathos of town-homes for nature-lovers dwells in the hearts of even these well-behaved little mortals.

'Please, ma'am, need we go home? 'Tis the far-off I want to look at', was politely whispered to me, and the glories of the sunset over my great view made it hard to say, 'I am afraid you must, dear, for it will be ten o'clock now before you reach Wapping.' [83]

No doubt it was hard to say, but she said it nevertheless: one should not, perhaps, belittle these sentiments, but nor should one allow oneself to be taken in by them. It is not just a question of the way in which the arcadian retreat remains nothing more than an 'afternoon out'. It is, as Raymond Williams puts it, the deception of 'the idea of an ordered and happier past set against the disturbance and disorder of the present. An idealisation, based on a temporary situation and on a deep desire for stability . . . [serving] to cover and to evade the actual and bitter contradictions of the time'.[84]

Correctional Arcadias must always return their victims to utility. But in the mood of present times, when utility itself is questioned, the pastoral tradition in social thought can appear as the answer in, and of, itself. Most clearly in Laing's anti-psychiatry the tradition persists in this novel form so that anti-psychiatry's solution to the deviant question is appropriately called an 'asylum' : a final, total retreat *from* the world. The good life, the whole life, the true life is thus seen to lie elsewhere in this 'post-industrial' transformation of the pastoral myth. Although even that novel twist provides a continuity within the tradition for, as George Steiner expresses its organising sentiment: 'Communion with God lies in the wilderness. The Redeemer comes from the hills and silent places; Satan is on the boulevard.' [85]

THE MACHINE AND THE GARDEN: THE BRITISH AND AMERICAN EXPERIENCE

Social-welfare ideologies inevitably succumb to this contradiction: are the practices which they undergird building a new world, or picking up the pieces? The two halves of this contradiction are not mutually exclusive, although they will obtain a different emphasis from different writers in the tradition. For example, sociological pastoral although its dominant concern has been with reclaiming runaways and drop-outs from the urban-industrial machine also contains the hope of a promised garden in the society of the future.

What I have done in the second part of this book is look at some of the contemporary ambiguities in social-work ideology, and then at the historical roots of the central ambiguities. It thus provides a sketchy history which is written with two purposes in mind. First, it hopes to show not only where we have come from, but also where we think we are going. And second, it helps to uncover some of the ideological foundations of the modern controversies which announced themselves particularly in misfit social thought, but which are also continued in the most dominant traditions of deviance theory. The utilitarian tradition of an Edwin Chadwick thus finds its continuation in the behavioural engineering of a B. F. Skinner. In his psychology we find an echo of the hopes of Josiah Wedgwood (an early factory disciplinarian) who wished to 'make such *machines* of the *men* as cannot err'.[86] The pastoral tradition, on the other hand, is continued in cottage-home movements, adventure playgrounds, free schools, outward-bound schemes and so on, and particularly in the ideas of community work and community action. Raymond Williams even goes so far as to suggest that community defence schemes against 'urban renewal' and the destruction of communities by motorway plans, and so on, continue (in the way in which the arguments are phrased) some of the tradition of resistance to the enclosure acts.[87]

These two traditions of pastoralism and utilitarianism provide the most convenient avenue to the understanding of welfare ideology. They also supply us with the dominant imagery for understanding what deviance and nonconformity is about: living proof of the refusal of human subjects to acquiesce to external domination, or lifeless human waste products. And what becomes clear when one looks at these two separate (but not entirely separate) lines of development in a historical perspective is that controversy within the field of deviance and welfare cannot be conducted in purely inward-looking, narrow professional terms, but must be connected to the wider domain of political and moral discourse.

What also needs to be said, although it can be deposited here only as a sort of footnote, is that the British and American experiences and traditions are quite different. It is possible, for example, that the tradition of sociological pastoral is much firmer in the United States than in Britain, where the agrarian myth and small-town populism are not so central in the imagery of political life. Richard Hofstadter writes, for example: 'The United States was born in the country and has moved to the city. From the beginning its political values and ideas were of necessity shaped by country life.'[88] In his book *The Machine in the Garden* Leo Marx identifies precisely that image – the industrial machine growing in the garden of virgin American territory – as preoccupying the American cultural tradition, and he writes of how 'the machine [so often appears] as a sudden, shocking intruder upon a fantasy of idyllic satisfaction'.[89] The character of the British and American Industrial Revolutions is quite different, however, and the American experience possibly provides the grass roots on which pastoral can take hold: we can recognise 'Merrie England' instantly as myth, whereas American small-town populism appears to have more substance. It is possible, for example, that the comparative difficulty in establishing the community-development idea in Britain can be attributed to these different traditions and experiences. We must also remember that these experiences, in which we find the origins of modern deviance theories and welfare ideologies, are not only the experiences of industrialisation and urbanisation, but also the experiences of a class and what it means to be a member of a class. This aspect is more solidly preserved in the British tradition of social welfare; in Britain the traditions of the labour movement, social democracy and socialism have more influence on the character of welfare ideologies than in the United States. This also introduces more complexity, for as it has developed the British social-democratic tradition preserves its own version of utilitarianism. Or rather, it has continued a complex of sentiments which Taylor, Walton and Young have described as 'ideological assumptions that can be traced not only to the Fabian translation of utilitarianism, but also to the legacy of Methodism in the early history of the Labour movement'.[90] These traditions of utilitarianism and Methodism cause the compassion in British welfare ideologies to be tinged with a punitive attitude, for 'Methodism has often been used as an ideology to castigate and segregate off members of local communities who persist in deviant or militant activities when others have desisted'.[91]

This British social-democratic tradition can for these reasons stand in an antagonistic relationship to the pastoralism implicit in such notions as 'community participation'. Replying to Wedgwood Benn's programme of a 'new politics', which had stressed the recently fashionable ideas of 'participation' and the 'de-centralisation' of government, Anthony Crosland could thus write in a Fabian pamphlet:

> I repeat what I have often said – the majority prefer to lead a full family life and cultivate their gardens. And a good thing too. . . . We do not necessarily want a busy bustling society in which everyone is politically active, and fussing around in an interfering and responsible (*sic*) manner, herding us all into participating groups.[92]

The 'garden' here, of course, is not the garden of a pastoral utopia but something into which 'lesser men' retreat while elites get on with the business of social-democratic governing.

There is, therefore, a complex web of conflicting and overlapping ideologies which surround the bare skeleton of the politics of conformity, order, deviance, welfare and reasonableness which the historical sketch in Part II of this book sets out. The picture is even more complex when the British and American traditions are contrasted, and there is no available theoretical framework which can pull all those complexities into a simple whole. We must ask, for example, to what extent the dominance of American criminology and deviance theories in the twentieth century has shaped the contours of the field, the selection of certain kinds of problems as interesting or important, and even the selection of certain kinds of social problems (and not others) as 'problems'.

C. Wright Mills has indicated how the American literature of the study of social problems is saturated with the values of small-town life. In his justly celebrated essay in the sociology of knowledge, 'The Professional Ideology of Social Pathologists', he conducted a survey of writers in the field and he found that 'all the authors considered (except one, who was foreign born) were born in small towns, or on farms near small towns, three-fourths of which were in states not industrialised during the youth of the authors'. He found, correspondingly, that the things identified as 'problems' in this literature 'typically concern urban behaviour' and that 'the operating criteria of the pathological are typically *rural* in orientation and extraction' :

> Most of the 'problems' considered arise because of the urban deterioration of certain values which can live genuinely only in a relatively homogeneous and primarily rural milieu. . . . When 'rural problems' are discussed, they are conceived as due to encroaching urbanisation. The notion of disorganisation is quite often merely the absence of that *type* of organisation associated with the stuff of primary-group communities having Christian and Jeffersonian legitimations. . . . The ideally adjusted man of the social pathologists is 'socialised' . . . [to] the norms of independent middle-class persons verbally living out Protestant ideals in the small towns of America.[93]

But in one important sense sociological excavations of the social and political traditions which underlie welfare ideologies are limited in their usefulness, and the sociology of knowledge is also limited in its ability to grasp the full implications of the theme of sociological pastoral. Pastoral does not take place on *actual* farms : its location is the mythical land of Arcadia. Pastoral does not relate back to actual times and customs as C. Wright Mills implies it does : its time is the Golden Age.

The pastoral tradition is a myth because it retrospectively and nostalgically celebrates values of community and brotherhood which, as far as we can gather, were never available to the mass of men and women, only to a small elite of landowners and the propertied. We can read in Mrs Barnett's account of her husband's life and work, for example, that she dreaded the arrival of underground-railway systems in London, which would bring with them 'rows of ugly villas such as disfigure Willesden' and 'would result in the ruin of the sylvan restfulness' of Hampstead. Confidently she writes : 'Therefore there was nothing else to do but enlarge the Heath.'[94] The heath would be enlarged, just as the commons had been enclosed, within the same unchanged, unequal set of property relations and life-chances : it is the absence of any sense of that actual history which betrays the myth in pastoral thought.

But the pastoral myth also preseves the place of study and practice in the field of deviance and welfare in moral and political discourse, linking the field to the crucial historical transition which shapes the character of its theories and ideologies. It is a place which must be remembered, in the sense of being put back together, if the real nature of deviance-control is to be understood and transformed in a way which, while it might not build an arcadian heaven on earth, will lay the social base for a fully human response to the deviant question.

8

CONCLUSION: SCIENTIFIC, MORAL AND POLITICAL DISCOURSE

Whatever happens, every individual is a child of his time; so philosophy too is its own time apprehended in thoughts. It is just as absurd to fancy that a philosophy can transcend its contemporary world as it is to fancy that an individual can overleap his own age, jump over Rhodes. If his theory really goes beyond the world as it is and builds an ideal one as it ought to be, that world exists indeed, but only in his opinions, an unsubstantial element where anything you please may, in fancy, be built.[1]

Hegel is not saying here that men should merely succumb to the fact that their thought is an expression of their time, but that social thought (which he calls philosophy) is already part of social reality and a part of men's collective attempts to maintain, or change, that reality. Hegel's position is also that thought should impose itself on reality, through the will of men, transforming material and social realities so that what is viewed as rational in social theory becomes realised in social practice. The thought of men, Hegel writes, and the will of men are not two separate entities: 'it must not be imagined that man . . . keeps thought in one pocket and will in another.'[2] Thought which does not realise its place in the world as practical action, and which does not connect up scholarly, scientific endeavour with the world of human, moral and political discourse, is idle thought.

The exploration of the connections between scientific discourse and moral–political discourse forms the backbone of this book. This first part shows how questions of politics and morality have inserted themselves into deviance theories in recent years. This development gives a jolt to the idea that the study of deviance and deviance-control is a simply technical, scientific matter. It disturbs the belief that social science should operate on problems as they are defined and thrown up by society.[3] It suggests that social science should also act responsibly and critically on the question of how social problems are defined, and that social welfare should not only confine itself to processing society's waste-products but should also interrogate the society which defines the deviant imagination as a waste-product. It proposes the alternative that misfits should be understood as men trying to place themselves in a world in which they are said to have no place.

But the misfit sociologies and the anti-psychiatries are children of their times. What Part I also shows is that the extent to which these new developments in deviance theory successfully connect up the field of deviance and welfare with moral and political discourse is limited. Their success depends to a considerable extent on the way in which they resonate sentimentally with the mood of some contemporary political debates: it is a success which depends, that is, on what I have called the smell of theory, a smell which must be distinguished from its substance. Perhaps 'smell' and 'substance' find some theoretical connection in the Frankfurt School critique of 'one-dimensional' society and modes of opposition to one-dimensionality. But, even so, it is difficult to extract the critical substance of that position from the smell of theory, and the Frankfurt critique is itself eventually 'drugstore-ised'.

To some extent, therefore, these new, critical developments are shadowy. But they nevertheless contain a complex and disturbing set of implications for the practice of deviance-control. They insist on a re-evaluation of both the theoretical and practical grounds on which social welfare is established, a re-evaluation which goes to the moral and political roots of the welfare state.

However, these radical theories do not find their radical practice. Their moral and political imperatives remain, by and large, things to be read about in books and scholarly essays. We say that where there is a will there is a way. But there is very little will, or perhaps no will at all, to practise the implications of the new deviance theories and undertake the revision which they require. The new approaches to deviance remain only as the theory of an unrealised practice, and their intelligence suffers as a consequence. For in the academic market place theories replace each other with an unending rapidity: they are coughed up and discarded, they fall prey to the spell of fashion, they are forgotten as soon as they are memorised, they become commodities to be hawked about from this place to that. And the new deviance theories have no guaranteed immunity from all this. Under conditions such as these Russell Jacoby may well be right when he claims that 'if inflated money seeks to overcome the falling rate of profit, inflated concepts [and theories] seek to overcome the falling rate of intelligence'.[4] It might be judged, for example, that in their attempt to assert their sympathy with the deviant the theories discussed in the first part of this book give themselves up uncritically to the deviant imagination. So that theories which concern madness assert their connection with craziness by becoming a little crazy themselves, and theories of deviance take their own deviant path. If that is so, then it is part of the difficulty of finding a place for the deviant's own voice in scientific discourse about his condition.

The second part of this book approaches the problem differently. A mistake which it is easy to fall into when trying to gain an appreciation of the moral and political slant which anti-psychiatry and the misfit sociologies put on deviance theory is to think of them as a 'politicisation' of the field of deviance. It is a mistake which is based on a recurrent myth of the welfare professions, namely that they act on a sphere of interest (the 'personal' sphere) which is entirely separate from the 'political' sphere. Part II, following from an account of how the political debate on welfare matters is handled in contemporary social work, goes some way towards exploding this myth. By looking at something of the history of welfare ideologies and deviance theories, I show that their foundations are explicitly political; and I argue that these practical and conceptual foundations are dictated by the requirements of a specific form of industrial society (that is, industrial capitalism) and that they are passed down to us in that form.

It is only by forgetting this decisive historical and political transformation which is their birth-place that the welfare professions can get along with an easy conscience with the business of technical–professional debate, a debate which is dislocated from the moral and political domain within which they act. It is the singular, and disconcerting, achievement of the new deviance theories that they re-open this area of moral and political discourse, posing the question of the relationship between the deviant and wider society. But what is surprising, and even embarrassing in its simplicity, is the way in which the 'radical' and 'counter-cultural' deviance theories of the 1960s appear to resurrect the main themes of the historical birth-place of social welfare. We find it in the idea of deviants as a class who might overturn the one-dimensional world (the historical correlate being the 'mob') and in the revitalisation of pastoral notions of a simple life as a viable alternative to the problems of urban-industrialism. In the reading of deviance theory which I have offered it is almost as if 'post-industrial' man had returned to some of the preoccupations of 'pre-industrial' society.

It would be too easy, however, and not at all accurate, to suggest that the new 'radical' twists of anti-psychiatry and the misfit sociologies only supply a continuation of the dominant traditions of deviance theory. For they also constitute an abrupt departure from the main traditions in that they give the deviant a voice, and they listen to his voice as that of a man who might be saying something – even something discomforting – about the world in which he lives with other men. The deviant's voice, in other words, is not devalued and discredited by virtue of his deviance. In the traditional approach to the misfit this is not the case: there he is voiceless, pickled and transformed into a reified object of no social worth. He is stared at by countless research scientists, but he is not asked to speak. In traditional theory the deviant is not a man like other men, and he is thought to have nothing to say which could make sense to reasonable and conforming men. It is this tradition which is shaped by the experiences of industrial capitalism in the first burst of its rapid growth. The main contours of deviance theories are already available by the mid-nineteenth century: it is there that scientific curiosity in the reified misfit is born.

This last statement must be emphasised, even in the face of a paucity of historical research on pre-capitalist deviance control which makes it no more than a roughly informed guess. There is, however, some supporting evidence, and, in his study of crime and public order in medieval England, John Bellamy describes how men of the time showed very little curiosity about the motivations and social origins of wrongdoers and wrongdoings. For example, he writes that Chief Justice Fortescue 'only got as far as speculating that England's many robberies indicated a rather praiseworthy determination not to be overawed by the law, an independence of spirit which gave and took hard knocks in good part'.[5] And a further indication can be obtained from the opinions of the Tudor chronicler Holinshed, as they are described by Bellamy:

> Holinshed believed that most persistent offenders were 'rogues', that is to say able-bodied men without employment. He argued that crimes were also commonly committed by two other groups. There were the 'young shifting gentlemen which oftentimes doo beare more port than they are able to maintaine' (i.e., live above their station) and the 'servingmen whose wages cannot suffice so much as to find them breeches'. Both types turned periodically to larceny to support themselves.[6]

By modern standards medieval criminology was obviously not very good, although it does appear to get to the moral knuckle. Some will find it comforting that we have left all this behind, and that a more solid scientific grasp of the problem has replaced common-sense observation and vague moralising. But it is a comfort only if one imagines that the moral–political problems of deviance-control have been finally settled, leaving the field open to neutral, technical specialists who 'know what is best' about deviance. It would also require some demonstration that the allegedly 'value free' speculations of science had measurably eliminated deviance, misery and unhappiness.

The second of these assumptions is highly questionable. And the first is a position which it is difficult, if not impossible, to hold to in the face of the critique of anti-psychiatry and the misfit paradigm. For what is called into question by their critique, and by the approach which I have adopted in this book, is precisely that relationship between the idea of professional technicians – the vast army of criminologists, penologists, social workers, psychiatrists, psychologists – and the troubled moral–political domain upon which they act, and the definitions of normality, worth and social value which they help to construct and enforce. It is necessary to state something, therefore, of the relationship between moral, scientific and political discourse in deviance and welfare theories, and some of the difficulties in establishing those relationships. It is a problem which is all the more urgent, and all the more difficult, when ideologies wrap themselves up in a scientific disguise: as when what are assumed to be simply technical arguments that deviance arises from monstrous conditioning, or genes which are somehow bent, further the powerful moral and political imperatives that deviants are essentially unlike other men – a race of 'city Arabs' as the nineteenth century put it, if a little more honestly.

The moral options available in deviance theories, fundamentally, are whether to view deviants as non-human, human but different, or indifferently human. Herbert Spencer could write in his *Principles of Sociology* of 'the garbage of the police and divorce courts' which he likened to 'the trivial details of table-talk'.[7] And it was a quality of less-developed intelligences and primitive minds, he thought, to concern oneself with such rubbish: Spencer reckoned that to feed such minds on the more 'concentrated diet' of scientific enquiry 'would be as impracticable as to feed a cow on meat'.[8] But for minds which defy Spencer's hard-headed utilitarianism, and which still claim to be critical intelligences, the question is still posed: and the question is whether to allow the misfit a voice in moral–political discourse and how to listen to him.

To raise the misfit's inarticulate voice to a level of coherent discourse is an immensely difficult task. It requires of us more than compassion, and more than a vaguely underdog sympathy. For example, misfit social thought is a stab in those directions, but it is always in danger of lapsing into a loose and hopeful romanticism. The task also requires more than just giving the deviant a 'fair hearing'. Mayer and Timms's book *The Client Speaks* gives us accounts, fair hearings, of working-class impressions of casework. But in Mayer and Timms's work when the client is asked to speak he is only asked to speak about the pre-determined goals and standards of social service: he is not asked to speak, and no attempt is made to help him, about the conditions of his life. Mayer and Timms can be said to give the client a fair hearing, therefore, but it is not a critical hearing. It thus continues the assumption that deviants have in some sort of way got it wrong and need to be put right: but it might be that they have got the conditions of their membership in this society quite right, and that their deviant conduct is an inarticulate commentary on those conditions. To give a further example: if working-class schoolchildren break up schools, a critical hearing will turn its attention to the nature of educational achievement and educational socialisation in a highly stratified class society, rather than looking only at the workings of the heads of 'mindless' vandals.

However, it is the spirit of scientific–technical professionalism which is largely dominant in contemporary theories of deviance and welfare. Even to the extent that in social work's professional ideology the question of why someone might choose to work in the occupation – working with the poor, with misfits and social out-casts – is described as a choice determined not by moral–political considerations, but by personality quirks. The social-work recruit is seen there as someone attempting to resolve (or 'work through') some problem of his own, and the moral–political considerations which might reasonably govern his, or her, choice of a career in the field of welfare are largely ignored.[9] This dominant spirit of technical professionalism also determines which questions should be asked about deviant conduct. Moral and political debate is not outlawed, but it is kept in its place, and the questions which are regarded as legitimate and 'useful' are questions with technical solutions. In doing this social welfare does not only forget its explicitly political history; it also imagines that certain questions (of a moral and political character) are already answered satis-factorily. But the question of what is right or wrong technically, although it has an importance in its own right, can only say what is right or wrong technically. It cannot decide how to act, what to do with professional technique when there are techniques to com-mand, whose side to be on when there are sides, or even how to judge whether there are sides to be taken. Technical thinking is abstract thinking. To pose a concluding question: what is the relationship between all this *talk* of research evidence, methodology, theory, technical know-how, and so on, and *action* in the world on the correction, restraint, liberty and life-chances of the deviant class?

The problem of 'homosexuality' and its 'aetiology' provides an illuminating case study on the career of a concept in the field of deviance and welfare. Szasz has mapped out some of the contours of the way in which the understanding of homosexuality emerged from a theological, moral debate into the civilising light of scientific medicine.[10] Accordingly, in enlightened circles, homosex-uality was no longer seen as an evil and came to be understood as a sickness. It is a decision on the homosexual which opens the way for technical debate on what is wrong with him, how he got to be the way he is, and how to correct his (or her) deviation. But the rules of the game can change, and it is a recent decision of the

American Psychiatric Association that homosexuality should no longer be classified as a mental disorder: officially, that is, the homosexual is not 'sick'. The journal *Mental Health* responded flippantly and somewhat sarcastically, writing of how 'in one great medical *breakthrough*, some 12,000,000 formerly *sick* citizens have become *well* – by fiat'.[11] In another response to the decision Bruce Voeller, spokesman for a militant American gay organisation, is quoted as saying, 'tell the world to cut the sickness crap and start helping us to get our rights'.[12] In this terse comment the client speaks. When deviance is put back into the moral and political world, a major problem becomes how to construct a world which can and will implement the moral and political programme of tolerance which welfare ideologies, forgetting their own real history, imagine that they represent.

NOTES AND REFERENCES*

CHAPTER 1

1. Evans-Pritchard (1956) pp. 84–5.
2. M. Douglas (1966) p. 39.
3. S. Cohen (1973a) *passim.*
4. Simmons (1969) p. 3.
5. Haug and Sussman (1969).
6. Spender (1953) pp. 33–4.
7. But see Chapter 6.
8. L. Taylor (1971) provides a good introductory text.
9. Bannister (1968) p. 181.
10. Gonldner (1971) p. 29.
11. Ibid. p. 31.
12. Ibid. p. 31.
13. For a discussion of this problem in relation to skid-row alcoholics, see Archard (1973).
14. Barthes (1973) pp. 15–25.
15. Particularly, Freud (1961); Durkheim (1952; 1964); Skinner (1973).
16. Taft (1942) p. 240.
17. Bonger (1969). For a critical account of Bonger's version of a Marxist criminology, see Taylor, Walton and Young (1973) ch. 7.
18. Empson (1966) p. 20.
19. Goodman (1960) p. 11.
20. Ibid. p. 11.
21. Bastide (1972) p. 9.
22. Ibid. pp. 9, 12.
23. Debout-Oleszkiewicz (1972) p. 73.

CHAPTER 2

1. Platt (1969) pp. 44–5.
2. Piedmont and Downey (1971).
3. Laing (1967) pp. 39–48.

* Full bibliographical details for titles cited in Notes and References are given, in alphabetical order, in the Bibliography, pp. 232–52.

4. Laing, Phillipson and Lee (1966); Laing (1961; 1969*a* and *b*; 1970).
5. Wynne *et al.* (1958); Bateson *et al.* (1956); Jackson (1968); Lidz *et al.* (1965); Ruesch and Bateson (1951); Watzlawick *et al.* (1968).
6. Schaffer *et al.* (1971); Searles (1965) p. 258.
7. Speck and Attneave (1973); Speck (1967*a* and *b*).
8. Pearson (1974*a*).
9. Laing and Esterson (1964, 1970); Esterson (1970).
10. Schatzman (1973).
11. Laing (1967) p. 136.
12. Compare H. S. Becker (1967*a*).
13. Cooper (1967); M. Barnett (1973); Lilly (1973); W. C. Schutz (1973) p. 11.
14. Laing (1968) p. 15.
15. Ibid. pp. 18–19.
16. Laing (1971) pp. 78 ff. Compare Fromm (1960) pp. 159 ff.
17. Sennett (1971). See also Ratner (1971) pp. 98 ff.
18. Laing and Esterson (1970) p. 12.
19. Laing (1961) p. ix.
20. Laing (1967) p. 87.
21. Ibid. p. 95.
22. See Szasz's works listed in the Bibliography, p. 249.
23. Szasz (1973*a*) pp. 23–4.
24. Szasz (1974) pp. 98–9.
25. Szasz (1973*b*) p. 201.
26. Ibid. pp. 200–1.
27. Szasz (1963) p. 212.
28. Szasz (1974) p. 10.
29. Szasz (1973) pp. 67–8.
30. Szasz (1965) ch. 6.
31. Szasz (1973*b*) p. 259.
32. Maddison (1973).
33. Price (1972) pp. 105–6.
34. Szasz (1962) p. 343.
35. Ibid. pp. 343–4.
36. Szasz (1965) p. 56.
37. Quoted in Leifer (1969) p. 197.
38. Ibid. p. 197.
39. Szasz (1965) pp. 269–70. This discussion is omitted from the 1971 paperback edition.
40. Ibid. p. 71.
41. Ibid. p. 268. This is also omitted from the 1971 edition.
42. Szasz (1973*a*) p. 139.

43. Quoted in Szasz (1965) p. 19.
44. D. Martin (1972) p. 129.
45. For philosophical discussions on this kind of distinction, see Margolis (1966); Flew (1973); Peters (1958); Szasz (1961).
46. Ryle (1963).
47. Szasz (1965) pp. 249–50.
48. Goffman (1969) p. 362.
49. Goffman (1968) p. 317.
50. Esterson (1970) p. 186.
51. Laing (1965) p. 23.
52. Esterson (1970) pp. 185–6.
53. Cooper (1970) p. 18.
54. Esterson (1970) p. 197.
55. Laing (1965) p. 28.
56. Sedgwick (1971); Friedenberg (1973).
57. Laing and Cooper (1971) pp. 24–5.
58. For example, Jourard (1968); C. R. Rogers (1961); Maslow (1973); Bannister and Fransella (1971).
59. Matson (1968) p. 44.
60. Quoted in Matson (1968) pp. 72–3.
61. For example, C. R. Rogers (1973) pp. 18–19.
62. Perls (1971) p. 32.
63. Matson (1968) pp. 141–2.
64. See Mungham and Pearson (1972); Mungham (1974). Some of the written expression of this radicalism can be traced in the periodicals *Social Policy, Case Con, Humpty Dumpty, Insurgent Sociologist, Red Rat* and *The Radical Therapist* (now *Rough Times*).
65. Reich (1972*b*) p. 66. Also Reich (1972*a*; 1948).
66. Particularly Marcuse (1972*a*; 1972*b*) and Chapter 4 below.
67. Different faces of the 'Freudian Left' are shown in P. A. Robinson (1972); King (1972); Roszak (1971); Roazen (1968); Brown (1966; 1968); Fromm (1960; 1963).
68. Laing (1967) p. 11.
69. Laing (1965) p. 12.
70. Esterson (1970) pp. 191, 224–5, 235. And Laing, Phillipson and Lee (1966) pp. 137–40.
71. Schatzman (1973) pp. 141–58.
72. Cooper (1967).
73. Laing (1968) p. 18.
74. Zilboorg (1935; 1941).
75. Szasz (1973*b*) p. 27.
76. Ibid. pp. 19–20.
77. Ibid. p. 64.

78. Ibid. pp. 90, 144.
79. Ibid. p. 314.
80. Ibid. p. 314.
81. Chesler (1974) p. 33.
82. Szasz (1973*b*) p. 126.
83. Szasz (1974) p. 77.
84. The approach to the sociology of deviance in J. D. Douglas (1972) is similar.
85. Foucault (1971).
86. Weis (1971) p. 51.
87. Szasz (1973*b*) p. 129.
88. Leifer (1969) p. 158.
89. Ibid. pp. 171, 180–1.
90. Szasz (1974) p. 85.
91. See the evidence from a behaviour-modification viewpoint summarised by Bandura (1970) pp. 81 ff., the communications analysis by Haley (1963) and the non-verbal communication studies by Scheflen (1963; 1965).
92. Sedgwick (1972) p. 222.
93. Agel (1971, 1973) and Radical Therapist Collective (1974).
94. Radical Therapist Collective (1974) pp. 7–8.
95. Robinson (1973).
96. See Laing (1972) and Barnes and Berke (1973).
97. M. Barnett (1973).
98. Cage (1968) p. 59.
99. Foucault (1971).
100. E. Becker (1964) pp. 9–10.
101. Ibid. p. 251.
102. Laing (1967) p. 107.
103. For an excellent illustration of conformity and non-conformity as a 'social accomplishment' see Parker (1974).
104. For two critics who take this view, see D. Martin (1972) and Coulter (1973).

CHAPTER 3

1. S. Cohen (1974) p. 23.
2. Hirst (1972) p. 29.
3. Schur (1971).
4. Ibid. pp. 128 ff.
5. Erikson (1966).
6. Hirst (1972) p. 54.
7. Pearson (1972, 1974*b*).
8. For example Schur (1971, 1973); Box (1971); Rock (1973*a*);

Taylor, Walton and Young (1973); S. Cohen (1971*a*); Gibbs (1966).

9. H. S. Becker (1963) pp. 8–9.
10. Lemert (1967) p. v. See also Lemert (1951).
11. Kitsuse (1968) pp. 19–20.
12. Erikson (1966) p. 6; and Erikson (1964) p. 11.
13. Lemert (1967) p. 17.
14. Genet (1967) p. 145.
15. Matza (1969) p. 80.
16. Scott (1969*a*).
17. Ibid. p. 4.
18. Ibid. p. 14.
19. Ibid. p. 121.
20. Ibid. p. 120. Also Scott (1970).
21. Reiss (1964).
22. H. S. Becker (1963) pp. 59–78; and H. S. Becker (1967*a*).
23. J. Young (1971*b*) pp. 27–8.
24. Scheff (1966). For an argument which contradicts Scheff, see Gove (1970).
25. Scheff (1968).
26. Balint (1957).
27. Kitsuse and Dietrick (1959).
28. Wilkins (1964).
29. See Maruyama (1960, 1963); and Wender (1968).
30. Shoham (1970).
31. Sartre (1964) pp. 17ff. The quotation is taken from the abbreviated account in Laing and Cooper (1971) pp. 71–2.
32. Goffman (1968) p. 126; and Schur (1973) p. 23.
33. For example, Sudnow (1965) and Cicourel (1968).
34. Schur (1964) p. 81. For an elaborate research analysis, see Stimson (1973).
35. H. S. Becker (1963) pp. 121–63.
36. Platt (1969).
37. H. S. Becker (1963) pp. 147–8
38. Dickson (1968).
39. Musto (1973).
40. Ibid. p. 255.
41. Ibid. p. 7.
42. Ibid. p. 7.
43. Ibid. p. 255.
44. Ibid. p. 255.
45. S. Cohen (1973*a*).
46. Ibid. p. 192. Compare this with the musical autobiography of the Mod phenomenon by The Who (1973).

47. Piliavin and Briar (1968); Garfinkel and Bittner (1967); D. Chapman (1968).
48. Schur (1973) p. 155.
49. Matza (1969) p. 9.
50. Ibid. p. 25.
51. Ibid. p. 17.
52. Debro (1970) p. 166.
53. Matza (1969) p. 24.
54. H. S. Becker (1963) pp. 41–58.
55. Taylor, Walton and Young (1973) p. 173.
56. Matza (1964) ch. 1.
57. Ibid. p. 11.
58. Ibid. p. 22.
59. Ibid. p. 29.
60. Taylor, Walton and Young (1973) pp. 180 ff.
61. Matza (1969) pp. 111–17.
62. Ibid. p. 110.
63. H. S. Becker (1964) p. 1.
64. Rock (1973*a*) p. 12.
65. J. Young (1971*a*) ch. 3.
66. S. Cohen (1971*a*) pp. 9–24.
67. Taylor, Walton and Young (1973) p. 140.
68. Schur (1973) pp. 135–9.
69. Schur (1971) pp. 115 ff.
70. *Times Literary Supplement* (June 1971) p. 633.
71. J. D. Douglas (1970) p. viii.
72. K. Marx (1961) p. 72.
73. Berger and Pullberg (1966) p. 60.
74. Berger and Luckmann (1971) p. 106.
75. Simmons (1969) p. 25.
76. Garfinkel (1967) pp. 37–8.
77. See Goldthorpe (1973) for an intelligent discussion of the matter.
78. Warren and Johnson (1972) p. 70.
79. J. D. Douglas (1970) p. 15.
80. Ibid. p. 19.
81. Habermas (1971) pp. 91 ff.
82. Ibid. p. 92.
83. Munday (1972) pp. 3–6.
84. Ibid. p. 4.
85. Becker (1967*b*) p. 241.
86. Matza (1969) p. 17.
87. Gouldner (1971) p. 379.
88. Ibid. p. 379.
89. Horton (1971) p. 187.

90. Gouldner (1971) p. 379.
91. Horton (1971) pp. 189, 187.
92. Gouldner (1968) p. 110.
93. Ibid. p. 104.
94. Ibid. p. 107.
95. Schur (1973); and J. Young (1971*a*) ch. 10.
96. Roman (1971).
97. Debro (1970) pp. 170–1.
98. Berger (1971) p. 2.
99. For a criticism of Berger's approach, see Walton and Gamble (1972) pp. 35–9.
100. Spitzer and Denzin (1968) p. 464.
101. Coulter (1973) p. 63.
102. Goffman (1972*a*) p. 147.
103. Weis (1971) pp. 39–40.
104. Ibid. p. 48.
105. S. Cohen (1974) p. 27.
106. Hagan (1973).
107. M. S. Davis (1971).
108. Gouldner (1971) p. 489.
109. S. Cohen (1974) pp. 27–8.

CHAPTER 4

1. Vaneigem (n.d.) p. 14.
2. For example: Freud (1961) XXI, pp. 64–145; Roszak (1971, 1972); Reich (1948, 1972*a*); Brown (1966, 1968); Reiche (1970); Deleuze and Guattari (1972); Gabel (1962); King (1972); Slater (1971); Kohn (1969); O'Neill (1972); Firestone (1972); Fromm (1960, 1963); Adorno (1967*a*, 1968); Jacoby (1972, 1973 *a* and *b*).
3. Marcuse (1968) pp. 19, 24.
4. E. Becker (1968) p. 271.
5. Mills (1959) pp. 170–6.
6. Debord (1970).
7. Quoted in a review of the 'post-industrial' theme by Bell (1971) p. 127.
8. Quoted in Roszak (1971) p. 11.
9. Marcuse (1968) p. 28.
10. Horkheimer (1947) p. 142.
11. Ibid. p. 159.
12. Adorno (1967*b*) p. 34.
13. Adorno (1974) p. 18. The translation is taken from Jay (1973) p. 277.

14. Marcuse (1972a) p. 21.
15. Orwell (1954) p. 25.
16. Ibid. pp. 126, 100, 115.
17. Ibid. p. 55.
18. Ibid. p. 104.
19. Ibid. p. 59.
20. Ibid. p. 51.
21. Ibid. p. 125.
22. Breines (1968) p. 136.
23. Ibid. p. 146.
24. Rubin (1970) pp. 109–10.
25. Marcuse (1972a) p. 42.
26. O'Neill (1972) ch. 4; Zijderveld (1972); Turner (1969); Feenberg (1971); Fiedler (1965).
27. Roszak (1972) p. 77.
28. W. C. Schutz (1973).
29. Marcuse (1972b) p. 16.
30. Ibid. p. 17.
31. Jay (1973) p. 103.
32. Marcuse (1972a) p. 25.
33. Ackerman and Jahoda (1950).
34. For an excellent history of this period see Jay (1973).
35. See, for example, the introductory comments by translators to Adorno (1967b, 1973a). The conceptual grounds of critical theory are set out in Schroyer (1973) and Wellmer (1970).
36. Adorno (1957).
37. Adorno et al. (1950).
38. See, particularly, Therborn (1970) and Jay (1972, 1973).
39. Horkheimer and Adorno (1973) pp. 4–5.
40. 'Traditional and Critical Theory' in Horkheimer (1972) p. 225.
41. Jay (1973) p. 261.
42. Skinner (1973).
43. Horkheimer and Adorno (1973) p. 28, and again on pp. 54 ff.
44. Marcuse (1972c) pp. 71–2.
45. Keniston (1968a).
46. Fiedler (1965).
47. 'White Panther Manifesto', reprinted in Stansill and Mairowitz (1971) p. 176.
48. See S. Weber (1970).
49. Roszak (1972).
50. Ibid. p. xxxiii.
51. Horkheimer and Adorno (1973) pp. 245–55.
52. Quoted in Jay (1973) p. 173.
53. Horkheimer (1947) p. 107.

54. Jacoby (1972) p. 22.

55. Quoted in Horkheimer (1947) p. 160.

56. Jay (1973) p. 291.

57. Horkheimer (1947) p. 94.

58. Adorno (1974) p. 50. For clear statements of Adorno's position on the question of 'negative' thought, see Adorno (1973c) pp. 27–8 and Adorno (1974) p. 247.

59. Adorno (1974) p. 50.

60. Particularly Marcuse (1970, 1972a).

61. Marcuse (1970) p. 69.

62. Ibid. pp. 69, 93.

63. Ibid. p. 78.

64. Horkheimer and Adorno (1973) p. 227.

65. Ibid. p. 231.

66. Jacoby (1970).

67. Habermas (1971) p. 43.

68. Ibid. pp. 42–3, emphasis added.

69. Haug and Sussman (1969).

70. S. Cohen (1973b) p. 120.

71. Horowitz and Liebowitz (1968).

72. Ibid. pp. 280, 283–4.

73. Ibid. p. 285.

74. Manifestos and statements by some of these organisations are available. See Mental Patients' Liberation Front (1971); Agel (1971) pp. 107–9; Mental Patients' Union (M.P.U.) (1973a, 1973b); Preservation of the Rights of Prisoners (PROP) (1973); Lawal et al. (1973); Stratton (1973). Also Rose (1974).

75. Horowitz and Liebowitz (1968) p. 280.

76. Ibid. p. 293.

77. Ibid. p. 288.

78. Quoted in S. Cohen (1973b), p. 122.

79. H. S. Becker (1963) p. 7.

80. Hobsbawm (1959) p. 2.

81. Goldman (1961). See also Ward (1973); S. Cohen (1968, 1971b); L. Taylor and Walton (1971); I. Taylor and Walton (1971); J. Martin (1961).

82. Lang (1974) and D. Reynolds (1975).

83. I. Taylor (1971a, 1971b).

84. Pearson (1975b).

85. For further directions in the social and political implications of youth behaviour and youth culture, see P. Cohen (1972); Clarke (1973); Jefferson (1973); Mungham and Pearson (1975); Parker (1974).

86. Hartley (1975).

87. Horowitz and Liebowitz (1968) p. 281.
88. Laing (1969*b*) p. 8.
89. Fanon (1970) p. 50.
90. Henley (1973) pp. 1–2.
91. F. Davis (1967) p. 12.
92. Agitprop Collective (1970) p. 51. Also, for further indications of the relationship between 'deviance', 'banditry' and 'politics', Lyman (1970); I. Taylor and P. Walton (1971); Rubin (1971); pp. 14–16.
93. Taylor, Walton and Young (1973) p. 187.
94. Ibid. p. 184.
95. 'Urban Gorilla Comes East' in Stansill and Mairowitz (1971) p. 171.
96. Reich (1972*b*) p. 66.
97. Situationist International (1967) p. 12.
98. Rock (1973*a*) pp. 103–4. Emphasis added.
99. Rubin (1970) p. 122.
100. Ibid. p. 4; and Hoffman (1971).
101. Leary (1970*a*).
102. Cooper (1967).
103. Matza and Sykes (1961).
104. For an application of the concept to leisure values and 'hippie' morality, see J. Young (1971*a*) chs 6–8; for a critical account, see Taylor, Walton and Young (1973) pp. 175 ff.
105. An account of the 'hippie personality' as 'antinomian' is to be found in Adler (1972).
106. See Hayter (1968); and Roszak (1972) especially ch. 8.
107. Durkheim (1964) pp. 65–73.
108. Erikson (1966) p. 12.
109. Scott (1972) p. 29.
110. Ibid. p. 29.
111. See Pearson (1974*b*) and Ewan (1972).
112. Sendak (1970).
113. Ibid.
114. This is a paraphrase of Reich (1972*a*) p. 19. Compare Howard Becker's statement: 'There is no reason to assume that only those who finally commit a deviant act actually have the impulse to do so. . . . At least in fantasy, people are much more deviant than they appear. Instead of asking why deviants want to do things that are disapproved of, we might better ask why conventional people do not follow through on the deviant impulses they have.' H. S. Becker (1963) pp. 26–7.
115. Dylan (1970).
116. Rock (1973*b*) p. 476.

117. Adorno (1973*b*) p. 57; also Adorno (1974) p. 49.
118. Liazos (1972); Thio (1973); Platt (1973, 1974). For a teaching syllabus along these lines, see Platt, Krisberg and Takagi (1973).
119. Gouldner (1968); Walton (1973); Mankoff (1971); Akers (1968); Taylor, Walton and Young (1973); Schervish (1973).
120. Weis (1971).
121. Lemert (1967) p. 17.
122. Debro (1970) p. 167; Weis (1971) p. 50.
123. See p. 70 above.
124. Walton (1973) p. 178.
125. Ibid. pp. 161, 179.
126. Gouldner (1971) p. 385.
127. Laing (1965) p. 12.
128. Goffman (1968) pp. 159 ff.
129. Ibid. pp. 60–5, 67–8.
130. Ibid. p. 68.
131. Ibid. p. 68.
132. Ibid. p. 68.
133. Goffman (1963) pp. 224–5.
134. Dawe (1973); Sennett (1973*b*); O'Neill (1972) ch. 2.
135. Taylor, Walton and Young (1973) pp. 139–40.
136. Hesse (1965) pp. 5–6.
137. Gouldner (1971) pp. 483, 485.
138. Ibid. p. 483.
139. Chevalier (1973) p. 56.
140. Cooper (1971) p. 44.
141. Strauss (1969) p. 27.
142. Leary (1970*b*) p. 63.
143. J. D. Douglas (1971) p. 269.
144. Ibid. pp. 251 ff.
145. Ibid. p. 327.
146. T. R. Young (1972) p. 69.
147. Ibid. p. 69.
148. Castaneda (1972; 1973*a*; 1973*b*).
149. R. Hughes (1972).
150. Don Juan's theory of socialisation is presented most systematically in Castaneda (1973*b*) pp. 8 ff.
151. Jacoby (1973*a*) p. 48.
152. Ibid. p. 39.
153. Gouldner (1969) p. 346; also see Gouldner (1971) pp. 73 ff.
154. Taylor, Walton and Young (1973) p. 221.
155. Ibid. p. 282. See also the argument around this point in the 'Review Symposium', *British Journal of Criminology*, vol. 13, no. 4 (1973) pp. 394–403.

156. E. Becker (1968) p. 364.
157. J. D. Douglas (1971) p. 324.
158. S. Cohen (1971*a*) p. 24.
159. T. R. Young (1971) p. 280.
160. Gouldner (1971) especially pp. 481–512, and Gouldner (1972).
161. Hobsbawm (1959) p. 60.

CHAPTER 5

1. B. C. Reynolds (1934) p. 125.
2. Wittgenstein (1971) p. 117.
3. A. Schütz (1964) II, p. 95.
4. E. C. Hughes (1971) II, p. 399.
5. See Chapter 3 above.
6. The mainstream ideology and culture of social work is best represented by the following works; Biestek (1961); Hollis (1964); Ferard and Hunnybun (1962); A. Garrett (1942); Hamilton (1951); Timms (1964, 1968); Perlman (1957); Bartlett (1970); Younghusband (1965, 1966).
7. Wooton (1959) pp. 271 ff.; Wilensky and Lebeaux (1965) pp. 314 ff.
8. Biestek (1961) p. 103.
9. See Pearson (1974*d*).
10. Mills (1943) p. 171.
11. Smalley (1967).
12. Woodroofe (1962).
13. Halmos (1965) pp. 160 ff.
14. Timms (1964) p. 61.
15. Scott (1969*b*); Deacon and Bartley (1974); Pearson (1974*d*).
16. Abel-Smith and Townsend (1965); and Rose (1974).
17. For a sketch of some of these developments see Seed (1973).
18. See his recitation of the familiar enough ideology of a 'post-political' society in the introduction to Halmos (1965). Although Halmos (1970*a*) p. xvii, disclaims this as his own belief, the later work (Halmos, 1970*b*) is predicated on the assumptions of the welfare professions *prior* to their radical interruption.
19. Towle (1973).
20. Lees (1971*a*) p. 371.
21. R. Bailey (1970); Deacon (1970); Keniston (1968*b*).
22. *Case Con*, no. 1 (1970) title page.
23. Nicolaus (1969) p. 154.
24. For example, National Association of Social Workers (1969); Bond (1971); Wineman and James (1969).

25. For accounts of some of the ambiguities of community work, see Rein (1970); Popplestone (1972); Cheetham and Hill (1973).
26. Mungham and Thomas (1974) p. 16.
27. Jacoby (1973a) p. 48.
28. See Chapter 4 above.
29. Perlman (1967, 1968, 1970) and Baker (1973); for criticism, Pearson (1974c).
30. Perlman (1973) p. 9.
31. Hobsbawm (1972) pp. 55–6.
32. Pearson (1975a); also Wilensky and Lebeaux (1965) pp. 319–22.
33. Gouldner (1971) p. 80.
34. B. C. Reynolds (1934) p. 127; Stevenson (1974) p. 2.
35. Halmos (1970b).
36. Meyer (1970) pp. 3–4; Bartlett (1970) p. 218.
37. Pearson (1975a).
38. North (1972) p. 284.
39. Ibid pp. 291–2.
40. Mayer and Timms (1970); Timms (1973); Rees (1973).
41. Pearson (1973).
42. Lees (1972).
43. Lees (1971b) p. 3. Emphasis added.
44. Wandor (1972). See also Reich and Teschitz (1973).
45. For example, Milligan (1973); Bradley *et al.* (1971); Hodges and Hutter (1974); Gay Liberation Front (G.L.F.) (1973).
46. M. Garrett (1974) p. 7. See also Weir (1974).
47. Mills (1959) p. 226.

CHAPTER 6

1. Matza (1969) p. 143.
2. Mailer (1963).
3. Leary (1970b) p. 67.
4. Ibid. p. 69. I have retained Leary's emphasis and spelling.
5. P. Rogers (1972) p. 167.
6. Foucault (1970) p. 132.
7. See Foucault (1971, 1973).
8. See Foucault (1970).
9. Foucault (1972) p. 40.
10. Foucault (1973) pp. ix ff.
11. Foucault (1970) p. 75, emphasis added.
12. See Foucault (1971) particularly pp. 228 ff.; and R. Williams (1973) pp. 183–4.
13. Radzinowicz (1966) p. 1.

14. Ibid. p. 59.
15. Quoted in Taylor, Walton and Young (1973) pp. 216–17.
16. Ibid. p. 216; and I. Taylor (1972) p. 633.
17. Taylor, Walton and Young (1973) p. 217.
18. Thomson (1971) p. 119.
19. Talbot (1971*b*).
20. Ibid. p. 101. See also Carpenter (1968) pp. 302–10.
21. *Report from the Select Committee on Prison Discipline, British Parliamentary Papers*, XVII (1968) p. 342.
22. May (1973) p. 12.
23. *Report from the Select Committee on Prison Discipline, British Parliamentary Papers*, XVII (1968) pp. 344, 345.
24. Mayhew (1967) II, p. 264.
25. *Report . . . on the Training of Pauper Children* (1841) p. 366, emphasis added.
26. See the discussion on pp. 75–6 above.
27. Quoted in Radzinowicz (1956*b*) p. 453. And for the same sentiment, see *British Parliamentary Papers*, XVII (1968) p. 471.
28. Radzinowicz (1966) p. 49.
29. For example, de Giustino (1972).
30. Mayhew (1967) I, p. 3.
31. Beames (1970) p. 5.
32. Chevalier (1973) p. 412.
33. Ibid, pp. 409–17.
34. Ibid. p. 412.
35. Ibid. p. 413.
36. Mayhew (1967) I, pp. 320 ff.
37. Beames (1970) p. 5.
38. Leigh (1971) p. 89.
39. *Report . . . Pauper Children* (1841) p. iii.
40. Particularly Mayhew (1967) I, pp. 6–102.
41. Ibid. I, p. 2. I have taken a few liberties with this quotation. Mayhew offers it as a definition of the 'wandering tribes in general'; it is followed, two paragraphs later, by a shorter definition of the 'wandering tribes of this country'. Apart from the question of length, the two statements are identical in spirit, and I have quoted from the fuller definition.
42. Thompson and Yeo (1973) p. 100.
43. See J. Young (1971*a*).
44. Mayhew (1967) III, pp. 432–3.
45. Thompson and Yeo (1973) p. 93.
46. Mayhew (1967) I, p. 320. The constancy of the 'space of knowledge' once more asserts itself here. Compare Mayhew's classification and David Matza's three-fold division of deviant careers

which, as he puts it, 'summarises . . . what we currently know about the process of becoming deviant'; namely, 'affiliation', 'affinity' and 'signification' (Matza, 1969, pp. 87 ff.). Mayhew's street-folk either *take* to the streets through a persistent affinity with that way of life; they are *bred* to an affiliation with the streets; or they are *driven* there, largely by forces of stigma and the severity of the Poor Laws (Mayhew, 1967, I, pp. 322–3).

47. Himmelfarb (1973) pp. 721–2.
48. Engels (1969) p. 84.
49. Beames (1970) p. 4; Macaulay (1883) IV, pp. 189–90; P. Rogers (1972) pp. 149 ff.
50. Beames (1970) pp. 1–4.
51. Talbot (1971*b*) p. 94.
52. Engels (1969) pp. 142–3; also Carpenter (1968) pp. 21 ff.
53. As in Thompson and Yeo (1973); Mayhew (1971*b*); Razzell and Wainwright (1973).
54. A 'pure finder' was a collector of dogs' dung, which was used in the process of tanning leather (Mayhew, 1967, II, pp. 142 ff.).
55. Benjamin (1973) p. 19.
56. Himmelfarb (1973) p. 708.
57. Mayhew (1967) I, p. iii.
58. Ibid. I, title page.
59. Ibid. IV, title page.
60. Himmelfarb (1973) p. 708.
61. Ibid. p. 717. However accurately it captures Victorian opinion and Victorian consciousness, Himmelfarb's argument stands in need of some correction in relation to the work of Henry Mayhew. Mayhew also conducted extensive surveys of workmen and artisans (see Thompson and Yeo, 1973; Mayhew, 1971*b*) although, for whatever reasons, he did not include these in his collected editions. Himmelfarb recognises the difficulty (p. 732 n. 17), but her argument does not encompass the breadth of Mayhew's researches.
62. Mayhew (1967) I, p. 4.
63. Ibid. I, p. 10.
64. Ibid. I, p. 20.
65. Himmelfarb (1973) p. 712.
66. Chevalier (1973) p. 77.
67. Ibid. pp. 56, 59.
68. Ibid. p. 370.
69. Himmelfrab (1973) pp. 726 ff.
70. Chevalier (1973) p. 59.
71. See above p. 151. In some of his drawings and sketches Victor Hugo made the deliberate (or unconscious) effort to merge the

characteristics of working people with those of animals. See Hugo (1967) XVII.

72. G. M. Young (1951) p. 17.
73. Kingsley is quoted in Thompson and Yeo (1973) p. 32; the excerpt from Ashley's diary is in Hodder (1886) II, p. 241.
74. Thompson (1968) p. 66.
75. See Rudé (1964, 1970); Hobsbawm (1959) ch. 7; Thompson (1968) pp. 66 ff.; P. Rogers (1972) pp. 98 ff.; Hobsbawm and Rudé (1973); Lefebvre (1973); D. Williams (1971); Hibbert (1958).
76. Stedman Jones (1971) p. 292.
77. Chevalier (1973) pp. 31–2.
78. P. Rogers (1972) p. 141. Also Marshall (1956) pp. 167–8; Engels (1969) pp. 70–6, 82–3; Kay-Shuttleworth (1970) pp. 24, 27–31, 36–7, 41; Gaskell (1968) pp. 79 ff.
79. Schoenwald (1973) p. 669.
80. Mayhew (1971a) pp. 276–9.
81. Briggs (1968) pp. 16–17.
82. Footnotes to the sewage metaphor in the following sentences would only be cumbersome. The images are taken from the different nineteenth-century works cited in this chapter
83. Mayhew (1967) II, pp. 154–5.
84. Hugo (n.d.) IV, p. 109.
85. Mayhew (1967) I, p. 101.
86. Osborne (1971) p. 17.
87. Ibid. pp. 9, 11.
88. Himmelfarb (1973) p. 719.
89. Chevalier (1973) p. 3.
90. May (1973) p. 18.
91. Quoted in Nisbet (1967) p. 29.
92. P. Rogers (1972) p. 253.
93. Mayhew (1967) II, p. 402.
94. Chevalier (1973) p. 109.
95. Hugo (n.d.) pp. 99, 105–6; and Hugo (1881) p. 450.
96. P. Rogers (1972) pp. 143–4; Himmelfarb (1973) pp. 730–1; Pearce and Roberts (1973).
97. P. Rogers (1972) p. 118.
98. Radzinowicz (1948) p. 406; and (1956a) pp. 1–29.
99. Radzinowicz (1948) p. 400.
100. P. Rogers (1972) pp. 99–166.
101. Stedman Jones (1971) *passim*; Thompson (1968) p. 895.
102. Beames (1970) p. 244.
103. Ibid. pp. 250, 260.
104. Brown (1968) ch. 15.

105. For example, Fromm (1960); Brown (1968) pp. 163–265; Steig (1970).
106. Schoenwald (1968, 1973).
107. Schoenwald (1973) pp. 669–70.
108. Ibid. pp. 669, 677–8.
109. For Chadwick, see Schoenwald (1973) and for Spencer, Schoenwald (1968).
110. Flinn (1965) p. 60.
111. Hugo (n.d.) pp. 99–100; Hugo (1881) p. 452; Mayhew (1967) II, pp. 383–464, and specifically p. 408.
112. *Report . . . on the Training of Pauper Children* (1841) p. xi.
113. Ibid. pp. 5, 8.
114. Schoenwald (1973).
115. *Report . . . on an Inquiry into the Sanitary Condition of the Labouring Population of Great Britain* (1842) p. 243; Flinn (1965) pp. 306–7. See also Baines (1835) pp. 481–2.
116. *Report . . . into the Sanitary Condition* (1842) pp. 244–5 (308). Throughout the following section footnotes refer to the original 1842 *Report*, with page references to Flinn's 1965 edition in brackets.
117. Ibid. pp. 245 ff. (308 ff.).
118. Ibid p. 274 (335).
119. Ibid. p. 274 (335).
120. Ibid. p. 234 (299).
121. Ibid. pp. 233–4 (298).
122. Ibid. p. 234 (299).
123. Ibid. pp. 234–5 (300).
124. Ibid. p. 235 (300).
125. Ibid. p. 232 (297).
126. Ibid. p. 267 (336–7).
127. Talbot (1971*b*) pp. 90–103.
128. Ibid. pp. 91, 93, 94.
129. Addams (1909) p. 92.
130. Ibid. pp. 83–106.
131. Talbot (1971*b*) pp. 99 ff.
132. *Report . . . into the Sanitary Condition* (1842) p. 276 (337).
133. Ibid. p. 276 (337).
134. Ibid. p. 277 (337).
135. Ibid. p. 277 (338).
136. Ibid. p. 277 (337).
137. Ibid. p. 277 (337).
138. Ibid. p. 132 (199).
139. Ibid. p. 133 (200).
140. Ibid. p. 134 (200).

141. Ibid. p. 132 (199).
142. Ibid. p. 203 (268).
143. Ibid. p. 201 (267).
144. Ibid. p. 201 (267).
145. Ibid. p. 201 (266).
146. Ibid. p. 203 (268). Emphasis added.
147. Ibid. p. 201 (266). Chadwick is explicitly anti-Malthusian : he writes that the political instabilities introduced by a predominantly youthful population condemn 'the dreadful fallacy which tends to an acquiescence in the continuance of the causes of pestilence and premature mortality as "correctives of the pressure of population" ' (p. 205 [270]). Compare Herbert Spencer's treatment of the same problem in Spencer (1961) pp. 309 ff.
148. Ibid. p. 202 (267).
149. Richter (1971) p. 28.
150. Briggs (1959) p. 61.
151. Thompson (1967) p. 57. Emphasis added.
152. McKendrick (1961) p. 55.
153. Briggs (1959) p. 61.
154. Ibid. p. 63.
155. Smelser (1959).
156. Quoted in Klingender (1972) p. 146.
157. Rudé (1970) pp. 131 ff.
158. Thompson (1968) p. 865.
159. R. Williams (1973).
160. Thompson (1967) pp. 93–4.
161. Ibid. p. 90. For some indication of the use of bells, clocks and fines in the early factory system and the suppression of talking, singing and even whistling in factories, see Fitton and Wadsworth (1958) pp. 232 ff.; S. J. Chapman (1904) pp. 218–19; Craig (1973) ch. 3 and pp. 115–16; Ure (1861) p. 15; K. Marx (1961) pp. 423–7; Engels (1969) pp. 205–8.
162. Bastide (1972), and Chapter 1 above.
163. For example, Barbu (1960).
164. Rudé (1970) p. 34.
165. Morgan (1974).
166. Stedman Jones (1971) p. 321.
167. Horowitz and Liebowitz (1968); and Chapter 4 above.
168. See Downes (1966) p. 121; P. Cohen (1972) pp. 26–7; White (1971).
169. Rudé (1970) p. 131.
170. Marshall (1962) p. 479.
171. Rudé (1964) ch. 13, and Rudé (1970).
172. Freire (1972) p. 28.

CHAPTER 7

1. R. Williams (1973) p. 32.
2. Ibid. p. 22.
3. Simmel (1950) p. 410.
4. See, for example, Gaskell (1968), which might be compared with Ure (1861) pp. 277 ff. and 374 ff. Benjamin (1973) also contains extended reference to nostalgia in the nineteenth century.
5. Simmel (1921) pp. 360–1.
6. Dickens (1969) ch. 2.
7. M. Weber (1970) pp. 261–2.
8. Ibid. p. 228.
9. Ibid. p. 229.
10. M. Weber (1930) pp. 181, 182.
11. Simmel (1950) p. 412.
12. Ibid. p. 413.
13. Ibid. p. 413.
14. Dickens (1969) p. 65.
15. Wadsworth and Mann (1931) pp. 476 ff.; S. J. Chapman (1904) pp. 76–8; Bythell (1969) pp. 181, 196, 198–203; Baines (1835) pp. 158–63.
16. Dickens (1969) p. 77.
17. R. Williams (1973) pp. 163–4.
18. Baines (1835) pp. 501–2.
19. Simmel (1950) pp. 411, 412, 414, 415.
20. Ibid. pp. 416–17.
21. Ibid. p. 417.
22. Ibid. p. 422.
23. Schmitt (1969) p. 15.
24. Ibid. p. 16.
25. Benjamin (1973) p. 168, and again p. 46. See also O'Neill (1972) pp. 24–37.
26. See Pearson (1974a) pp. 145–7.
27. See Horton (1964); Jacoby (1973a).
28. Nisbet (1969) p. ix. Emphasis added.
29. Benjamin (1973) p. 48; R. Williams (1973) pp. 227–9.
30. R. Williams (1973) pp. 229, 227.
31. Ibid. p. 156; also R. Williams (1974) p. 30.
32. Goffman (1971) pp. 139, 146 ff., 157.
33. Ibid. pp. 150–2.
34. Ibid. pp. 169, 175, 183, 184.
35. Ibid. pp. 184, 188–9, 191; Goffman (1962, 1970).
36. Brittan (1973) p. 153.

37. Goffman (1972*b*); and Dawe (1973).
38. Lyman (1973) p. 360.
39. Lerner (1972) p. 145.
40. Lyman (1973) p. 364.
41. Goffman (1972*b*) p. 386.
42. Ibid. pp. 386–8.
43. Sennett (1973*b*) p. 31.
44. See Chapter 4 above, pp. 107–10.
45. Sennett (1973*a*) pp. 51 ff.
46. Ibid. ch. 2, and pp. 61–6; and Sennett (1970) pp. 105, 216–17.
47. Ibid. p. 65.
48. Ibid. p. 137.
49. Ibid. p. 157.
50. Lerner (1972) pp. 245–6.
51. J. Young (1974).
52. Laing (1971) p. 43.
53. Ibid. p. 46.
54. Wolf (1974) p. 726.
55. West (1957) p. 106. The idea of *Miss Lonelyhearts* as pastoral
    was suggested to me by Lerner (1972).
56. Platt (1969) p. 61. See also pp. 36–43, 61–6.
57. Quoted in Teeters and Reinemann (1950) p. 62.
58. Burt (1944) pp. 265, 519.
59. N. McLain, 1901, quoted in Platt (1969) p. 66.
60. Nisbet (1967) p. 46.
61. Nisbet (1943) pp. 156, 162.
62. Nisbet (1967) pp. 46–7.
63. Nisbet (1969) p. 78.
64. Dennis (1958) pp. 200–1.
65. Barnett (1918) II, pp. 313, 314.
66. Ibid. I, pp. 122, 125.
67. Ibid. I, pp. 118–19.
68. Ibid. I, p. 297.
69. Ibid. I, pp. 141–2.
70. Quoted ibid. I, p. 29.
71. Hill (1970) pp. 89–90.
72. Ibid. p. 90.
73. Ibid. pp. 90, 92.
74. Ibid. p. 93.
75. Addams (1909) pp. 116–17.
76. Ibid. pp. 131–2.
77. Mayo (1949) pp. 8, 14, 67.
78. Addams (1909) p. 107.
79. Ibid. pp. 110–11.

80. Ibid. pp. 111–12.
81. R. Williams (1973) p. 94.
82. Barnett (1918) II, p. 249.
83. Ibid. I, p. 289.
84. R. Williams (1973) p. 45.
85. Steiner (1973) p. 7.
86. Quoted in McKendrick (1961) p. 34.
87. R. Williams (1973) pp. 291, 292.
88. Hofstadter (1960) p. 23.
89. L. Marx (1964) p. 29.
90. Taylor, Walton and Young (1974).
91. Ibid.
92. Crosland (1971) p. 13. See also Benn (1970).
93. Mills (1943) pp. 166–7, 174–5, 180.
94. Barnett (1918) II, p. 312. A fuller account of Mrs Barnett's involvement in the Hampstead Suburb scheme can be read in Creese (1966) ch. 10. Creese's exposition of the matter is generous and sympathetic, but he nevertheless judges that in view of the prices of the homes offered for sale Mrs Barnett's ambition to create a classless community 'was no more that a pious hope' (p. 238).

CHAPTER 8

 1. Hegel (1942) p. 11.
 2. Ibid. p. 226.
 3. For an extended discussion of this point, see Habermas (1971) chs 4–6, and (1974) pp. 3 ff.
 4. Jacoby (1973*b*) p. 41.
 5. Bellamy (1973) p. 31.
 6. Ibid. p. 31.
 7. Spencer (1906) I, p. 79.
 8. Ibid. p. 79.
 9. See Pearson (1973, 1975*a*).
10. Szasz (1973*b*).
11. *Mental Health*, vol. 58, no. 1 (1974) p. 3.
12. *Gay News*, no. 46 (May 1974) p. 20.

BIBLIOGRAPHY

B. Abel-Smith and P. B. Townsend, *The Poor and the Poorest* (Bell, 1965).

N. W. Ackerman and M. Jahoda, *Anti-semitism and Emotional Disorder* (Harper & Row, 1950).

J. Addams, *The Spirit of Youth and the City Streets* (Macmillan, 1909).

N. Adler, *The Underground Stream: New Life Styles and the Antinomian Personality* (Harper & Row, 1972).

T. W. Adorno, 'The Stars Down to Earth: the *Los Angeles Times* Astrology Column. A Study in Secondary Superstition', *Jahrbuch für Amerikastudien*, vol. 2 (1957) pp. 19–88.

T. W. Adorno, 'Sociology and Psychology, Part 1', *New Left Review*, no. 46 (1967*a*) pp. 67–80.

T. W. Adorno, *Prisms*, trans. S. and S. Weber (Spearman, 1967*b*).

T. W. Adorno, 'Sociology and Psychology, Part 2', *New Left Review*, no. 47 (1968) pp. 79–97.

T. W. Adorno, *Negative Dialectics*, trans. E. B. Ashton (Seabury Press, 1973*a*).

T. W. Adorno, 'Correspondence with Walter Benjamin', *New Left Review*, no. 81 (1973*b*) pp. 55–80.

T. W. Adorno, *Philosophy of Modern Music*, trans. A. G. Mitchell and W. V. Bromster (Seabury Press, 1973*c*).

T. W. Adorno, *Minima Moralia*, trans. E. F. N. Jephcott (New Left Books, 1974).

T. W. Adorno, E. Frenkel-Brunswick *et al.*, *The Authoritarian Personality* (Harper & Row, 1950).

J. Agel (ed.), *The Radical Therapist* (Ballantine, 1971).

J. Agel (ed.), *Rough Times* (Ballantine, 1973).

Agitprop Collective, *Bust Book: The People v. Regina* (Action Books, 1970).

R. L. Akers, 'Problems in the Sociology of Deviance', *Social Forces*, vol. 46, no. 4 (1968) pp. 455–65.

P. Archard, 'Sad, Bad or Mad: Society's Confused Response to the Skid-row Alcoholic', in *Contemporary Social Problems in Britain*, ed. R. V. Bailey and J. Young (Saxon House, 1973) pp. 127–43.

N. Armistead (ed.), *Reconstructing Social Psychology* (Penguin, 1974).

R. Bailey, 'Social Workers as Social Policemen', Sixth National Deviancy Conference, University of York (2–3 October 1970).

R. V. Bailey and M. J. Brake (eds), *Radical Social Work* (Edward Arnold, 1975).

R. V. Bailey and J. Young (eds), *Contemporary Social Problems in Britain* (Saxon House, 1973).

E. Baines, *History of the Cotton Manufacture in Great Britain* (Fisher, Fisher & Jackson, 1835).

R. Baker, 'The Challenge for British Casework', *Social Work Today*, vol. 4, no. 10 (1973) pp. 290–3.

M. Balint, *The Doctor, His Patient and the Illness* (Pitman, 1957).

A. Bandura, *Principles of Behaviour Modification* (Holt, Rinehart & Winston, 1970).

D. Bannister, 'The Logical Requirements of Research into Schizophrenia', *British Journal of Psychiatry*, vol. 114 (1968) pp. 181–8.

D. Bannister and A. Fransella, *Inquiring Man* (Penguin, 1971).

Z. Barbu, *Problems of Historical Psychology* (Routledge & Kegan Paul, 1960).

M. Barnes and J. Berke, *Mary Barnes: Two Accounts of a Journey Through Madness* (Penguin, 1973).

M. Barnett, *People, Not Psychiatry* (Allen & Unwin, 1973).

S. A. Barnett, *Canon Barnett: His Life and Work*, 2 vols (Murray, 1918).

R. Barthes, *Mythologies*, trans. A. Lavers (Paladin, 1973).

H. M. Bartlett, *The Common Base of Social Work Practice* (National Association of Social Workers, 1970).

R. Bastide (ed.), *Les Sciences de la Folie* (Mouton, 1972).

G. Bateson *et al.*, 'Toward a Theory of Schizophrenia', *Behavioural Science*, vol. 1, no. 4 (1956) pp. 251–64.

T. Beames, *The Rookeries of London* (Cass, 1970).

E. Becker, *The Revolution in Psychiatry* (Free Press, 1964).

E. Becker, *The Structure of Evil* (Braziller, 1968).

H. S. Becker, *Outsiders* (Free Press, 1963).

H. S. Becker (ed.), *The Other Side* (Free Press, 1964).

H. S. Becker, 'History, Culture and Subjective Experience: an Exploration of the Social Bases of Drug-induced Experiences', *Journal of Health and Social Behaviour*, vol. 8 (1967*a*) pp. 163–76; reprinted in *Sociological Work*.

H. S. Becker, 'Whose Side are We on?', *Social Problems*, vol. 14 (1967*b*) pp. 239–47; reprinted in *Sociological Work*.

H. S. Becker, *Sociological Work* (Allen Lane, 1970).

D. Bell, 'Post-industrial Society: the Evolution of an Idea', *Survey*, vol. 17 (1971) pp. 102–68.

J. Bellamy, *Crime and Public Order in England in the Later Middle Ages* (Routledge & Kegan Paul, 1973).

W. Benjamin, *Charles Baudelaire: A Lyric Poet in the High Era of Capitalism* (New Left Books, 1973).

A. W. Benn, *The New Politics: a Socialist Reconnaissance*, Fabian Tract no. 402 (1970).

P. L. Berger, 'Sociology and Freedom', *American Sociologist*, vol. 6, no. 1 (1971) pp. 1–5.

P. L. Berger and T. Luckmann, *The Social Construction of Reality* (Penguin, 1971).

P. L. Berger and S. Pullberg, 'Reification and the Sociological Critique of Consciousness', *New Left Review*, no. 35 (1966) pp. 56–71.

F. P. Biestek, *The Casework Relationship* (Allen & Unwin, 1961).

N. Bond, 'The Case for Radical Casework', *Social Work Today*, vol. 2, no. 9 (1971) pp. 21–3.

W. Bonger, *Criminality and Economic Conditions* (Indiana University Press, 1969).

S. Box, *Deviance, Reality and Society* (Holt, Rinehart & Winston, 1971).

N. Bradley, L. Danchik *et al.*, *Unbecoming Men: a Men's Consciousness Raising Group Writes on Oppression and Themselves* (Times Change Press, 1971).

P. Breines, 'Marcuse and the New Left in America', in *Antworten auf Herbert Marcuse*, ed. J. Habermas (Suhrkamp Verlag, 1968).

P. Breines (ed.), *Critical Interruptions* (Herder & Herder, 1970).

A. Briggs, *The Age of Improvement 1783–1867* (Longmans, 1959).

A. Briggs, *Victorian Cities* (Penguin, 1968).

A. Brittan, *Meanings and Situations* (Routledge & Kegan Paul, 1973).

N. O. Brown, *Love's Body* (Vintage, 1966).

N. O. Brown, *Life Against Death: The Psychoanalytical Meaning of History* (Sphere, 1968).

C. Burt, *The Young Delinquent*, 4th ed. (University of London Press, 1944).

D. Bythell, *The Handloom Weavers* (Cambridge University Press, 1969).

J. Cage, *A Year from Monday* (Calder & Boyars, 1968).

M. Carpenter, *Reformatory Schools for the Children of the Perishing and Dangerous Classes and for Juvenile Offenders* (Woburn, 1968).

C. Casteneda, *The Teachings of Don Juan* (Penguin, 1972).

C. Castaneda, *A Separate Reality* (Penguin, 1973*a*).

C. Castaneda, *Journal to Ixtlan* (Bodley Head, 1973*b*).

D. Chapman, *Sociology and the Stereotype of the Criminal* (Tavistock, 1968).

S. J. Chapman, *The Lancashire Cotton Industry* (Manchester University Press, 1904).

J. Cheetham and M. Hill, 'Community Work: Social Realities and Ethical Dilemmas', *British Journal of Social Work*, vol. 3, no. 3 (1973) pp. 331–48.

P. Chesler, *Women and Madness* (Allen Lane, 1974).

L. Chevalier, *Labouring Classes and Dangerous Classes,* trans. F. Jellinek (Routledge & Kegan Paul, 1973).

A. Cicourel, *The Social Organisation of Juvenile Justice* (Wiley, 1968).

J. Clarke, 'The Skinheads and the Study of Youth Culture', Fifteenth National Deviancy Conference, University of York (September 1973).

P. Cohen, 'Subcultural Conflict and Working Class Community', *Working Papers in Cultural Studies*, no. 2 (1972) pp. 5–51.

S. Cohen, 'Who Are the Vandals?', *New Society*, no. 324 (1968) pp. 872–8.

S. Cohen (ed.), *Images of Deviance* (Penguin, 1971*a*).

S. Cohen, 'Directions for Research on Adolescent Group Violence and Vandalism', *British Journal of Criminology*, vol. 11, no. 4 (1971*b*) pp. 319–40.

S. Cohen, *Folk Devils and Moral Panics* (Paladin, 1973*a*).

S. Cohen, 'Protest, Unrest and Delinquency: Convergences in Labels and Behaviour', *International Journal of Criminology and Penology*, vol. 1 (1973*b*) pp. 117–28.

S. Cohen, 'Criminology and the Sociology of Deviance in Britain', in *Deviance and Social Control*, ed. P. Rock and M. McIntosh (Tavistock, 1974) pp. 1–40.

J. D. Colfax and J. L. Roach (eds), *Radical Sociology* (Basic Books, 1971).

D. Cooper, 'Comment to R. V. Speck, "The Politics and Psychotherapy of Mini- and Micro-groups" ', Dialectics of Liberation Congress, London (July 1967); available on record, Intersound Recordings DL5.

D. Cooper, *Psychiatry and Anti-Psychiatry* (Paladin, 1970).

D. Cooper, *The Death of the Family* (Allen Lane, 1971).

J. Coulter, *Approaches to Insanity* (Martin Robertson, 1973).

D. Craig, *The Real Foundations: Literature and Social Change* (Chatto & Windus, 1973).

W. L. Creese, *The Search for Environment* (Yale University Press, 1966).

A. Crosland, *A Social Democratic Britain*, Fabian Tract no. 404 (1971).

F. Davis, 'Why All of Us May Be Hippies Someday', *Trans-action*, vol. 5, no. 2 (1967) pp. 10–18.

M. S. Davis, 'That's Interesting: Towards a Phenomenology of Sociology and a Sociology of Phenomenology', *Philosophy of the Social Sciences*, vol. 1 (1971) pp. 309–44.

A. Dawe, 'The Underworld-view of Erving Goffman', *British Journal of Sociology*, vol. 24, no. 2 (1973) pp. 246–53.

B. Deacon, 'The Warfare State', *Case Con*, no. 1 (1970) pp. 4–7.

B. Deacon and M. Bartley, 'Becoming a Social Worker', in *Crisis in Social Work*, ed. H. Jones (Routledge & Kegan Paul, 1974).

G. Debord, *Society of the Spectacle* (Red & Black, 1970).

S. Debout-Oleszkiewicz, 'Les Sciences Dictées par la Folie: La Théorie de Charles Fourier', in *Les Sciences de la Folie*, ed. R. Bastide (Mouton, 1972).

J. Debro, 'Dialogue with Howard S. Becker', *Issues in Criminology*, vol. 5, no. 2 (1970) pp. 159–79.

D. de Giustino, 'Reforming the Commonwealth of Thieves: British Phrenologists and Australia', *Victorian Studies*, vol. 15, no. 4 (1972) pp. 439–61.

G. Deleuze and F. Guattari, *L'Anti-Oedipe: Capitalisme et Schizophrénie* (Les Éditions de Minuit, 1972).

N. Dennis, 'The Popularity of the Neighbourhood-Community Idea', *Sociological Review*, vol. 6 (1958) pp. 191–206.

C. Dickens, *Hard Times* (Penguin, 1969).

D. T. Dickson, 'Bureaucracy and Morality: an Organisational Perspective on a Moral Crusade', *Social Problems*, vol. 16 (1968) pp. 143–57.

J. D. Douglas (ed.), *Deviance and Respectability* (Basic Books, 1970).

J. D. Douglas, *American Social Order* (Free Press, 1971).

J. D. Douglas, 'The Experience of the Absurd and the Problem of Social Order', in *Theoretical Perspectives on Deviance*, ed. R. A. Scott and J. D. Douglas (Basic Books, 1972).

M. Douglas, *Purity and Danger* (Routledge & Kegan Paul, 1966).

D. Downes, *The Delinquent Solution* (Routledge & Kegan Paul, 1966).

E. Durkheim, *Suicide*, trans. J. A. Spaulding and G. Simpson (Routledge & Kegan Paul, 1952).

E. Durkheim, *The Rules of Sociological Method*, trans. S. A. Solovay and J. H. Mueller (Free Press, 1964).

T. Duster, *The Legislation of Morality* (Free Press, 1970).

B. Dylan, *New Morning*, CBS 6900 (1970).

H. J. Dyos and M. Wolff (eds), *The Victorian City*, 2 vols (Routledge & Kegan Paul, 1973).

W. Empson, *Some Versions of Pastoral* (Penguin, 1966).

F. Engels, *The Condition of the Working Class in England* (Panther, 1969).

K. T. Erikson, 'Notes on the Sociology of Deviance', in *The Other Side*, ed. H. S. Becker (Free Press, 1964) pp. 9–22.

K. T. Erikson, *Wayward Puritans* (Wiley, 1966).

A. Esterson, *The Leaves of Spring* (Tavistock, 1970).

E. E. Evans-Pritchard, *Nuer Religion* (Oxford University Press, 1956).

S. Ewan, 'Charles Manson and the Family. Authoritarianism and the Bourgeois Conception of "Utopia": Some Thoughts of Charlie Manson and the Fantasy of the *Id*', *Working Papers in Cultural Studies*, no. 3 (1972) pp. 33–45.

F. Fanon, *A Dying Colonialism* (Penguin, 1970).

A. Feenberg, 'Technocracy and Rebellion', *Telos*, no. 8 (1971) pp. 21–42.

M. L. Ferard and N. K. Hunnybun, *The Caseworker's Use of Relationships* (Tavistock, 1962).

L. A. Fiedler, 'The New Mutants', *Partisan Review*, vol. 32, no. 4 (1965) pp. 505–25.

S. Firestone, *The Dialectic of Sex* (Paladin, 1972).

R. S. Fitton and A. P. Wadsworth, *The Strutts and the Arkwrights 1758–1830: a Study of the Early Factory System* (Manchester University Press, 1958).

A. Flew, *Crime or Disease?* (Macmillan, 1973).

M. W. Flinn (ed.), *Report on the Sanitary Condition of the Labouring Population of Great Britain* (Edinburgh University Press, 1965).

M. Foucault, *The Order of Things* (Tavistock, 1970).

M. Foucault, *Madness and Civilisation*, trans. R. Howard (Tavistock, 1971).

M. Foucault, *The Archaeology of Knowledge*, trans. A. M. Sheriden Smith (Tavistock, 1972).

M. Foucault, *The Birth of the Clinic: an Archaeology of Medical Perception*, trans. A. M. Sheridan Smith (Tavistock, 1973).

P. Freire, *Cultural Action for Freedom* (Penguin, 1972).

S. Freud, *Civilisation and its Discontents*, in *The Standard Edition of the Complete Psychological Work of Sigmund Freud*, vol. xxi, trans. and ed. J. Strachey (Hogarth, 1961) pp. 64–145.

E. Z. Friedenberg, *Laing* (Fontana, 1973).

E. Fromm, *Fear of Freedom* (Routledge & Kegan Paul, 1960).

E. Fromm, *The Sane Society* (Routledge & Kegan Paul, 1963).

E. Fromm, *The Crisis of Psychoanalysis* (Cape, 1971).

J. Gabel, *La Fausse Conscience* (Les Éditions de Minuit, 1962).

H. Garfinkel, *Studies in Ethnomethodology* (Prentice-Hall, 1967).

H. Garfinkel and E. Bittner, ' "Good" Organisational Reasons for "Bad" Clinic Records', in H. Garfinkel, *Studies in Ethnomethodology* (Prentice-Hall, 1967).

A. Garrett, *Interviewing: its Principles and Methods* (Family Service Association of America, 1942).

M. Garrett, 'Women's Work', *Case Con*, no. 15 (1974) pp. 7–9.

P. Gaskell, *Artisans and Machinery* (Cass, 1968).

Gay Liberation Front, *Psychiatry and the Homosexual* (Pomegranate Press, 1973).

J. Genet, *The Thief's Journal* (Penguin, 1967).

J. P. Gibbs, 'Conceptions of Deviant Behaviour: the Old and the New', *Pacific Sociological Review*, vol. 9, no. 2 (1966) pp. 9–14.

E. Goffman, 'On Cooling the Mark out: Some Aspects of Adaptation to Failure', in *Human Behaviour and Social Processes*, ed. A. M. Rose (Routledge & Kegan Paul, 1962).

E. Goffmas, *Behaviour in Public Places* (Free Press, 1963).

E. Goffman, *Asylums* (Penguin, 1968).

E. Goffman, 'The Insanity of Place', *Psychiatry*, vol. 32, no. 4 (1969) pp. 357–88.

E. Goffman, *Strategic Interaction* (Blackwell, 1970).

E. Goffman, *The Presentation of Self in Everyday Life* (Penguin, 1971).

E. Goffman, 'Mental Symptoms and Public Order', in *Interaction Ritual* (Penguin, 1972*a*).

E. Goffman, *Relations in Public* (Penguin, 1972*b*).

N. Goldman, 'A Socio-psychological Study of School Vandalism', *Crime and Delinquency* (1961) pp. 221–30.

J. H. Goldthorpe, 'A Revolution in Sociology?', *Sociology*, vol. 7, no. 3 (1973) pp. 449–62.

P. Goodman, *Growing Up Absurd* (Vintage, 1960).

A. W. Gouldner, 'The Sociologist as Partisan: Sociology and the Welfare State', *American Sociologist*, vol. 3, no. 2 (1968) pp. 103–16.

A. W. Gouldner, 'The Unemployed Self', in *Work*, ed. R. Fraser, vol. 2 (Penguin, 1969).

A. W. Gouldner, *The Coming Crisis of Western Sociology* (Heinemann, 1971).

A. W. Gouldner, 'The Politics of the Mind', *Social Policy*, vol. 2, no. 6 (1972) pp. 5–21, 54–8.

W. R. Gove, 'Societal Reaction as an Explanation of Mental Illness: an Evaluation', *American Sociological Review*, vol. 35, no. 5 (1970) pp. 873–84.

J. Habermas, *Toward a Rational Society*, trans. J. J. Shapiro (Heinemann, 1971).

J. Habermas, *Theory and Practice*, trans. J. Viertel (Heinemann, 1974).

J. Hagan, 'Labelling and Deviance: A Case Study in the "Sociology of the Interesting"', *Social Problems*, vol. 20, no. 4 (1973) pp. 447–58.

J. Haley, *Strategies of Psychotherapy* (Grune & Stratton, 1963).

P. Halmos, *The Faith of the Counsellors* (Constable, 1965).

P. Halmos, *The Faith of the Counsellors*, new ed. (Schocken, 1970*a*).

P. Halmos, *The Personal Service Society* (Constable, 1970*b*).

G. Hamilton, *Theory and Practice of Social Casework*, 2nd ed. (University of Columbia Press, 1951).

B. Hartley, 'Son of Alf Garnett', in *British Working Class Youth Culture*, ed. G. Mungham and G. Pearson (Routledge & Kegan Paul, 1975).

M. R. Haug and M. B. Sussman, 'Professional Autonomy and the Revolt of the Client', *Social Problems*, vol. 17 (1969) pp. 153–61.

A. Hayter, *Opium and the Romantic Imagination* (Faber, 1968).

G. W. F. Hegel, *The Philosophy of Right*, trans. T. Knox (Oxford University Press, 1942).

N. M. Henley, 'Power, Sex and Non-verbal Communication', *Berkeley Journal of Sociology*, vol. 18 (1973) pp. 1–26.

H. Hesse, *Steppenwolf* (Penguin 1965).

C. Hibbert, *King Mob* (Longmans, Green & Co., 1958).

O. Hill, *The Homes of the London Poor* (Cass, 1970).

G. Himmelfarb, 'The Culture of Poverty', in *The Victorian City*, ed. H. J. Dyos and M. Wolff, vol. 2 (Routledge & Kegan Paul, 1973) pp. 707–36.

P. Q. Hirst, 'Marx and Engels on Law, Crime and Morality', *Economy and Society*, vol. 1, no. 1 (1972) pp. 28–56.

E. J. Hobsbawm, *Primitive Rebels* (Manchester University Press, 1959).

E. J. Hobsbawm, *Bandits* (Penguin, 1972).

E. J. Hobsbawm and G. Rudé, *Captain Swing* (Penguin, 1973).

E. Hodder, *The Life and Work of the Seventh Earl of Shaftesbury*, 3 vols (Cassell, 1886).

A. Hodges and D. Hutter, *With Downcast Gays* (Pomegranate Press, 1974).

A. Hoffman, *Steal This Book* (Grove Press, 1971).

R. Hofstadter, *The Age of Reform* (Vintage, 1960).

F. Hollis, *Casework: A Psychosocial Therapy* (Random House, 1964).

M. Horkheimer, *Eclipse of Reason* (Oxford University Press, 1947).

M. Horkheimer, *Critical Theory*, trans. M. J. O'Connell *et al.* (Herder & Herder, 1972).

M. Horkheimer and T. W. Adorno, *Dialectic of Enlightenment,* trans. J. Cumming (Allen Lane, 1973).

I. L. Horowitz and M. Liebowitz, 'Social Deviance and Political Marginality: toward a Redefinition of the Relation between Sociology and Politics', *Social Problems*, vol. 15, no. 3 (1968) pp. 280–96.

J. Horton, 'The Dehumanisation of Anomie and Alienation: A Problem in the Ideology of Knowledge', *British Journal of Sociology*, vol. 15 (1964) pp. 283–300.

J. Horton, 'The Fetishism of Sociology', in *Radical Sociology*, ed. J. D. Colfax and J. L. Roach (Basic Books, 1971) pp. 171–93.

E. C. Hughes, *The Sociological Eye*, 2 vols (Aldine-Atherton, 1971).

R. Hughes, 'The Sorcerer's Apprentice', *Time* (6 November 1972) p. 64.

V. Hugo, *Oeuvres Complètes, Romans* IX (Hetzel & Quantin, 1881).

V. Hugo, *Œuvres Complètes*, 18 vols (Le Club Française, 1967).

V. Hugo, *Works,* vol. 4, *Les Miserables,* Book 5 (Nottingham Society, n.d.).

D. D. Jackson (ed.), *Human Communication,* 2 vols (Science and Behaviour Books, 1968).

R. Jacoby, 'Reversals and Lost Meanings', in *Critical Interruptions,* ed. P. Breines (Herder & Herder, 1970) pp. 60–73.

R. Jacoby, 'Negative Psychoanalysis and Marxism : Towards an Objective Theory of Subjectivity', *Telos,* no. 14 (1972) pp. 1–22.

R. Jacoby, 'The Politics of Subjectivity : Slogans of the American New Left', *New Left Review,* no. 79 (1973*a*) pp. 37–49.

R. Jacoby, 'Laing, Cooper and the Tension in Theory and Therapy', *Telos,* no. 17 (1973*b*) pp. 41–55.

M. Jay, 'The Frankfurt School in Exile', *Perspectives in American History,* vol. 6 (1972) pp. 337–85.

M. Jay, *The Dialectical Imagination* (Heinemann, 1973).

T. Jefferson, 'The Teds – a Political Resurrection', Fifteenth National Deviancy Conference, University of York (21–3 September 1973).

S. M. Jourard, *Disclosing Man to Himself* (Van Nostrand, 1968).

J. P. Kay-Shuttleworth, *The Moral and Physical Condition of the Working Classes* (Cass, 1970).

K. Keniston, *Young Radicals* (Harcourt Brace Jovanovich, 1968*a*).

K. Keniston, 'How Community Mental Health Stamped out the Riots (1968–1978)', *Trans-action* (July–August 1968*b*) pp. 21–9.

R. King, *The Party of Eros* (University of North Carolina Press, 1972).

J. I. Kitsuse, 'Societal Reaction to Deviant Behaviour', in *Deviance: the Interactionist Perspective,* ed. E. Rubington and M. S. Weinberg (Macmillan, 1968) pp. 19–29.

J. I. Kitsuse and D. C. Dietrick, 'Delinquent Boys : a Critique', *American Sociological Review,* vol. 24, no. 2 (1959) pp. 208–15.

F. D. Klingender, *Art and the Industrial Revolution* (Paladin, 1972).

M. L. Kohn, *Class and Conformity* (Dorsey, 1969).

R. D. Laing, *The Self and Others* (Tavistock, 1961).

R. D. Laing, *The Divided Self* (Penguin, 1965).

R. D. Laing, *The Politics of Experience* (Penguin, 1967).

R. D. Laing, 'The Obvious', in *The Dialectics of Liberation,* ed. D. Cooper (Penguin, 1968) pp. 13–33.

R. D. Laing, *Self and Others,* 2nd ed. (Penguin, 1969*a*).

R. D. Laing, *The Politics of the Family* (Canadian Broadcasting Company, 1969*b*).

R. D. Laing, *Knots* (Tavistock, 1970).

R. D. Laing, *The Politics of the Family and Other Essays* (Tavistock, 1971).

R. D. Laing, 'Metanoia : Some Experiences at Kingsley Hall, London', in *Going Crazy*, ed. H. M. Ruitenbeek (Bantam, 1972) pp. 11–21.

R. D. Laing and D. Cooper, *Reason and Violence*, 2nd ed. (Tavistock, 1971).

R. D. Laing and A. Esterson, *Sanity, Madness and the Family* (Tavistock, 1964).

R. D. Laing and A. Esterson, *Sanity, Madness and the Family*, new ed. (Penguin, 1970).

R. D. Laing, H. Phillipson and A. R. Lee, *Interpersonal Perception* (Tavistock, 1966).

T. Lang, 'Alienated Children : the Psychologies of School Phobia and their Social and Political Implications', in *Reconstructing Social Psychology*, ed. N. Armistead (Penguin, 1974) pp. 174–88.

N. Lawal *et al.*, *The Criminal and Society* (PROP, 1973).

T. Leary, *The Politics of Ecstasy* (Paladin, 1970a).

T. Leary, *Jail Notes* (Douglas, 1970b).

R. Lees, 'Social Work, 1925–50 : the Case for a Reappraisal', *British Journal of Social Work*, vol. 1, no. 4 (1971a) pp. 371–9.

R. Lees, 'Politics and Social Deprivation', *Social Work Today*, vol. 2, no. 18 (1971b) pp. 3–5.

R. Lees, *Politics and Social Work* (Routledge & Kegan Paul, 1972).

G. Lefebvre, *The Great Fear of 1789*, trans. J. White (New Left Books, 1973).

R. Leifer, *In the Name of Mental Health* (Science House, 1969).

J. Leigh, 'Juvenile Offenders and Destitute Pauper Children', in *Meliora, Second Series*, ed. C. J. C. Talbot (Cass, 1971) pp. 81–9.

E. M. Lemert, *Social Pathology* (McGraw-Hill, 1951).

E. M. Lemert, *Human Deviance, Social Problems and Social Control* (Prentice-Hall, 1967).

L. Lerner, *The Uses of Nostalgia* (Chatto & Windus, 1972).

A. Liazos, 'The Poverty of the Sociology of Deviance : Nuts, Sluts and Preverts, *Social Problems*, vol. 20, no. 1 (1972) pp. 103–20.

T. Lidz, S. Fleck and A. R. Cornelison, *Schizophrenia and the Family* (International Universities Press, 1965).

J. C. Lilly, *The Centre of the Cyclone* (Paladin, 1973).

P. Lomas, *True and False Experience* (Allen Lane, 1973).

S. M. Lyman, 'Red Guard on Grant Avenue', *Trans-action*, vol. 7, no. 6 (1970) pp. 21–34.

S. M. Lyman, 'Civilisation, Contents, Discontents, Malcontents', *Contemporary Sociology*, vol. 2, no. 4 (1973) pp. 360–6.

T. B. Macaulay, *The History of England*, 4 vols (Longmans, 1883).

N. McKendrick, 'Josiah Wedgwood and Factory Discipline', *Historical Journal*, vol. 4, no. 1 (1961) pp. 30–55.

S. C. Maddison, 'Mindless Militants? Psychiatry and the University', in *Politics and Deviance*, ed. I. Taylor and L. Taylor (Penguin, 1973) pp. 111–35.

N. Mailer, 'The White Negro: Superficial Reflections on the Hipster', in *Advertisements for Myself* (Corgi, 1963) pp. 241–59.

M. Mankoff, 'Societal Reaction and Career Deviance: a Critical Analysis', *Sociological Quarterly*, vol. 12 (Spring issue, 1971) pp. 204–18.

H. Marcuse, *One Dimensional Man* (Sphere, 1968).

H. Marcuse, *Five Lectures: Psychoanalysis, Politics and Utopia*, trans. J. J. Shapiro and S. Weber (Beacon Press, 1970).

H. Marcuse, *An Essay on Liberation* (Penguin, 1972*a*).

H. Marcuse, *Eros and Civilisation* (Abacus, 1972*b*).

H. Marcuse, *Counter-Revolution and Revolt* (Allen Lane, 1972*c*).

J. Margolis, *Psychotherapy and Morality* (Random House, 1966).

D. Marshall, *English People in the Eighteenth Century* (Longmans, 1956).

D. Marshall, *Eighteenth Century England* (Longmans, 1962).

D. Martin, 'R. D. Laing: Psychiatry and Apocalypse', in *Going Crazy*, ed. H. M. Ruitenbeek (Bantam, 1972) pp. 129–60.

J. Martin, *Juvenile Vandalism* (C. C. Thomas, 1961).

M. Maruyama, 'Morphogensis and Morphostasis', *Methodos*, vol. 12, no. 48 (1960) pp. 251–96.

M. Maruyama, 'The Second Cybernetics: Deviation-amplifying Mutual Causal Processes', *American Scientist*, vol. 51 (1963) pp. 164–79.

K. Marx, *Capital*, 1 (Foreign Publishing House, 1961).

L. Marx, *The Machine in the Garden* (Oxford University Press, 1964).

A. Maslow, *The Farther Reaches of Human Nature* (Penguin, 1973).

F. W. Matson, *The Broken Image* (Braziller, 1968).

D. Matza, *Delinquency and Drift* (Wiley, 1964).

D. Matza, *Becoming Deviant* (Prentice-Hall, 1969).

D. Matza and G. M. Sykes, 'Juvenile Delinquency and Subterrannean Values', *American Sociological Review*, vol. 26, no. 5 (1961) pp. 712–19.

M. May, 'Innocence and Experience: the Evolution of the Concept of Juvenile Delinquency in the Mid-nineteenth Century', *Victorian Studies*, vol. 17, no. 1 (1973) pp. 7–29.

J. E. Mayer and N. Timms, *The Client Speaks* (Routledge & Kegan Paul, 1970).

H. Mayhew, *London Labour and the London Poor*, 4 vols (Cass, 1967).

H. Mayhew, 'Home is Home, Be it Never so Homely', in *Meliora, First Series*, ed. C. J. C. Talbot (Cass, 1971*a*) pp. 258–80.

H. Mayhew, *Voices of the Poor: Selections from the 'Morning Chronicle' 1849–50*, ed. A. Humphreys (Cass, 1971*b*).

E. Mayo, *The Social Problems of an Industrial Civilisation* (Routledge & Kegan Paul, 1949).

Mental Patients' Liberation Front, 'A Statement', *Radical Therapist*, vol. 2, no. 4 (1971) p. 24.

Mental Patients' Union, 'Statement of the M.P.U.', *Case Con*, no. 13 (1973*a*) p. 25.

Mental Patients' Union, *Declaration* (London : mimeo, 1973*b*).

C. H. Meyer, *Social Work Practice: a Response to the Urban Crisis* (Free Press, 1970).

D. Milligan, *The Politics of Homosexuality* (Pluto Press, 1973).

C. W. Mills, 'The Professional Ideology of Social Pathologists', *American Journal of Sociology*, vol. 49, no. 2 (1943) pp. 165–80.

C. W. Mills, *The Sociological Imagination* (Oxford University Press, 1959).

I. Morgan, 'Paupers and Bureaucrats', *Social Work Today*, vol. 5, no. 2 (1974) pp. 54–6.

B. Munday, 'What is Happening to Social Work Students?' *Social Work Today*, vol. 3, no. 6 (1972) pp. 3–6.

G. Mungham, 'Social Workers and Political Action', in *Social Work in Crisis*, ed. H. Jones (Routledge & Kegan Paul, 1974).

G. Mungham and G. Pearson, 'Radical Scholarship and Radical Action', Eleventh National Deviancy Conference, University of York (September 1972).

G. Mungham and G. Pearson (eds), *British Working Class Youth Culture* (Routledge & Kegan Paul, 1975).

G. Mungham and P. A. Thomas, 'Lay Advocacy', *New Society*, vol. 27, no. 587 (1974) p. 16.

D. Musto, *The American Disease: Origins of Narcotics Control* (Yale University Press, 1973).

National Association of Social Workers, 'The Social Worker as Advocate : Champion of Social Victims', *Social Work*, vol. 14, no. 2 (1969) pp. 16–22.

M. Nicolaus, 'Remarks at ASA Convention', *American Sociologist*, vol. 4, no. 2 (1969) pp. 154–6.

R. A. Nisbet, 'The French Revolution and the Rise of Sociology in France', *American Journal of Sociology*, vol. 49, no. 2 (1943) pp. 156–64.

R. A. Nisbet, *The Sociological Tradition* (Heinemann, 1967).

R. A. Nisbet, *The Quest for Community* (Oxford University Press, 1969).

M. North, *The Secular Priests* (Allen & Unwin, 1972).

J. O'Neill, *Sociology as a Skin Trade* (Heinemann, 1972).

G. Orwell, *Nineteen Eighty-Four* (Penguin, 1954).

S. G. Osborne, 'Immortal Sewerage', in *Meliora, Second Series*, ed. C. J. C. Talbot (Cass, 1971) pp. 7–17.

H. Parker, *View from the Boys: a Sociology of Down-town Adolescents* (David & Charles, 1974).

F. Pearce and A. Roberts, 'The Social Regulation of Sexual Behaviour and the Development of Industrial Capitalism in Britain', in *Contemporary Social Problems in Britain*, ed. R. V. Bailey and Y. Young (Saxon House, 1973) pp. 51–72.

G. Pearson, 'Misfit Sociology: a Study in Scholarship and Action', Eleventh National Deviancy Conference, University of York (September 1972).

G. Pearson, 'Social Work as the Privatised Solution to Public Ills', *British Journal of Social Work*, vol. 3, no. 2 (1973) pp. 209–28.

G. Pearson, 'Prisons of Love: the Reification of the Family in Family Therapy', in *Reconstructing Social Psychology*, ed. N. Armistead (Penguin, 1974*a*) pp. 137–56.

G. Pearson, 'Misfit Sociology and the Politics of Socialisation', in *Critical Criminology*, ed. I. Taylor, P. Walton and J. Young (Routledge & Kegan Paul, 1974*b*).

G. Pearson, 'The Fetish of Method', *Social Work Today*, vol. 5, no. 3 (1974*c*) pp. 85–7.

G. Pearson, 'The Politics of Uncertainty: a Study in the Socialisation of the Social Worker', in *Towards a New Social Work*, ed. H. Jones (Routledge & Kegan Paul, 1974*d*).

G. Pearson, 'Making Social Workers: Bad Promises and Good Omens', in *Radical Social Work*, ed. R. V. Bailey and M. J. Brake (Edward Arnold, 1975*a*).

G. Pearson, ' "Paki-bashing" in a North Lancashire Cotton Town: a Case and its History', in *British Working Class Youth Culture*, ed. G. Mungham and G. Pearson (Routledge & Kegan Paul, 1975*b*).

H. H. Perlman, *Social Casework: A Problem-Solving Process* (University of Chicago Press, 1957).

H. H. Perlman, 'Casework is Dead', *Social Casework*, vol. 48, no. 4 (1967) pp. 22–5.

H. H. Perlman, 'Can Casework Work?', *Social Service Review*, vol. 42, no. 4 (1968) pp. 435–47.

H. H. Perlman, 'Casework and the "Diminished Man" ', *Social Casework*, vol. 51, no. 4 (1970) pp. 216–24.

H. H. Perlman, 'Social Casework in Social Work', in *Casework Within Social Work*, ed. G. Parker (University of Newcastle Press, 1973) pp. 7–18.

F. Perls, *Gestalt Therapy Verbatim* (Bantam, 1971).

R. S. Peters, *The Concept of Motivation* (Routledge & Kegan Paul, 1958).

E. B. Piedmont and K. J. Downey, 'Revolutions in Psychiatry : or, the Emperor's New Clothes', *International Journal of Social Psychiatry*, vol. 17, no. 2 (1971) pp. 111–21.

I. Piliavin and S. Briar, 'Police Encounters with Juveniles', in *Deviance: the Interactionist Perspective*, ed. E. Rubington and M. S. Weinberg (Collier-Macmillan, 1968) pp. 137–45.

A. M. Platt, *The Child Savers* (University of Chicago Press, 1969).

A. M. Platt, 'Prospects for a Radical Criminology in the United States', European Group for the Study of Deviance and Social Control, Florence (13–16 September 1973).

A. M. Platt, 'The Triumph of Benevolence : the Origins of the Juvenile Justice System in the United States', in *Crime and Justice in America*, ed. R. Quinney, new ed. (Little Brown, 1974).

A. M. Platt, B. Krisberg and P. Takagi, 'The New Criminology : a Course Outline', *Newsletter: Union of Radical Criminologists*, vol. 1, no. 1 (Berkeley School of Criminology, California, 1974).

G. Popplestone, 'Collective Action among Private Tenants', *British Journal of Social Work*, vol 2, no. 3 (1972) pp. 369–86.

Preservation of the Rights of Prisoners, *Statement by London Group of PROP and Prisoners' Charter* (PROP, 1973).

J. H. Price, *Psychiatric Investigations* (Butterworth, 1972).

Radical Therapist Collective, *The Radical Therapist* (Penguin, 1974).

L. Radzinowicz, *A History of English Criminal Law*, 3 vols (Stevens, 1948, 1956*a*, 1956*b*).

L. Radzinowicz, *Ideology and Crime* (Heinemann, 1966).

C. Ratner, 'Principles of Dialectical Psychology', *Telos*, no. 9 (1971) pp. 83–109.

P. E. Razzell and R. Wainwright (eds), *The Victorian Working Class . . . Letters to the 'Morning Chronicle'* (Cass, 1973).

S. Rees, 'No More than Contact! Perspectives and Outcome in Social Work', Fifteenth National Deviancy Conference, University of York (21–3 September 1973).

W. Reich, *Listen, Little Man!* (Noonday Press, 1948).

W. Reich, *The Mass Psychology of Fascism*, trans. V. R. Carfagno (Souvenir Press, 1972*a*).

W. Reich. *The Sexual Struggle of Youth* (Socialist Reproduction, 1972*b*).

W. Reich and K. Teschitz, *Selected Sex-Pol Essays 1934–37* (Socialist Reproduction, 1973).

R. Reiche, *Sexuality and Class Struggle* (New Left Books, 1970).

M. Rein, 'Social Work in Search of a Radical Profession', *Social Work*, vol. 15, no. 2 (1970) pp. 13–28.

A. J. Reiss, 'The Social Integration of Queers and Peers', in *The Other Side*, ed. H. S. Becker (Free Press, 1964) pp. 181–210.

B. C. Reynolds, 'Between Client and Community: a Study of Responsibility in Social Casework', *Smith College Studies in Social Work*, vol. 5, no. 1 (1934) whole issue.

D. Reynolds, 'When School Breaks the Truce', in *British Working Class Youth Culture*, ed. G. Mungham and G. Pearson (Routledge & Kegan Paul, 1975).

D. Richter, 'The Role of Mob Riot in Victorian Elections', *Victorian Studies*, vol. 15, no. 1 (1971) pp. 19–28.

P. Roazen, *Freud: Political and Social Thought* (Vintage, 1968).

P. Robinson, *Asylum*, 16 mm. film (1973).

P. A. Robinson, *The Sexual Radicals* (Paladin, 1972).

P. Rock, *Deviant Behaviour* (Hutchinson, 1973*a*).

P. Rock, 'Review of R. Scott and J. Douglas (eds), *Theoretical Perspectives on Deviance*', *Sociology*, vol. 7, no. 3 (1973*b*) pp. 476–7.

C. R. Rogers, *On Becoming a Person* (Houghton Mifflin, 1961).

C. R. Rogers, *Encounter Groups* (Penguin, 1973).

P. Rogers, *Grub Street: Studies in a Subculture* (Methuen, 1972).

P. M. Roman, 'Labelling Theory and Community Psychiatry', *Psychiatry*, vol. 34, no. 4 (1971) pp. 378–90.

H. Rose, 'Up against the Welfare State: the Claimant Unions', in *The Socialist Register 1973*, ed. R. Miliband and J. Saville (Merlin Press, 1974) pp. 179–203.

T. Roszak, *The Making of a Counter-Culture* (Faber, 1971).

T. Roszak, *Where the Wasteland Ends* (Faber, 1972).

J. Rubin, *Do it!* (Simon & Schuster, 1970).

J. Rubin, *We Are Everywhere* (Harper & Row, 1971).

G. Rudé, *The Crowd in History* (Wiley, 1964).

G. Rudé, *Paris and London and the Eighteenth Century: Studies in Popular Protest* (Fontana, 1970).

J. Ruesch and G. Bateson, *Communication: The Social Matrix of Psychiatry* (Norton, 1951).

G. Ryle, *The Concept of Mind* (Penguin, 1963).

J.-P. Sartre, *Saint Genet*, trans. B. Frechtman (W. H. Allen, 1964).

L. Schaffer, L. C. Wynne *et al.*, 'On the Nature and Sources of the Psychiatrist's Experience with the Family of the Schizophrenic', in *Changing Families*, ed. J. Haley (Grune & Stratton, 1971).

M. Schatzman, *Soul Murder* (Allen Lane, 1973).

T. J. Scheff, *Being Mentally Ill* (Aldine, 1966).

T. J. Scheff, 'Negotiating Reality: Notes on Power in the Assessment of Responsibility', *Social Problems*, vol. 16, no. 1 (1968) pp. 3–17.

A. E. Scheflen, 'Communication and Regulation in Psychotherapy', *Psychiatry*, vol. 26, no. 2 (1963) pp. 126–36.

A. E. Scheflen, 'Quasi-courtship Behaviour in Psychotherapy', *Psychiatry*, vol. 28, no. 3 (1965) pp. 245–57.

P. G. Schervish, 'The Labelling Perspective: its Bias and Potential in the Study of Political Deviance', *American Sociologist*, vol. 8, no. 2 (1973) pp. 45–57.

P. J. Schmitt, *Back to Nature: the Arcadian Myth in Urban America* (Oxford University Press, 1969).

R. L. Schoenwald, 'Town Guano and *Social Statics*', *Victorian Studies*, vol. 11, supplement (1968) pp. 691–710.

R. L. Schoenwald, 'Training Urban Man: a Hypothesis About the Sanitary Movement', in *The Victorian City*, vol. 2, ed. H. J. Dyos and M. Wolff (Routledge & Kegan Paul, 1973) pp. 669–92.

T. Schroyer, *The Critique of Domination* (Braziller, 1973).

E. M. Schur, 'Drug Addiction under British Policy', in *The Other Side*, ed. H. S. Becker (Free Press, 1964) pp. 67–83.

E. M. Schur, *Labelling Deviant Behaviour* (Harper & Row, 1971).

E. M. Schur, *Radical Non-Intervention: Re-thinking the Delinquency Problem* (Prentice-Hall, 1973).

A. Schütz, *Collected Papers*, II (Martinus Nijhoff, 1964).

W. C. Schutz, *Joy: Expanding Human Awareness* (Penguin, 1973).

R. A. Scott, *The Making of Blind Men* (Russell Sage, 1969a).

R. A. Scott, 'Professional Employees in a Bureaucratic Structure', in *The Semi-Professions and their Organisation*, ed. A. Etzioni (Free Press, 1969b).

R. A. Scott, 'The Construction of Conceptions of Stigma by Professional Experts', in *Deviance and Respectability*, ed. J. D. Douglas (Basic Books, 1970) pp. 225–90.

R. A. Scott, 'A Proposed Framework for Analysing Deviance as a Property of Social Disorder', in *Theoretical Perspectives on Deviance*, ed. R. A. Scott and J. D. Douglas (Basic Books, 1972) pp. 9–35.

R. A. Scott and J. D. Douglas (eds), *Theoretical Perspectives on Deviance* (Basic Books, 1972).

H. F. Searles, *Collected Papers on Schizophrenia and Related Subjects* (Hogarth, 1965).

P. Sedgwick, 'R. D. Laing: Self, Symptom and Society', *Salmagundi*, no. 16 (1971) pp. 5–37; reprinted as *Laing and Anti-Psychiatry*, ed. R. Boyers (Penguin, 1972).

P. Sedgwick, 'Mental Illness *is* Illness', *Salmagundi*, no. 20 (1972) pp. 196–224.

P. Seed, *The Expansion of Social Work in Britain* (Routledge & Kegan Paul, 1973).

M. Sendak, *Where the Wild Things Are* (Puffin Picture Books, 1970).

R. Sennett, *Families Against the City* (Harvard University Press, 1970).

R. Sennett, 'Review of R. D. Laing, *The Politics of the Family*', *New York Times Book Review* (3 October 1971) pp. 2–3, 40–1.

R. Sennett, *The Uses of Disorder* (Penguin, 1973*a*).

R. Sennett, 'Two on the Aisle', *New York Review of Books*, vol. 20, no. 17 (1 November 1973*b*) pp. 29–31.

S. Shoham, *The Mark of Cain: The Stigma Theory of Crime and Social Deviation* (Israel University Press, 1970).

G. Simmel, 'Sociology of the Senses: Visual Interaction', in *Introduction to the Science of Sociology*, ed. R. E. Park and F. W. Burgess (University of Chicago Press, 1921) pp. 356–61.

G. Simmel, *The Sociology of Georg Simmel*, trans. and ed. K. H. Wolff (Free Press, 1950).

J. L. Simmons, *Deviants* (Glendessary Press, 1969).

Situationist International, *Ten Days That Shook the University* (Situationist International, 1967).

B. F. Skinner, *Beyond Freedom and Dignity* (Penguin, 1973).

P. E. Slater, *The Pursuit of Loneliness* (Allen Lane, 1971).

R. E. Smalley, *Theory for Social Work Practice* (Columbia University Press, 1967).

N. J. Smelser, *Social Change in the Industrial Revolution* (Routledge & Kegan Paul, 1959).

R. V. Speck, 'Psychotherapy of the Social Network of a Schizophrenic Family,' *Family Process*, vol. 6, no. 2 (1967*a*) pp. 208–14.

R. V. Speck, 'The Politics and Psychotherapy of Mini- and Micro-groups', Dialectics of Liberation Congress, London (July 1967*b*); available on record, Intersound Recordings DL5.

R. V. Speck and C. Attneave, *Family Networks* (Pantheon, 1973).

H. Spencer, *The Principles of Sociology*, 2 vols (Williams & Norgate, 1906).

H. Spencer, *The Study of Sociology* (University of Michigan Press, 1961).

S. Spender, *World Within World* (Readers' Union Ltd, 1953).

S. P. Spitzer and N. K. Denzin (eds), *The Mental Patient* (McGraw-Hill, 1968).

P. Stansill and D. Z. Mairowitz (eds), *BAMN: Outlaw Manifestos and Ephemera 1965–1970* (Penguin, 1971).

G. Stedman Jones, *Outcast London* (Oxford University Press, 1971).

M. Steig, 'Dickens' Excremental Vision', *Victorian Studies*, vol. 13, no. 3 (1970) pp. 339–54.

G. Steiner, 'The City Under Attack', *Salmagundi*, no. 24 (1973) pp. 3–18.

O. Stevenson, 'Editorial', *British Journal of Social Work*, vol. 4, no. 1 (1974) pp. 1–2.

G. V. Stimson, *Heroin and Behaviour* (Irish University Press, 1973).

B. Stratton, *Who Guards the Guards?* (North London PROP, 1973).

A. L. Strauss, *Mirrors and Masks* (Sociology Press, 1969).

D. Sudnow, 'Normal Crimes', *Social Problems*, vol. 12 (1965) pp. 255–76.

T. S. Szasz, *The Myth of Mental Illness* (Harper & Row, 1961).

T. S. Szasz, 'Bootlegging Humanistic Values through Psychiatry', *Antioch Review*, vol. 22 (1962) pp. 341–9.

T. S. Szasz, *Law, Liberty and Psychiatry* (Macmillan, 1963).

T. S. Szasz, *Psychiatric Justice* (Collier Macmillan, 1965; Collier Books, 1971).

T. S. Szasz, *Ideology and Insanity* (Calder & Boyars, 1973*a*).

T. S. Szasz, *The Manufacture of Madness* (Paladin, 1973*b*).

T. S. Szasz, *The Second Sin* (Routledge & Kegan Paul, 1974).

D. R. Taft, *Criminology*, 1st ed. (Macmillan, 1942).

C. J. C. Talbot (Viscount Ingestre), *Meliora, or Better Times to Come, First and Second Series*, 2 vols (Cass, 1971*a*).

C. J. C. Talbot, 'Social Evils : Their Causes and Their Cure', in *Meliora, Second Series*, ed. C. J. C. Talbot (Cass, 1971*b*) pp. 90–103.

I. Taylor, 'Soccer Consciousness and Soccer Hooliganism', in *Images of Deviance*, ed. S. Cohen (Penguin, 1971*a*) pp. 134–64.

I. Taylor, ' "Football Mad" : a Speculative Sociology of Football Hooliganism', in *A Reader in the Sociology of Sport*, ed. E. Dunning (Cass, 1971*b*) pp. 352–77.

I. Taylor, 'The Criminal Question in Contemporary Social Theory', *The Human Context*, vol. 4, no. 3 (1972) pp. 633–40.

I. Taylor and L. Taylor (eds), *Politics and Deviance* (Penguin, 1973).

I. Taylor and P. Walton, 'Hey, Mister, This Is What We Really Do : Some Observations on Vandalism in Play', *Social Work Today*, vol. 2, no. 10 (1971) pp. 8–9.

I. Taylor, P. Walton and J. Young, *The New Criminology* (Routledge & Kegan Paul, 1973).

I. Taylor, P. Walton and J. Young (eds), *Critical Criminology* (Routledge & Kegan Paul, 1974).

L. Taylor, *Deviance and Society* (Nelson, 1971).

L. Taylor and P. Walton, 'Industrial Sabotage : Motives and Meanings', in *Images of Deviance*, ed. S. Cohen (Penguin, 1971) pp. 219–45.

N. G. Teeters and J. O. Reinemann, *The Challenge of Delinquency* (Prentice-Hall, 1950).

G. Therborn, 'A Critique of the Frankfurt School', *New Left Review*, no. 63 (1970) pp. 65–96.

A. Thio, 'Class Bias in the Sociology of Deviance', *American Sociologist*, vol. 8, no. 1 (1973) pp. 1–12.

E. P. Thompson, 'Time, Work-discipline and Industrial Capitalism', *Past and Present*, vol. 38 (1967) pp.56–97.

E. P. Thompson, *The Making of the English Working Class* (Penguin, 1968).

E. P. Thompson and E. Yeo (eds), *The Unknown Mayhew* (Penguin, 1973).

A. Thomson, 'Prevention is Better than Cure', in *Meliora, Second Series*, ed. C. J. C. Talbot (Cass, 1971) pp. 118–29.

N. Timms, *Social Casework: Principles and Practice* (Routledge & Kegan Paul, 1964).

N. Timms, *The Language of Social Casework* (Routledge & Kegan Paul, 1968).

N. Timms, *The Receiving End* (Routledge & Kegan Paul, 1973).

C. Towle, *Common Human Needs*, new ed. (Allen & Unwin, 1973).

V. W. Turner, *The Ritual Process* (Routledge & Kegan Paul, 1969).

A. Ure, *The Philosophy of Manufactures*, 3rd ed. (Bohn, 1861).

R. Vaneigem, *The Revolution of Everyday Life* (Situationist International, n.d.).

A. P. Wadsworth and J. de L. Mann, *The Cotton Trade and Industrial Lancashire 1600–1780* (Manchester University Press, 1931).

P. Walton, 'The Case of the Weathermen: Social Reaction and Radical Commitment', in *Politics and Deviance*, ed. I. Taylor and L. Taylor (Penguin, 1973) pp. 157–81.

P. Walton and A. Gamble, *From Alienation to Surplus Value* (Sheed & Ward, 1972).

M. Wandor, 'The Small Group', in *The Body Politic: Writings from the Women's Liberation Movement in Britain 1969–1972* (Stage One, 1972) pp. 107–15.

C. Ward (ed.), *Vandalism* (Architectural Press, 1973).

C. B. Warren and J. M. Johnson, 'A Critique of Labelling Theory from the Phenomenological Perspective', in *Theoretical Perspectives on Deviance*, ed. R. A. Scott and J. D. Douglas (Basic Books, 1972) pp. 69–92.

P. Watzlawick, J. H. Beavin and D. D. Jackson, *Pragmatics of Human Communication* (Faber, 1968).

M. Weber, *The Protestant Ethic and the Spirit of Capitalism*, trans. T. Parsons (Allen & Unwin, 1930).

M. Weber, *From Max Weber*, trans. and ed. H. H. Gerth and C. W. Mills (Routledge & Kegan Paul, 1970).

S. Weber, 'Individuation as Praxis,' in *Critical Interruptions*, ed. P. Breines (Herder & Herder, 1970) pp. 22–59.

A. Weir, 'The Reproduction of Labour Power', *Case Con*, no. 15 (1974) pp. 3–6.

J. G. Weis, 'Dialogue with David Matza', *Issues in Criminology*, vol. 6, no. 1 (1971) pp. 33–53.

A. Wellmer, *The Critical Theory of Society* (Herder & Herder, 1970).

P. H. Wender, 'Vicious and Virtuous Circles: the Role of Deviation-amplifying Feedback in the Origin and Perpetuation of Behaviour', *Psychiatry*, vol. 31, no. 4 (1968) pp. 309–24.

N. West, *Complete Works* (Secker & Warburg, 1957).

D. White, 'Brum's Mobs', *New Society*, vol. 18, no. 473 (1971) pp. 760–3.

The Who, *Quadrophenia*, (1973) Track Records 2657 013.

H. L. Wilensky and C. N. Lebeaux, *Industrial Society and Social Welfare* (Free Press, 1965).

L. T. Wilkins, *Social Deviance* (Tavistock, 1964).

D. Williams, *The Rebecca Riots* (University of Wales Press, 1971).

R. Williams, *The Country and the City* (Chatto & Windus, 1973).

R. Williams, *The English Novel* (Paladin, 1974).

D. Wineman and A. James, 'The Advocacy Challenge to Schools of Social Work', *Social Work*, vol. 14, no. 2 (1969) pp. 23–32.

L. Wittgenstein, *Tractatus Logico-Philosophicus* (Routledge & Kegan Paul, 1971).

E. Wolf, 'Review of H. Landsberger (ed.), *Rural Protest*', *New Society*, vol. 27, no. 598 (1974) p. 726.

K. Woodroofe, *From Charity to Social Work* (Routledge & Kegan Paul, 1962).

B. Wooton, *Social Science and Social Pathology* (Allen & Unwin, 1959).

L. C. Wynne *et al.*, 'Pseudo-mutuality in the Family Relations of Schizophrenics', *Psychiatry*, vol. 21, no. 3 (1958) pp. 205–20.

G. M. Young, 'Mid-Victorianism', *History Today*, vol. 2 (January 1951) pp.11–17.

J. Young, *The Drugtakers* (Paladin, 1971*a*).

J. Young, 'The Role of the Police as Amplifiers of Deviance, Negotiators of Reality and Translators of Fantasy', in *Images of Deviance*, ed. S. Cohen (Penguin, 1971*b*) pp. 27–61.

J. Young, 'Working Class Criminology', in *Critical Criminology*, ed. I. Taylor, P. Walton and J. Young (Routledge & Kegan Paul, 1974).

T. R. Young. 'The Politics of Sociology: Gouldner, Goffman and Garfinkel', *American Sociologist*, vol. 6, no. 4 (1971) pp. 276–81.

T. R. Young, *New Sources of Self* (Pergamon, 1972).

E. Younghusband (ed.), *Social Work with Families* (Allen & Unwin, 1965).

E. Younghusband (ed.), *New Developments in Casework* (Allen & Unwin, 1966).

A. C. Zijderveld, *The Abstract Society* (Penguin, 1972).

G. Zilboorg, *The Medical Man and the Witch during the Renaissance* (Johns Hopkins Press, 1935).

G. Zilboorg, *A History of Medical Psychology* (Norton, 1941).

OFFICIAL PUBLICATIONS

Report . . . on the Training of Pauper Children (H.M.S.O., 1841).

Report . . . on an Inquiry into the Sanitary Condition of the Labouring Population of Great Britain (H.M.S.O., 1842).

Report from the Select Committee on Prison Discipline, in *British Parliamentary Papers*, Prison Discipline, 1850 (632) vol. XVII (Irish University Press, 1968).

INDEX